My Horsy Life

My Horsy Life

An unconventional equine memoir

Janet Rising

Matador
9 Priory Business Park,
Wistow Road, Kibworth Beauchamp,
Leicestershire. LE8 0RX
Tel: 0116 279 2299
Email: books@troubador.co.uk
Web: www.troubador.co.uk/matador
Twitter: @matadorbooks

ISBN 978 1800460 195

British Library Cataloguing in Publication Data.
A catalogue record for this book is available from the British Library.

Printed and bound in the UK by TJ Books Limited, Padstow, Cornwall
Typeset in 11pt Minion Pro by Troubador Publishing Ltd, Leicester, UK

Matador is an imprint of Troubador Publishing Ltd

To everyone who has ever ridden
at the riding school at the top of the hill

Contents

Introduction

MOST EQUESTRIAN MEMOIRS TELL of an epic struggle to achieve international equestrian glory, of memories sprinkled with names of familiar and famous equestrian heroes.

Not this one.

This is a tale of a working-class, pony-less child who learned to ride in the suburbs, who made do with riding in dribs and drabs, out hacking, grabbing rides where she could regardless of the suitability of her mounts. Despite being born to a non-equestrian family I refused to allow lack of opportunity and funds to prevent me from pursuing my passion for all things equine.

I learned to ride at a large and amazing riding school, with an instructor whose unorthodox teachings shaped my equestrian career – and whose exploits share this memoir. I have been lucky – and determined enough – to work with horses and donkeys before spending two decades as editor of *Pony*, the magazine for young riders.

This book is neither instruction manual, not is it designed to recommend. It records my experiences, thoughts, observations, conclusions and equestrian memories of – and it is important to stress this – times now gone. I hope some will resonate with you and bring back happy memories of your own. If, on the other hand, you find your eyes rolling and your tongue clicking in outrage and indignation at the exploits I have recorded then please remember that it is merely an account of one horsy life. Mine.

That is all.

It begins

SOME GIRLS ARE DESTINED to grow up loving horses, to the bewilderment of their families with no ties to the land, with no immediate memory of equine involvement. Where does this obsession come from, from where does it take root? Born in the late 1950s I was such a girl and, if you are reading this, the chances are that you were, too.

I can't remember exactly when this obsession took hold of me, but even before I started school I was known by my family as *the one who loved horses*.

'She loves horses,' my parents would say, rolling their eyes, almost embarrassed by the peculiarity, all links with equines in their own past lost and forgotten. '*We have no idea where she gets it from. Janet's pony mad!*' they would laugh, as though it were an affliction, a virus, something

I'd picked up. And maybe it was, perhaps it is. It was something they were sure I would grow out of, something to endure until the next phase. Only there was no next phase. Horses were it. We were all stuck with it.

Some horse-struck girls, as their parents assure them, do as they are told and grow out of their equine love affair but others, the hardcore ones, the ones for whom nothing but horses will satisfy their mysterious craving, begin a journey that lasts a lifetime, a love that nothing will overtake or can ever replace.

Parents are horrified by it: the expense, the obsessing, the dirt and the smell, and the dread of a horsy daughter growing up into the worst of black sheep, a *horsy woman*. Broken fingernails, hairs on jumpers, a whiff of dung about her, forever in jodhpurs, a booming voice, the mannish manner, the cliché of the domineering animal type, a woman to which no man would be attracted, the shame of a grandchildren-less future a horrifying possibility. Surely it shouldn't – *couldn't* – happen to *their* dear daughter, to their family. The horror, the dread, the nightmare! Couldn't she take up something more ladylike – ballet, for example, or ballroom dancing? Anything but horses, please God, anything! What had they done to deserve this? Where did it come from, how did it begin?

It may have started with the bell. Perfectly conditioned as any of Pavlov's dogs, its peal would cause me to leap up, beg a crust of bread or an apple and rush outside to the road, straining to catch sight of her, long of mane and short of tail, perfection in equine form…

Angela: the rag-and-bone man's horse.

Dapper was how you would describe Mr D, the rag-and-bone man, dressed in his suit, his trilby hat raised in deference to his customers. The sound of the bell and the clip-clop of his dark brown mare's silver shoes inviting housewives to bring out their rags and other treasures no longer wanted to be weighed and priced. Recycling, before it became the fashion. Mr D could recognise a child in love and was kind enough to always slow Angela – strange choice of name, unquestioned at the time – to a halt and allow me to offer her the treat, watching and hearing her jaws move as my hand softly stroked the thin white stripe on her face, and juice from the apple, mingling with equine saliva, ran into my fingers. A real-live horse! Outside our house! Gobbing on my hand! I can remember the feel of my heart beating painfully against my ribs at the encounter, my face aching from a smile wider than I produced for anything else.

It was doubly kind of Mr D to indulge my addiction for neither rag nor bone was ever forthcoming from our house, our sole contribution to his round limited to dubious top-up fuel for his horse. Anything we had that was past its original usefulness was dispatched to my father's shed where it would reappear – whole or in part – unrecognised, morphed into something else.

How I longed to have been born a century before, to be surrounded by horses pulling carriages, ridden along the road, hauling carts full of coal and delivering goods from the butcher and the dairy. Our coal was delivered by lorry, the coalmen black from their trade and smelling of coal dust, carrying sacks through our house to the bunker in the garden. My mother covered the carpet with towels and mats, dancing in obvious distress, praying the men wouldn't brush their charcoal coats against the wallpaper in our narrow hallway.

I hadn't the sense to realise that had I been born in the previous century, not only would I have witnessed cruelty to many of those horses slaving in their role as machinery keeping the wheels of industry turning, but I would have been running around London without shoes, without a bed of my own and with a body racked with rickets. The chances of me riding in a carriage a hundred years ago were as slim as they were in the days I strained to hear the clip-clop of Angela's hooves on the tarmac.

But growing up in the 1960s, my room was a shrine to all things equine. My original, grey-flocked Sindy horse and its plastic palomino partner, Thunderbolt; my tiny Britains and Timpo models, all 400 of them, safe in their home-made cardboard stables in the cupboard behind my bed, every name recorded in a notebook. And then there were my other model horses, the in-between sizes bought from Woolworths with preciously saved pocket money. There were pictures of horses on the walls, horse transfers on the door, a prized horse brass, and pages and pages full of my failed efforts to capture a likeness of the most noble of creatures in pencil and paint. Real horses and ponies were not available to me and so then, as today, I filled my bedroom with images and artefacts depicting all things horse.

Several decades later, when I was privileged to hold the post of editor of *Pony* magazine, readers would send letters with photographs of their bedrooms to demonstrate that they had *the horsiest bedroom in the world!* Rosettes, model horses, posters, drawings, bits and pieces of pony kit such as brushes, halters – even rugs – covered every surface, regardless of whether or not the owner had a real pony of their own. One girl had even painted a full-size pony looking out over his stable on *her* bedroom door. We were so impressed we included it as a make in the magazine, showing other readers how they, too, could have a pony in their bedroom.

Now you can buy duvet covers and pillowcases smothered in images of horses; you can hang horsy wallpaper on your walls. There are life-size furry models to ride – even fake-fur heads of unicorns with twirling, golden horns, much like the glassy-eyed, severed stags heads you see in country house hotels – only less moth-eaten and less, well, dead. Horsy bedrooms continue to this day, parents closing the door on the evidence of their offspring's lunacy with a sigh. But now, as then, posters of horses may be preferable to posters of pop stars, evidence of a daughter growing up too fast.

Many parents despair that their offspring's selfies always include a pony, but I feel they are fixating on the negative, when there are so many positives to be had. Riding teaches you resilience (you need to be determined and follow through) and negotiating skills (a pony rarely agrees with your crazy, celebrity-induced ideas). Caring for a pony teaches you responsibility (he relies on you for his welfare), that you are not always going to get your own way (get used to it) and that you are not the centre of the universe (get used to it).

Riding instils a respect in those with more experience (your instructors), as well as an appreciation of sportsmanship (you're not always going to win – and sometimes you're *never* going to), not to mention teamwork (it's not all about you). In addition, ponies are very good at teaching you that sulking, showing off and stamping your foot cuts little ice (get a handle on your feelings). If this isn't enough to get doubting parents onside, they could consider that a love of ponies will often delay a girl's interest in the opposite sex. Okay, it's expensive, but a pony will keep a daughter younger for longer than if her interest was in boys.

If passion for her pony is for the long haul, rather than a passing phase, a young girl's four-legged chum will teach the most important lesson of all: how to love.

Before I could afford regular riding lessons, and before I was old enough to go to the riding school every waking moment, Saturday was still my most looked-forward-to day of the week. Not only because there was no school, not only because *Champion the Wonder Horse* galloped across the TV screen in the morning, but because the western series *Bonanza* was scheduled for the evening, and I – purely because of its abundance of horses – was allowed to stay up and watch. Did I love Little Joe because he rode a piebald to die for, or did I love the piebald because of Little Joe? At least, I assumed it to be *pie*, rather than *skew*, but I would have to wait for the arrival of colour TV in our house at the end of the next decade, the 1970s, to confirm it.

In the meantime, there were western films to watch, full of horses which could gallop for miles and for hours without getting out of breath, whether chasing villains or pulling a stagecoach. Cowboy horses, cavalry horses, painted Indian horses and (drum roll) the glamorous Trigger, ridden by Roy Rogers. Later there was even a whole programme, half-an-hour of pure escapism, for people like me. *The White Horses*, imported from Yugoslavia, told the story of Julia who rode her uncle's Lipizzaner horses, especially her favourite, Boris. Oh to be Julia! The theme tune had the perfect canter beat, so with it ringing around my head I ran and galloped and jumped show jumps made from household bits and bobs, and pieces of old wood from the shed in the garden, heroine to my own story and prompted by television coverage of show jumping at Hickstead, and the Horse of the Year Show at Wembley. (I never walked anywhere – bloody evidence of the tumbles I took galloping on my imaginary horse shone through the knees of my shredded tights like scars won in battle.) I wanted to be Marion Coakes with her wonder-pony, the 14.2hh Stroller. Glued to our black-and-white TV, thrilled and in awe, I watched as the pair won a silver medal at the Mexico Olympic Games against horses two-, three-hands bigger than brave, little Stroller – Marion Coakes beating all but one of the men, carrying on what Pat Smythe had started, kicking off equality in sport for a generation, and inspiring pony books for generations to come. There were horses for the horse-starved if you knew where to look – if only from afar.

When I was about eight years old, I was awarded a book for good attendance to Sunday School. Tearing off the wrapping to reveal my prize I gazed upon a dust jacket showing a straight-backed rider on an impossibly long-legged black pony, a red rosette fluttering from his bridle: *Jill's Gymkhana*. God, or at least his staff on earth, did indeed work in mysterious ways. It was as though The Almighty was endorsing my interest – or maybe I just banged on about ponies at Sunday School as much as I did everywhere else.

Jill's Gymkhana by Ruby Ferguson changed my life. Because Jill Crewe, heroine of her own story, proved I wasn't alone, because Jill Crewe was *me*. She loved horses (tick). She couldn't afford one (tick). She whiled away the hours wishing, and hoping, and feeding other people's horses from the other side of fences (tick). I had thought I was the only one so afflicted, but it turned out there were more like me. I wasn't alone.

Sadly, any affinity I had with Jill lasted only for as long as the end of chapter one. In the next Jill did get a pony – and that's when, like a forgotten clock, the ticking stopped. That I couldn't have a pony wasn't just true, it was true with knobs on. It was *so* true that after many earnest attempts to plead my case I acknowledged that it was a lost cause and stopped asking. We didn't even have a car – a pony was out of the question. It wasn't *buying* a pony that was the problem, my mother explained, but the cost of *keeping* it for a pony could never have lived at our home, even if I had known how to look after it. Sacks of coal could be taken through the house to reach the garden, but even I realised that a pony could not.

Unlike Jill we didn't have an orchard. We had no shed in which a manger and cobbles lurked, waiting for me to tear out all the rubbish and reveal its wonderful secret. Our garden was long and thin, flanked by identical gardens on either side, the shed at the end full of my father's motorbikes, tools and things that would one day come in useful. True, we lived adjacent to Green Belt, where the sprawl of housing built in the 1930s, 1950s and 1960s stopped abruptly as it met fields and trees stretching into the Essex countryside, where the gentry from London used to flock to their country seats, but whose country seats had become unappreciated, fallen into disrepair and torn down. From my elder sister's room at the back of the house, past our garden full of my father's lovingly grown dahlias and vegetables, we could look over the rooftops to the fields and forests beyond. I didn't realise at the time, but my parents had, unwittingly, moved from the East End of London to the most perfect place for their pony-mad daughter. I just had to wait a little longer before I could find that out.

Until then, there were always holidays…

We went to Clacton. I vividly remember this because of the photograph we have of my sister and I each astride a pony. Because on holiday, by the sea, there were always pony rides and it was these precious pony rides, snatched moments of pony heaven, for which I saved my holiday money with the zeal of a Dickensian miser. At Clacton, on a large stretch of grass overlooking the sea, tied to the rail when I turned up with my precious, pony ride sixpence, was Little Joe's piebald. All the other ponies receded from my gaze as I stared at the equine vision of black and white with mounting excitement. I was going to ride Little Joe's horse!

Except that because I was small and the pony wasn't, my elder sister got to ride it. I was hoisted aboard the cutest, fluffiest chestnut pony with a mane you could hide in while my sister lived my dream. It is the only picture we have of me on a pony where I am wearing a scowl – and you can only *just* make it out as the ponies are far, far away, visible only from the fetlocks up, the sky dominating the top half of the image. My father hadn't really been looking at the ponies when he pointed his camera but had instead focused on the wrong thing – his own daughters. Parents, what are they like?

But there were other photographs from other holidays, and one was of me aboard the skewbald Texas at a holiday camp in Bournemouth. I had clocked Texas as I'd galloped around the camp on my imaginary horse, knees braced, and had fallen in love. By this time I had learned the ropes and I waited, shaking my head as other ponies became available, waiting for the skewbald to return from taking a rival camper for a ride. Only Texas would do. The girl who led me allowed my father to hold him (my dad always liked animals, and wasn't scared to get up close and personal, whereas my mum was more cautious) while she took a picture. And she got it better – at least you could see all of us, rather than the surrounding area – portrait, rather than landscape. After that, whenever I galloped around the camp on my own two feet, it was Texas I imagined beneath me.

Pony rides comprised being hoisted aboard, your feet pushed into the stirrups or, if they were too long, the leathers, a child barely older than yourself casually leading you to a designated point before turning around and retracing their steps. Sometimes the leader – probably bored and keen to mix things up a bit – might ask whether you fancied a trot and I would nod furiously, clutching the pommel, anxious to maximise my experience.

Recently, I went to a riding school's open day where pony rides were on offer. The parents queued to sign a disclaimer. The riders were all fitted with hats. Eventually, after all this time-consuming red tape the be-hatted, signed-off child was lifted up on to the saddle. The ponies were led by two capable and powerful teenagers, one either side. No trotting. No holding the reins. More chance of flying through the air than a parent being allowed to hold the pony while someone took a photograph. I'm not judging, just telling it like it was. Not for the first time I was grateful to have lived during a different time. I take heart in the certain knowledge that despite the best efforts of H&S, some of those children will have been bitten by the bug. They have the ride of their lives ahead of them.

Our stays at holiday camps along the south coast were eagerly awaited and duly recorded with images I still cherish. On donkeys, on ponies, grinning and elated at being astride an equine at last, albeit for the briefest of moments. I sat upright, my heels rammed down, having learned from Jill how it should be done. I held the reins as best I could, before sliding off and offering my mount a sugar lump filched from a seaside café, my palm flat, thumb tucked in, keen to demonstrate my knowledge. Even ponies in fields were fair game, called over with the rustle of more half-inched sugar (before you hit the keyboard, I now know never to feed strange ponies), the camera recording the moment as I stroked and patted, my face beaming fit to burst.

When I wasn't hunting down real ponies on holiday I sought out bookshops, handing over half-a-crown (a sacrifice of several pony rides) for more Jill books, read from cover-to-cover in our caravan or chalet at night. These were paperbacks, with none of the beautiful illustrations by Caney as in my *Jill's Gymkhana*, but this minor detail could be overlooked – at least the words hadn't been mucked about with. Jill still had Black Boy and Rapide, even if she sported a black bob on the cover, and Rapide appeared to have morphed into a chestnut with a flaxen mane. In my mind they were still exactly as Caney depicted them, the ponies with flicked-over tails and expressive faces, Jill and her chums all elephant-ear jodhpurs and fierce lipstick. When I couldn't find a Jill book I discovered *The Silver Brumby* series by Elyne Mitchell, *Three Ponies and Shannan* and many of the other Pullein-Thompsons' books. My holidays were filled with ponies – even if they were not always the real thing.

Back home, living on the edge of Green Belt meant that equines were never far away (the area is still one of the most heavily equine-populated places in the country) and we often saw horses and ponies in fields when we were out walking as a family. I'd attempt to entice them over to the fence but mostly they ignored me, or if they did take a chance that I might have some tit-bit for them, they would soon wander off again when they found out I had called them over on false pretences, or for a mere handful of grass. I had to get my horsy fix elsewhere.

I joined Brownies; I flew up to Guides. One day, after a Guides meeting in the Scout hut along the road from our usual church hall, we all streamed out of the hut to a surprise. A pony, pale palomino, led by a man waiting to turn it out in the Scout's field as soon as it was empty of little girls. I wasn't the only one drawn to the fairy horse and the man, magically, amazingly, made all my dreams come true by offering three of us hanging around, obviously smitten and stroking his pony's silver mane, a ride.

No saddle, no reins, just a leg-up onto a warm, golden back, the man leading the pony by its halter along at walk, then a bouncy, giggling trot before we slid off, patting the pony and thanking its owner, pale hairs clinging to our navy skirts. When I told my mother, I couldn't understand why she didn't share my joy. She asked me questions: How many others had been with me? Who was this man? Had Brown Owl been there? Where did this ride take place? How long had it lasted? I now appreciate why she was so agitated but at the time, in my innocence, it had been just a simple act of kindness by someone who, like Mr D the rag-and-bone man, recognised a passion he shared. And that, of course, could have made for a huge problem, leaving myself vulnerable to anyone with their own agenda.

How many random acts of kindness are now withheld, how many nuggets of golden memories lost because of the few who have ruined it for the rest? I can still remember how it was to ride that beautiful, fairy-like pony, to feel his body heat radiate through my legs, and I'm still grateful for the opportunity. It fuelled my hunger for horses. It helped to keep me going through the drought.

The Library Holiday Club, attended when I was nine, was where I met my friend Jan. When I tell anyone she is my oldest friend, Jan, quite rightly, corrects me: she is the friend I have *known the longest*. Drawn together by our mutual love of horses, we scoured the shelves for pony books. And there they were, hardback Hodder & Stoughton Jills, the whole set, beautifully illustrated by Caney, just like my *Jill's Gymkhana*. And Caney's talent drew me to the cover of *A Tale of Two Horses*, the story of the explorer Aimé Tschiffely and his brave Criollos, Mancha and Gato, the book written in his horses' words. We discovered *My Friend Flicka* and K M Peyton, who by writing *Fly-by-Night*, confirmed why I couldn't keep a horse in my garden. And then, amongst the reference books, we found instruction manuals about how to care for horses and how to ride, the information within them greedily devoured. It was another world this one of horses, riding, hunting and shows, of the Pony Club and London mews, of Drum Horses and the Household Cavalry – even the Spanish Riding School of Vienna.

My grandparents bought me the *Princess Tina Pony Books*, a *Sindy Book of Horses*, sticker books and instruction books into which I dived, hungry for knowledge, losing myself, absorbing everything I could about breeds, riding, saddlery, building my own library. How come it all went into my head and stayed there when I couldn't grasp algebra, and I could never remember the names of countries on the globe? The *I-Spy book of Horses and Ponies* became my constant companion, although I rarely had the opportunity to tick all the horses and ponies it urged me to spy. It would all come in useful, I knew, for when I could have a pony of my own.

So I read about Jill and her ponies, coveting her adventures with Ann Derry and Diana Bush. I learned that dreams could come true – but only for other people because I was still without a real pony, still making hobby horses from old socks and broom handles on which I jumped hoes and fold-up chairs in the garden, and sitting on the banisters and imagining myself astride Champion, getting my fix any way I could. I sewed rugs for my Sindy horse and Thunderbolt, I added to my collection of models of various sizes. I even made my own riders for my tiny Britains models, tracing Jill from the cover of her book before pencilling her onto cardboard, sticking two outlines together from the waist up so they could sit safely astride. The indentations where I pressed my pencil on the book can still be felt by a passing hand.

I owned a whole riding school in the cupboard behind my bed, but I still didn't have a real pony of my own and without riding lessons, I wasn't even a rider.

The riding school
at the top of the hill

Y OU NEEDED TO TAKE a left past the fish-n-chip shop next to the toy shop where I bought my model ponies and keep walking past the 1950s bungalows and the fringes of the council estate on the opposite side of the road. At the crossroads, you'd take another left between the two schools and continue up the hill past the allotments, where houses were limited to one side of the road, and all traces of modern sprawl gave way to fields. If you kept walking past the pub you reached the summit, where an ancient and picturesque village opened out before you. Here then, you seemed to step not only into a world away from the urban sprawl of modernity, but into another time.

Essex is flat. So say those whose main view of the county is restricted to the back end of a lorry as they whiz

– or more usually, crawl – along the A13, but the hill to the village is steep, causing legs to complain at the novelty. The reward for your effort is great, however, as you can see why medieval royalty chose this spot to build their palace. No-one, friend in need of hospitality, or foe on the make, could creep up on you unseen. The village is over 340 feet above sea level.

From the village green you can still look down over fields, over the backs of grazing horses and ancient buildings to towns and cities in Essex, and even Kent beyond. Behind the bus stop, where I would later wait with my friends in summer and winter, in daylight and after dark, for the sighting of the rare and welcome bus to appear from around the corner and take us home, there remains the big dip in the ground, the ducking pond where villagers took delight in the ritual humiliation of scolds and gossips – and possibly even put suspected witches to the test.

There's the pub, of course, and the impressive Victorian house which used to be the vicarage, behind which are fields where more horses lived, but of the village shop with its corrugated roof, where we supplemented our diet with Mr Kipling apple pies and frozen Arctic Rolls, there remains no trace.

But there is, as you would expect, a church – not as old as you might suppose but still beautiful and serene, facing the bus stop, dominating the green, surrounded by the graves of villagers long gone, and those more recently lost and missed, with room still for villagers whose allegiance to this place will extend beyond their final breath. Beside the church, behind the houses, behind its high brick walls and a clock tower and just visible from the bus stop is what you have come to see: the riding school, the riding school at the top of the hill.

During the nineteenth century, a big house was built on the ruins of the medieval palace, facing west where the setting sun takes its time to sink behind the long-standing forests in the distance. Were it not for the ancient redwoods along the avenue, majestic sentinels along the ridge towards London, you would have had a good view of the capital city; it is only fifteen miles away, Canary Wharf even closer. When I was a teenager, Docklands and Canary Wharf didn't exist, the Shard not even a twinkle in its architect's eye. London is nearer now, creeping and growing like a sly and artful enemy, a smile on its face, glinting in the sun, promising riches to those who succumb to its charms. How long before it arrives, sudden and unwelcome, at the riding school at the top of the hill?

The old and beautiful coach house which belonged to the big house remains, the only evidence that it ever existed. It had, since the 1930s, been home to the riding school. With its high walls built in a quadrangle, large wooden gates, beautiful cobbled yard, the groom's house built into the bricks, water trough in the corner and window boxes full of marigolds, it still stands solid and proud, at the pinnacle of the hill. There were eight stalls for the carriage horses, some of the original tiles still clinging to the walls, red paint showing through the black on the woodwork. Turned into looseboxes, the pillars between which the horses would have been tied are still intact. There were two huge cage boxes – probably for hunters or hacks. Opposite the groom's house was a large room with high windows, which would have housed the harness and saddlery and, on either side of the gates, two high interiors without windows at all, where the carriages would have been stored, the tall, heavy doors now open, the space converted to more looseboxes. Beyond the main yard was a lower yard: pigsties converted to pony boxes, a row of wooden stables for liveries and a tiny paddock, as well as a tractor shed and workshop.

It was here, in the late 1960s, where I had my first riding lesson on a little chestnut pony called Penny. Lasting for a magical half-hour I was led, hatless, in my slacks and school shoes, around the back of the riding school and down the steep back lane by someone I thought looked very efficient but who was probably about thirteen. The countryside opened up before us as we traversed between the riding school's fields – those for the liveries on the left, another for the school horses on the right. I tried to remember all I had learned from my books as Penny clip-clopped along the tarmac road, which morphed into a dirt track as it passed the working farm which incorporated another big livery yard with evidence of yet more horses, its green and golden fields stretching into the distance. It took exactly half-an-hour to walk and trot from the school, to the farm and back again, my leader puffing as we climbed the steep hill back to the yard. My first lesson came to an end but my legal high continued for days.

Penny crunched my offered sugar lump and I floated off on air to wait at the bus stop where I enjoyed an out-of-body experience. Yes, I was there with my father, and yet I was still on Penny, still watching her small, pricked, chestnut ears ahead of me, holding the reins, feeling the hard leather of the saddle between my knees. I even looked forward to my backside aching – as my family laughingly told me it would. Bring it on. Every ache would prove I had actually been *riding*. Every twinge would stir memories of half-an-hour which had to last me for at least a fortnight until I could save enough pocket money for a repeat performance.

Five shillings, two-weeks' pocket money, well spent, but it was as though I had paid the devil, or rather, I knew what it felt like to sell the devil my soul. That first hit held me in its grip – the magical horses and ponies, the beautiful cobbled yard with its huge doors and promises of wondrous things beyond. And imagine, somebody actually lived in the grooms' quarters in the yard! I was hooked – as if there could have been any doubt about it – and I vowed that every coin I gained in future would go straight to the riding school at the top of the hill. There was no question of my parents paying for lessons; if I wanted to ride badly enough, I would have to save up to fund my new hobby myself, end of.

My first ride had provided the hold the riding school now had over me. It was my supplier, my pusher, feeding the habit of a willing nine-year-old victim, hungry for more.

There was no going back.

Wish you were here... part one

I'LL NEVER KNOW HOW I managed to persuade my parents to let me go on a riding holiday. After three years of intermittent riding lessons and hacks I was hungry for a more inclusive experience, if only temporarily. I had, of course, read about riding holidays in pony books so I knew what they were about. The heroines always had the most fantastic time sleeping under the stars or in barns with their mounts, cantering on sandy beaches, spending every moment bonding with their super ponies and like-minded friends without the tiresome interference of grown-ups telling them to wash their hands before lunch or insisting that they be careful. Their riding holidays were full of midnight feasts, exciting adventures and jolly japes. Being a sucker for a well-spun yarn and with no experience to the contrary, I knew a riding holiday would be the most amazing experience *ever*. I was in no doubt that it would change my life. How could I get myself on one? I had to work it somehow!

I had been on a couple of camping jaunts with the Guides so you'd think I'd have gleaned something from the experience – namely that living outdoors didn't measure up to the jolly time hyped up by the *Famous Five* or those depicted in pony books. At Guide camp there were midges which saw you only as food. *Your* food was either burnt or raw. Freshly self-dug latrines were not places around which to hang. It was too much to expect canvas to keep out the cold of a raw summer night in England, and a midnight hike was neither romantic nor bracing when the hikers were caught in a torrential thunderstorm, eventually returning to their tents soggy, cold and wondering whether it wasn't time to move on from Guiding. And this was before the days of outdoor clothing and walking boots. We hiked in our uniforms of blue shirts and navy skirts and normal, stout shoes. Child abuse, I think they'd call it now.

My companion during these Guides camps was a girl called Elizabeth. She lived nearby with her younger brother and her parents (he large, she small), who were a big noise round at the local community centre. The first time I went to her house I wondered what had happened to it – the kitchen sink and all available surfaces were crammed with dirty crockery and partially-eaten meals. Clothes littered every surface in the through-lounge (very in at the time was the through-lounge) and were heaped up, rather hopefully, on a rarely troubled ironing board.

You had to move things to sit down. You had to move more things to see the floor. Elizabeth's idea of packing was to open a suitcase, screw all her clothes up tightly and throw them in, sitting on the lid until the lock clicked. I was, even at the tender age of twelve, shocked.

Of course, as a grown-up I realise what a thankless task housework is. *Nobody* notices when you've done it, *everybody* notices when you haven't. Even twelve-year-olds.

To make up for the disarray, their house boasted a colour television. Oh the decadence! I would always wrangle a trip to Elizabeth's on Monday nights so I could see *The High Chaparral* in all its glory – having graduated from Little Joe and his piebald in *Bonanza*, not to mention Trampas and Steve on their buckskin and bay in *The Virginian*. Even the sound seemed enhanced when the screen wasn't bogged down in shades of grey. Now Blue Cannon (and his pale palomino) was the object of my desire, and Elizabeth had a thing for Manolito. Hindsight makes me wonder how I could ever have fallen for anyone so wet, and I now realise what a sleezy know-it-all Manolito was, but that was then, and this is now. Different times. I was but a child.

On the early evening before my first Guide camp, Elizabeth and her father turned up on our doorstep, the car still running, expectant looks adorning their faces. Camp, they insisted, began today. Now! Why wasn't I ready?

My mother went into meltdown – didn't camp start tomorrow? She was sure it did! But no, insisted Elizabeth's father, used to fighting his corner on community centre committees and puffing, rather importantly, on a cigar, today was most definitely the day!

We rushed around, apologising and throwing all my stuff into a holdall. How could we have got it wrong? My mother wasn't used to confrontation, especially with male members of the human race and so, with a rushed goodbye, I joined Elizabeth in the back seat of her father's car and we set off to the campsite. Upon our arrival we could plainly see that everywhere was still in a state of preparation – tents still to be erected, an absence of blue-robed Guides on site, no Brown Owl, no nobody, no nothing. Except us. My mother didn't see the funny side and neither, quite honestly, did I. Good job it was only a journey of eight miles or so.

A lesson learned: READ THE INSTRUCTIONS and never be afraid to argue with someone who insists they are right, no matter what bloody gender they are. There must be some sort of law that states that the more someone argues they are right, the more likely they are to be wrong. If there isn't, there should be.

So what of riding holidays, I hear you ask. Well, at least four classified pages of each and every one of my *Pony* magazines (dutifully ordered at the newsagent every month and read, word-for-word, cover-to-cover) were crammed with advertisements for riding holidays at about the time I was swooning over Blue Cannon, and Elizabeth's father was busy being right until proven wrong. Pony-mad children were spoilt for choice. Pony-owning children didn't need to go on a riding holiday as they had a pony at their disposal twenty-four-seven but if, like me, your contact with ponies was restricted to a lesson every fortnight and an extra hack out on your summer holiday, the idea of having a pony nobody but you rode for a week was a dream come true – for six days, anyway. But even though riding holiday centres were springing up like mushrooms all over the country in response to demand, my choice of where to go – and even whether I'd be able to go at all – was limited and in dispute.

For a start, I had to persuade my parents, and at least Girl Guide camp had paved the way for a few days away from the loving bosom of my family. A few pounds for GG camp was nothing to the prices riding holiday centres were asking, which explained why everyone with several acres, some ponies and the desire to make a few quid had decided that offering riding holidays meant money in the bank.

Trekking seemed to be the cheapest option – between twelve and fifteen pounds a week to plod around the Brecon Beacons or the wilds of Scotland. This didn't appeal; I didn't want to plod. By now I was cantering on my lessons and eager to expand my riding prowess, such as it was. Wales and Scotland were too far away, anyway. A riding holiday proper, as read about in pony books, with instruction, hacking and the thrill of a gymkhana at the end of the week, was way more expensive, say eighteen pounds – up to twenty-five for the very top riding schools. I don't know what my dad was earning in 1970 but my hourly riding lessons were twelve shillings (60p, God, I'm old) and my pocket money was only five bob (25p), so you can probably work out for yourself that a riding holiday was a whole chunk of money. A vast, huge, whopping chunk. Added to that was the problem of actually getting there because we still didn't have a car.

Ahhh, but Elizabeth's father did…

Elizabeth was dead keen. We perused the adverts and realised that there was only one kind of riding holiday that would do for us – western riding! We would be able to live out our *High Chaparral* fantasies. Excitement went into overdrive and – surprise, surprise, my long-suffering parents, once the logistics of getting me to a riding centre were taken out of the equation, agreed to the idea. We could start looking for a suitable centre.

Too late – we'd jumped the gun and had already sent for details. Our first choice was a so-called ranch situated in not-so-difficult-to-get-to Hampshire. The brochure was an A4 folded leaflet in hurts-your-eyes yellow with a stylised image of a western rider on the front. Inside, photographs of the proprietor wearing a grin like a split melon and riding her cow pony in all the gear, and someone else wearing a poncho and riding bareback, enticed prospective holiday makers to get in the mood. '*Ride Western, English and Injun in the New Forest*,' it said. Guests would 'experience riding on real western saddles on well-schooled horses and ponies trained in western and English style'. All this for twenty pounds a week. Considerably more than a twelve-pound trekking holiday but oh, so much more exciting. So worth it! But were we?

Amazingly, my parents agreed to the extra expense. My mother in particular, took a huge leap of faith – her younger daughter entrusted to the care of complete strangers – thinking back I'm astonished she agreed. But she did, and with the deposit stumped up and sent off, I spent the next couple of months bouncing off walls. A real riding holiday! Western riding! Injun riding! (Stuff the English style, I could do that at the riding school.) Not only would I be with horses and ponies for a whole week – live, sleep, breathe, etc – but I would be able to ride in a real western saddle, ride one-handed, neck reining, all that malarkey. It was as though all my wishes were being granted at once. God had come up trumps again!

The great day came at last. My mother choked back the tears (a week seemed a long time to let her daughter go), I sat in the back of Elizabeth's dad's car and my friend and I gazed out of the windows as the countryside morphed into cowboy country: the New Forest!

In the Forest, way off the beaten track, down a dirt road with no houses in sight, Elizabeth's parents pulled up at the very English-looking, blue-and-white painted bungalow surrounded by a few dusty corrals in the middle of nowhere, spat out their offspring, her friend and their luggage onto the gravel drive, hastily turned the car around and sped off for home, unable to see us for the dust, their attitude to their daughter's time away from home being somewhat different to my mother's.

We were shown to our accommodation. Bunkhouse it was not. Rather, a basic caravan with two bunks, two beds already occupied by two geeky-looking girls two years older than us, the other, much more streetwise older girls having baggsied all the rooms in the bungalow... sorry, bunkhouse. Doubts seeped in. I couldn't see any horses; I couldn't see the smiling proprietor. What I could see was a rather large number of resident cats all missing their tails (by design, it turned out, the owner being a keen breeder of Manx). What would dawn on me later was that we had been well and truly fitted up.

Supervision was the sole responsibility of two girls whose collective ages may or may not have just about totalled, say, thirty-two. The one in charge was smiley, confident and quite professional in her manner. The other (probably a working pupil being paid diddly-squat) was sullen and less forthcoming – the negative to the other's positive. But hey, we were there, we would meet our ponies tomorrow! In the meantime we were shown the tuck shop (a cupboard housing chocolate bars, sweets, postcards and stamps for sale at vastly inflated prices), the sitting room (with paintings of horses on the walls), the tack room (full of wonderful western saddles, which generated some excitement) and the dining table where our evening meal was served.

Did I say evening meal? Hardly. Jam sandwiches. A few biscuits. Perhaps the real meals would begin tomorrow, we thought. They didn't. Limp white bread stuck together with preserved strawberries was the basic fare every night – and we spent quite a lot of time fishing out cat hairs stuck in the jam. I had a sneaky suspicion that the state of the kitchen wasn't too far removed from the one in Elizabeth's house. The only time we caught sight of our hostess (beaming smile as seen on the cover noticeable by its absence) was when she was coming and going – though not necessarily in that order. She clearly wanted nothing to do with her 'guests.' She certainly didn't want to feed them much.

But we did ride in the western saddles – at least I did for several days. I also rode in English tack (which I felt was a cop-out) and for one very long, four-hour ride we rode bareback, or 'injun' (politically incorrect now, of course, but that was 1970-speak for Native Americans), and was amazed when my legs didn't fall off.

I picked up muck from the corrals with my bare hands, I cleaned tack, I threw money at the tuck shop when hunger pangs growled, and Elizabeth and I organised a midnight feast in the caravan with our two nerdy companions. I don't know why everyone in books does it: it was pretty grim. We only had sweets and biscuits to eat, I could hardly keep my eyes open and the fact that I couldn't clean my teeth again (the bathroom being in the bunga... bunkhouse) bothered me. It was nothing like the midnight feasts I had read about. A let down doesn't begin to describe it.

Wednesday afternoon was billed as free time – but who wants free time on a riding holiday? Not the guests, that's for sure, but it must have been for the benefit of the two polar opposites in charge. With the afternoon stretching ahead of us, the streetwise girls who were stationed in the bunga... sodding *bunkhouse*, decided we'd all hitchhike to the closest town/village. So we did, picked up by some young, over-excited and dodgy-looking geezers in a van, into which we all bundled. We then mooched around the village, which resembled a ghost town, for a bit (it was early closing day, remember when that was the norm?) and it was hardly the great metropolis anyway, before hitching back to the ranch. What were we thinking? What was the management (I use the term loosely) thinking? Nobody asked us where we might be going. Nobody enquired where we'd been. Nobody even missed us. Duty of care? Pah! It was a concept yet to be conceived. Quite honestly, twenty quid seems expensive now, considering the effort put in.

On the Tuesday, I received a letter from my mother, telling me things that were going on at home and how much she and my father were missing me. I got one every day until I left on the Saturday (I probably managed to send her a solitary postcard which arrived after I got home). One of the streetwise girls got hold of them and so, of course, I was ridiculed as a being a mummy's girl. I wasn't impressed at the time, but now I think how lovely it was of my mum to have bothered to write every day. She obviously missed me, and I think it speaks volumes about how parents worry and think about their offspring, when their offspring have no bloody idea, and are off being led into the clutches of van drivers by older girls.

So what did I learn from my western riding holiday? I learned to be punctual because to arrive anywhere late means losing out to the streetwise early birds and sleeping in a caravan. I learned that hitchhiking probably isn't the best idea streetwise girls might have, but at least it gets you out. I learned that it is compulsory to be dumped into a water trough for a laugh, and that tying someone up to a tree and branding them with cold, wet, ash is considered hysterical – providing it isn't you being branded. I learned not to believe everything I read in glossy brochures and that *riding holiday* can sometimes be code for getting someone else to clear up your horses' mess, and eat food you wouldn't serve to the cat. In short, I learned that you don't always get what you pay for. I don't think I learned much about riding, come to think of it, but it was still pretty amazing to be around horses all day, every day.

And I still remember some of them: small, tubby, grey Baby, glamorous and unimaginatively named Pally the palomino (not ridden by the guests, obviously), dappled grey Feather and dark brown Comanche. It wasn't the best riding holiday in the world, but I had a whale of a time and it remains fresh in my mind, as my account testifies.

Four years after my western vacation I went on another riding holiday in the New Forest. I can't remember how much it cost (considerably more than twenty quid, anyway) but it was at a smartly run establishment with qualified and caring staff and offering well organised lessons, treasure hunts, quizzes, rosettes for various tasks and a gymkhana, as all good riding holidays should. This time I went with my friend Jill, a fellow rider at the riding school, and I know we had a great time, were fed well and learned a lot. And that's all I can remember. I can't recall any details of the people, of the events – or even the horses, which is the oddest thing of all.

Can I remember everything about the bad riding holiday because it was bad, or because it was the first one I had been on? Did the fact that we all went feral add to the memory? Why was the homogenised, safe – yet brilliant – riding holiday I experienced later erased from my memory?

I don't know what this says about me, or about experiences in general. I only know that it's true.

Learning to be useful

JUST RIDING WAS NEVER enough. I longed to be a helper at the riding school at the top of the hill. I could see that other girls, older, more experienced, were running here and there, being ordered about by Rose, leading horses out for clients, mucking out and learning more and more. I wanted to be like that.

Rose was the riding school's manageress, in total and complete charge of *everything*. Rose first rode there in 1944, light relief from her work in an ammunition factory. She joined the school full-time when the war ended (it was that, she would tell us, or run away to the circus). After her employer died in the early 1960s, Rose took over the total running of the school for his widow and family, moving into the grooms' quarters, the door to which opened out onto the cobbled yard like some magical portal to another world. It was during that decade that riding became popular with the masses living on the housing estates nudging the Green Belt, and demand saw the school grow from one which offered the occasional hack, to a fully fledged riding school with hacks, lessons and livery services.

Rose was of the old school, a tough woman in a tough job, ruling with the absolute power of a dictator. There was no democracy at the riding school at the top of the hill – you did as Rose told you or you left. When I got to know her better, I would learn of her hidden depths, of her wicked sense of humour and her desire to make riding fun and accessible to everyone, demonstrating a softer side to nervous riders, young and old. When I was twelve, having graduated from half-hour rides to the hour hacks, and then the lessons after school, I was the lowest of the low and needed to make an impression – I needed to learn all there was to learn. My ambition was to be one of the girls who helped at the yard, the girls to whom Rose shouted, 'Saddle up my horse, and don't take all day about it!'

So, like others about my own age, I began staying behind after my ride, lurking around in the hope that one of the staff, or the older girls who were looked upon as helpers, would hand me a horse or ask me to do something – anything! And this was allowed, this staying behind, this hanging around in order to increase your skills, to improve your knowledge. Slave labour, some might say, but they would have been wrong because until you were useful, you were a liability. It was more like free babysitting.

We were lucky that Rose encouraged us to stay and learn because for most riding schools today it is a liability too far, and once you have finished your lesson you must go, or join a stable management class where skills learned one week with one horse may be forgotten by the next, or prove more challenging with a different horse or pony. It is repetition that ensures that what you learn turns into an instinctive response, and the more horses you have at your disposal with which to learn, the more knowledge you acquire – and the more information goes in and stays in. We were gaining valuable experience.

There was a gradual turnover of helpers, the older, valued girls (for it was mostly girls) gradually replaced by new apprentices, each group banding together in solidarity, culture and age. When you become adult, a couple of years here or there make no difference to your friendships but when you are a teenager it matters. I and my compatriots (there were no fewer than sixteen helpers-in-waiting in our age and inexperience bracket) had little in common with the existing group of older, more useful girls who smoked in secret, wore fashionable clothes and their hair long, and who had boyfriends as well as ponies of their own. They rode out together, or took their ponies to the outdoor school and set up a few jumps, their transistor radios belting out Led Zeppelin and Carole King as they sat casually in their saddles, flicking back their hair, able to do as they pleased. It was my riding holiday all over again – they were the cool kids on the yard, valued by Rose for their ability to help. We were shy, inept and pathetically eager.

But being pathetically eager paid off, the cool helpers handing you a quiet horse to take to the trough before ordering you to lead it around the yard to keep it warm as they mucked out its stable in winter. You'd be shown how to put on a head collar to save them time, told how to lead the horse through the door, to mind its hips, to mind your feet (or if they didn't tell you, the horse took it upon himself to teach you anyway), and then sent off to empty the wheelbarrow, wobbling across the cobbles, making sure it didn't get away from you as you steered it down the slope towards the muck skip, praying you didn't turn it over – or if you did, that Rose wouldn't be about to witness it.

If you got to the yard before the first ride of the day, you'd be handed a brush and told to groom Jimmy or Mischief. Only for Rose, catching sight of the result as you led out Mischief, bursting with pride at your handiwork and ready to receive compliments, to shout across the yard, 'Who groomed this Mischief? Come on girls, it can't go out like this! Look, it's got all the dirt around its eyes from when it was a foal!' As Mischief was about twenty-seven at the time this was clearly an exaggeration (Rose's speciality), but you got the gist, cringed with embarrassment, and vowed to do better next time.

As I spent more and more time at the riding school at the top of the hill – sometimes going on hacks, other times having lessons in the school – helping out and trying to get noticed for all the right reasons rather than drawing attention to my ineptitude, instead of feeling more intertwined with horses and horsy people, it sometimes felt that the gap was widening. The girls who had ponies were in a completely different league to me, oblivious to the suffering of the poor and pony-less around them. Proximity to ponies made not having one even worse because now I was riding the real thing, my imaginary horses, in my imaginary stables, were impossible to conjure up for an imaginary ride. My fantasies now took the form of one of the pony-owners lending me their pony for lessons, sharing with the no-hoper that was me. This never happened. The older girls seemed instead to look down from an even greater height – they didn't mean to be unkind, they just couldn't put themselves in my position, and why should they? Once they had a pony, any memories of life before being a pony owner faded, and they had their own, pony-owning pals with whom they mingled and rode.

There was always the feeling of being on the periphery of something special yet just out of reach. Of not quite belonging, of longing to be included in some magical club, membership of which had yet to be granted. I was an outsider when I longed to be within the hallowed circle. The fact that there were horses everywhere I looked in the fields surrounding the riding school at the top of the hill made it worse. It seemed there were literally dozens of horses just doing nothing all day, when they could have been fulfilling my dreams. There wasn't a field without horses grazing it, no area where horses did not frequent. I had to serve my apprenticeship in sight and sound of horses and ponies I could not touch, of horses and ponies banned to me. It was like getting a starving man to serve at a banquet, forbidden to taste that which he served.

My compatriots and I, all in the same boat and dreaming the same dreams, had to serve our apprenticeships. We had to stick at it until we were useful, until we knew enough to be of value. We didn't seem to appreciate how lucky we were in that we were poised, with knowledge there for the soaking-up, in a place where things could, and would, get better. Fast-tracking your way to knowledge and acceptance seemed to depend on having your own pony so we had no choice but to wait and bide our time, painful as it was. Things could only get better, even though we had pain to negotiate first.

As with all apprenticeships, you always started with the shit jobs and worked your way up, and at the riding school at the top of the hill there were two particularly shit jobs that had to be included on every potential helper's portfolio.

The first made use of your legs.

It is a universal fact, undocumented in any equestrian manual but nevertheless acknowledged by all people horsy, that a horse's ability to hear is directly proportional to the amount of grass in its field. The same horses who, late last summer were waiting for you by the field gate in the early morning, swishing their tails at the flies, having trawled, disappointed, through dusty and yellowing grass all night, throwing you a look which says, *Finally! About time! What time do you call this?* will, at the beginning of spring, when the grass has turned lush and green, be barely spotted at the far end of the field at any time of the day or night, tails deliberately turned in your direction and demonstrating what is known in the industry as *cocking a deaf-un*.

Greeted at the weekend by all her horses at the wrong end of a ten-acre field, some still in bed and dozing, any ideas of a day's work firmly at the back of their minds, Rose would moan loudly before looking around at all her hovering helpers, selecting one which she thought looked speedy, and might be the least useful when it finally came to putting on head collars. Delighted to be singled out for a special task the newbie would eagerly step forward, trembling with excitement and anticipating their chance to shine. Pointing to the equine specks in the distance, Rose would describe the special task for which this expendable member had been selected.

'Ere, Girlie, hop about and be a bit useful. Run down the end of the field behind those horses and send them up this way – and don't take all day about it, we've a ride to get out in a couple of hours.'

And off would go the sacrificial helper in an anticlimactic run, disappointment seeping from every pore but still heading off down the hill as fast as they could, anxious to turn it around, to do a good job and be noticed. I know this because on more than one occasion the poor unfortunate was me.

By the time you were half-way down the field you were wheezing like a broken-winded cab horse, but you didn't dare stop – mainly because you could still hear Rose bellowing at you to hurry up. Running behind the horses you'd have to whoop and throw your arms about in an effort to get them up and on the move. If you were lucky, and looked scary enough, you might set them off at a canter. If they were too full of grass, or recognised a pathetic loser when they saw one, they might half-heartedly meander up the field, stopping now and again to snatch another few blades in the manner of the unimpressed, behaviour punctuated by Rose yelling at you to get a bloody move on, and reminding you that we didn't have all day. You were, in effect, a human sheepdog, dashing back and forth, tongue lolling, straining to hear Rose tell you 'that'll do'.

If you somehow managed to make it back to the gate before everyone else had forgotten you and gone up with the horses then Rose, realising that charity might be in order if oxygen wasn't to be administered in the very near future and explanations offered to a bereaved and furious parent, would instruct a couple of people to shove you, lifeless and pathetic, your lungs still heaving, onto the back of a horse, which would cart you up the hill to the yard like a casualty of war. There, instead of lying down in a darkened room for several hours, you'd be handed a dandy brush and instructed to groom Sunshine.

As we got wise to this, and more proficient, we'd take a head collar with us, hoping to snare a horse which might be lying down, negating the need to vault on. If you weren't very good at vaulting, and I never was, and if the other horses around you decided to gallop off up the field, your chosen mount might refuse to wait and go without you, pulling the rope out of your hand as herd instinct kicked in. This would earn you another stiff lecture from Rose for letting go and allowing the rope to endanger one of her horses. As your skills were honed and if you timed it right, you could clamber aboard before the horse got up and enjoy a canter up the field.

Not only did we gain a longer ride this way, but we were saved the possibility of collapse, not to mention a future heart or wind condition.

The second shit job – sorry, *initiative* – was designed to test your nerve.

Being the *gate person* involved working the field gate for those better (and braver) than you at fastening a head collar in haste (or even just throwing a lead rope around an equine neck) when it was time for the liveries to come in. As they all came in at the same time there was some – let's call it, for the sake of argument, *jostling* – as a horse higher up the pecking order might decide to plough through the others who had got to the gate first. This made the exercise more exciting and tested your nerve, as did slamming the gate on any horse un-collared but still determined to make it through. Gate people were always recognisable by the splattering of mud from flying hooves on their clothes. And hair. And face, coupled with a wide-eyed, traumatised expression, and fear of any sudden movements, or noises behind them.

Another important facet to this task was to *never complain*. It was as well to remember that it was never a good thing to show fear or disappointment when in the company of Rose. Rose held stoicism in high esteem, citing as an example the case of an ancient woman who had continued hunting despite a broken leg, her plaster cast worn as a badge of honour. That the same woman was famous for wearing a lavender-coloured bonnet whenever she followed hounds, and was obviously a couple of brushes short of a grooming kit, was greatly played down.

Once, during the winter, somebody (Rose describing her as someone who, despite being a bit limp, might possibly be useful as a gate person) got it so spectacularly wrong, it was a wonder they didn't get themselves killed. (Rose was always telling us it was a wonder we hadn't *got ourselves killed*, somehow pushing all responsibility for anything that had happened firmly onto our shoulders, not unlike when folk accuse women of getting themselves pregnant.)

We first suspected something might be amiss when, after negotiating the gate and securing the first few horses in their stables, the entire yard was suddenly awash with loose horses dashing here and there, diving for their stables unaided. After seeing them into all the right places we returned to give the gate keeper a piece of our minds, only to discover her gone. Except she wasn't; she was face-down under the gate over which all the horses, unimpressed by her pretence at authority and ignoring her feeble attempts to dissuade them, had galloped, taking the gate off its hinges as they followed through. Injury had been averted due to the abundance of liquid mud in the gateway into which the gate person had been squashed, in the manner of a doomed woolly mammoth into a swamp. Hauling her out was accompanied by a noise like a giant welly being sucked off a leg stuck in the mire – only much louder – and we checked her airway and slapped her on the back in admiration for not only staying alive, but conscious throughout the ordeal. Respect!

When we told Rose there had been an incident, she was alarmed. Which of her horses were hurt? When we explained she visibly relaxed, her only concern that the gate person hadn't made a fuss. Stoicism, you see. But she hadn't, and she lived, and – miraculously – she still rides to this day. One initiation test well and truly passed, proving forever the theory that what doesn't kill you makes you stronger (or possibly brings on amnesia).

Due to the teachings of Rose I can sum up my whole attitude to life in eight words, a mere twenty-four letters: *Get on with it. Don't make a fuss.* Not too shabby a mantra to live by.

And so we learned. We learned how to lead horses here and there, to ignore the terrifying eagerness of hungry horses as we hastily tipped short feeds into mangers instead of dropping the bucket and running for our lives. Lunchtime was a frantic ten-minute feeding frenzy with Rose ordering us to 'stand back and let the dog see the rabbit' as she dished out feeds into buckets, handing them to the waiting helpers and telling them to get a move on as the horses kicked their doors in a loud show of solidarity. The menu was limited: oats, oats, oats – with an occasional scattering of pony nuts or a sprinkling of bran, dampened down with half-a-scoop of soaked sugar beet. None of the bewildering array of feeds available now.

We learned from Rose as she tried, without success, to obey the instructions on feed sacks *to open pull string* that whoever invented such a useless method that *didn't* open sacks should have been sewn up in one. We learned how to groom all over, not just the easy bits that might not kick or bite, and to tack up without leaving the mane and forelock sticking up like a brush or the noseband wonky.

We learned to stack a wheelbarrow correctly, building up the four corners so that we could get more on, rather than heaping it all in like a pyramid so everything slid off onto the yard. This meant fewer trips to the muck heap, increasing productivity, and the handles were held low over the cobbles to minimise juddering and straw loss. We learned to sweep properly, instead of *using that broom like a pencil* as Rose berated us or *worrying the head off it* – and to return all the tools to their rightful place when we were done. Should there be any doubt as to who was doing the right thing Rose would shake her head and tell us, 'Well, *one* of us is mad, and *I* feel all right.'

We put on New Zealand rugs, and we took them off again, wet and muddy, when the horses came in, making ourselves wet and muddy in the process. We learned the skill of tightening girths without a horse catching us with angry teeth, altered clients' stirrup leathers, showed them how to hold the reins. We remembered to turn off the tap to the water trough before it flooded the yard (understatement was never one of Rose's strong points and any spilt water – maybe we'd used a split bucket in which to soak the sugar beet – was a *flood*; horses didn't tank off with their riders, they *disappeared over the horizon as though their tails were alight*; the weather was never cold, rather it was *like Siberia* – although, to be fair, when the wind blew in from the east, that part of Essex did get the fall-out of the icy blasts from exactly there), and we made sure Tiger, the outside dog, was shut in his kennel before the liveries came in from the field. If we didn't, Rose would return incensed from one of the two nearby livery yards she ran, demanding to know why she was the only person who could hear that dog barking, and why no-one had thrown a house brick at it (for the record bricks, house or otherwise, were never thrown at the dog).

Occasionally, we even cleaned tack.

I knew how to clean tack – I'd read all about it in the manuals. Turned out I was wrong. You *didn't* use tepid water, you *didn't* make sure the leather didn't get too wet. Instead, you dunked all the bridles into a bucket of steaming water into which a good measure of Fairy Liquid had been squeezed and left them to soak until the water turned dark grey and cold and you could scour off the grease. If the bits on the bridles weren't sewn on then the billets and buckles were so stiff you could happily waste a day trying to get them apart, with only broken nails and a loss of temper to show for it. So nothing did get taken apart, Rose being convinced we'd only put everything back together wrong anyway. And although the leather may not have been as soft and as supple as the manuals described, we did get the grease and sweat off, and it was a rather nice, burnt-treacle colour as a bonus.

The only bits we ever saw were snaffles, with the occasional Pelham and Kimblewick thrown in to mix it up a bit. We were dimly aware of double bridles, but they were considered quite exotic, and we were not to be trusted with such complicated metalwork.

The saddles did not receive the same extreme treatment as the bridles but were cleaned in the more conventional manner. There was quite a variety: leather lined, serge lined, linen lined – even a felt saddle for Mossy the Shetland.

Sunshine's saddle had a crupper, which needed careful fitting, and as Starlight's saddle boasted old-fashioned, closed stirrup bars, her stirrups were of the safety kind, with rubber bands on the outside. Knee and thigh rolls were conspicuous by their absence – no such luxuries had been invented – and there were hardly any full panelled saddles in evidence. Flat-seated half-panel saddles were the norm, with girths in a choice of leather or string. The seats of most of the saddles were highly polished from the rubbing of a thousand riders' bums, resisting saddle soap, not needing it anyway. It was quite a collection – and every saddle regularly got a new horse or pony every twenty years or so. Rose even had a side saddle hidden away in her hallway, which she would haul out every now and again so that we could have a go on an obliging, if bewildered, school horse.

When saddles and bridles appeared in black leather, instead of the more normal tan (everyone soaked their new tan leather in neatsfoot oil to darken it down, the resulting stain on your breeches considered preferable to subjecting your poor horse to wearing orange), Rose wasn't impressed. Black leather, she told us, was for harness horses, brown for riding. Later, when I worked at a show yard, I learned that the way to get the reddish leather in-hand bridles to shine was to use boot polish from the get-go. Once saddle soap had touched them, it was game over as far as a shine was concerned. Unless you're the Household Cavalry, boot polish is a total no-no for riding tack, of course.

What we never saw at the riding school at the top of the hill was a gadget of any kind, if you don't count grass reins. The mere mention of draw reins could have serious consequences, causing Rose to, what we might today call, *go off on one*. Gadgets were the very devil and, Rose told us fiercely, caused more problems than they might solve. She liked to see horses moving freely, unencumbered by restrictive tack – heck, her horses never even wore anything more complicated than a cavesson noseband, and some bridles were missing even those.

Rose's philosophy was that her horses should have the freedom to protest if their riders were below par, allowed to pull at the reins to give their riders a hint, lifting their heads in order to grass-up a rider's over-enthusiastic use of the hand. She deplored the use of over-harsh bits and the severe and tightly-fitted nosebands which now seem to be the norm. I'd dare to go so far as to suggest that putting a horse into an unnecessarily severe bit before lacing him into a tight noseband to prevent him from opening his mouth, or otherwise protesting against his rider's poor hands, might be considered today's bearing rein. Rose preferred to see her horses moving freely, rather than witness clumsy attempts to get them on the bit. She knew that over-zealous hands, or a novice rider obsessed with rein contact, can sour a horse, making him reluctant to go forward.

I quite like the naked look you get when a horse's bridle is missing its noseband – and the fact you can stroke your hand down along the whole length of the horse's face without interruption. The picture is further improved by a curb bit which keeps the cheekpieces in the right place, and horses so attired remind me of old paintings where nosebands were not so fashionable as they are now. It particularly suits a horse with a blaze as there is nothing to break up the white line. On the other hand, a noseband can do wonders for the look of a horse, but only if its width is suitable for the shape of the horse's head (rule of thumb: the coarser the head, the wider and flatter the noseband), and fitted so that it balances the face. Too high and the horse looks like he's all nose, too low and he looks too long in the face. Too narrow a noseband makes him look as though he's borrowed a bridle from his smaller, more petite, sister.

So the tack at the riding school at the top of the hill was plain and without frills. We may not have learned much about the different types of tack available – although there was nothing like the bewildering variety on offer nowadays, it was all fairly traditional – but I'm certain the horses appreciated its simplicity.

It took two or three years of watching, learning and doing for me to become less of a hindrance around the yard at the riding school at the top of the hill, and more of a help. My progress was not always steady: there were hiccups and setbacks like a board game, but gradually the ladders outweighed the snakes. The inaugural part of my apprenticeship was coming to an end.

From school to work

WHEN THE SCHOOL HOLIDAYS hit, there was no question of what I might do with my time. No whining that I was bored, no pestering to be entertained. Indeed, whenever my mother told me to keep a certain day free because we were visiting relatives, or they were visiting us (and it wouldn't hurt me, I was assured, to put on a skirt and look like a girl for once) I seethed with injustice. A day spent away from the riding school was, in my book, a day wasted.

School – real school, attended from nine-to-four, Monday-to-Friday – was a huge, purpose-built comprehensive school (an oxymoron if ever there was one) which took an entire term for pupils to familiarise themselves with its layout: two halls, two gyms, a swimming pool and PE block, science block, domestic science and home economics block, two food halls, sixth form block – it went on and on like a rambling Edwardian pile, except this 1960s-built monstrosity was made from breeze block, glass and panels of vibrant blue. Writing about it now it sounds okay, but CSEs, where pupils were graded instead of passing or failing, gave some teachers a get-out-of-jail card so rather than making an effort to pull everyone up to pass O levels, the bar sank lower and lower, and pupils considered borderline were offered dual entry into both exams. It was the beginning of the 'nobody loses' culture, the system designed to cater for all (in)abilities, and failing those who might have gone on to higher things if they'd only been encouraged, not to mention the disruptive pupils, let down by the lack of specialist attention they needed to excel – or even to just get by.

Thankfully, for me anyway, what the school lacked in its educational prowess, it made up for by its location. I could, from my sister's bedroom window, see the tallest classrooms towering above the houses behind ours, and on a summer's evening we might hear strains of the school orchestra practising 'The Skye Boat Song', which seemed to be the only non-hymn music teacher Mr H could play on the piano. But it wasn't its close proximity to our house that appealed, but rather the open countryside beyond it, and this provided a distraction from all the droning on and arguing in the classroom, the sarcasm, yawning, clock-watching, rubber band flicking, hair pulling, name calling, chalk and board rubber hurling (by the teachers), pleas for silence and threats of detention. To escape the mayhem, I would gaze out of the windows at horses grazing in the distance. Quite often, those turned out in the fields adjacent to the school would push their way through the fence and run around the vast school fields, all the pupils galloping after them during break like primitive cavemen intent on bringing one down and dragging it off to the domestic science block as a fresh ingredient for cookery classes, or perhaps to the science block for dissection.

One square field sloped down on three sides like a vast Hickstead Derby Bank to the exterior fences (not unlike the ones seen in old prisoner of war movies, minus – surprisingly – the lookout posts and lights). This provided the perfect hiding place from teachers' eyes for snogging, smoking and torture of fellow pupils, such as the *grass treatment*, where several large boys would pin down a smaller boy and stuff grass into all facial orifices. This would be administered for some minor indiscretion – perhaps having failed to produce a protection-racket payment of a fag, for example. If you tut-tut at such bullying then I must point out that, in our defence, the teachers led by example, sarcasm being their weapon of choice, my favourite being the question, asked prior to the Christmas holidays, *Nicholls, have you combed your hair in 1973?*

But every teacher had his or her speciality, such as Miss T who, clad in low-fronted, tight-fitting dresses, spent each lesson draped over the edge of a desk from whence she flirted with the boys. Some of the teachers seemed to be there in body, if not always in spirit, as with one maths teacher who, in the totally self-absorbed way that is often peculiar to those gifted in the numerical, spent most lessons cocooned in his own bewilderment, surplus to requirements. At the beginning of every lesson the poor man would enquire how we had got on with our homework. This provided an opportunity for a pupil to raise their hand and confess that yes, Sir, they had struggled with question one. Mr P would then cover the blackboard with question one's workings out, while we, behind him, hastily scribbled it all down in our books. The class would work its way through all the homework questions in the same manner, giving Mr P cause to remark, in our next lesson, how well we had done for a class who professed itself confused by the homework he had set. Impressive by its cunning it may have been, but hardly useful if you wished to actually learn something.

Our headmaster was a short man. If he had cause to speak to a pupil for some minor digression, and had difficulty hearing them he would, as he asked them to repeat themselves, bend lower and lower at each request so the pupil would be compelled to follow him as though they were tied together, until they would both be bent over like question marks examining the floor.

My favourite subject, not surprisingly, was English, and the best teacher was Mr Frencham, who took no prisoners and kept classes focused and on track. When asked by the careers adviser what I wanted to do when I left school I, in my naivety, thought she actually wanted to know so I had no hesitation in boldly declaring that I intended either to work with horses or be a writer – preferably both. I don't remember speaking in a foreign language (my German vocabulary was limited to listing breakfast items and *auf und ab gehen*, in case I should ever need to teach a German tourist to rise to the trot) but maybe I had a bit of a moment, which would explain why, instead of offering suggestions about how I might pursue said careers, several leaflets regarding working in a building society or a bank were shoved in my direction, the so-called advisor's job done, all responsibility behind her. Thinking back, I wonder whether she was on commission from the financial sector – she certainly had nothing to offer pupils outside her limited brief. Or maybe she thought I was taking the piss. Even then, in the early 1970s, it was expected that girls would work for only a few years before starting a family, so her title should perhaps have been taken with a pinch of salt.

I could, if I were in the right classroom four storeys up, just make out the tiny shapes of horses on the 2.30pm hacks from the riding school at the top of the hill walking down the big hill, and trotting up again on their return journey. I'd sigh with envy and fail to register what the teacher had just asked me, *again*.

I did my best to shoe-horn horses into every project.

Instructed to take something into school about which to talk during my O Level English Oral exam I pulled off the big one: Heather kindly lent me her pony Misty, and Jill (my second holiday companion who attended a different school) accompanied us on a lovely chestnut Arab mare called Tina that she regularly rode. I couldn't ask anyone who went to my school as, inexplicably, truancy – when eventually noticed – was actually frowned upon. Out on the playing field I told my classmates about horses, using

Misty as my model, answering their questions. Once concluded, Misty's bucking display (you only had to put your hand behind the saddle for Misty to go bronco on you) was appreciated more than anything I had said.

I had done it: I had actually managed to take a horse to school, a snub to all those teachers who had written all my school reports on the same, unoriginal theme proclaiming, *Janet would do well to realise there are more important things in life than horses.*

My comprehensive school enjoyed a shorter life span than my horsy career for it is no more – the classrooms, the gyms, the swimming pool all gone, a waste of facilities levelled, probably due to a change in government policy or local council budgets. No evidence of it now exists, a few sorry certificates the only proof that I had ever attended – those and my un-cherished memories.

By the time I was about fourteen I was a teacher, of sorts, myself. As we got more proficient under Rose we'd be tasked with taking the half-hours. I had come full-circle, accompanying new riders on their first exciting venture into the world of riding. I was a riding teacher! I took this very seriously. Some of my fellow helpers looked upon the half-hours as a total bore-chore, heading for the safety of the barn or noiselessly backing into a stable whenever they spied a likely rider approaching the yard (the half-hours went out at any time of the day, as and when they turned up: there was no set time) or, if they hadn't been quick enough on the uptake and had got caught, they mooched along, not bothering too much with the rider – but I couldn't do that. I remembered the thrill of my early lessons and, totally empathising with the riders' eagerness to learn, I would do my best. And I found there was quite a lot I could tell them, even as we walked up and down the back lane.

I would show them how to hold the reins correctly, getting them sitting tall and central, legs in the right position. I would explain about steering from side-to-side – impressing upon them never to forget that the pony's mouth was on the other end of the reins. I got them to halt without leaning backwards or forwards, then asked them to use their legs to get their pony to walk on again. Then trotting – 'hold on to the pommel, count the steps, *one-two*, *one-two*, now replace with *up-down*, *up-down*, keep the legs back, push the hips forward, you're getting it! Now sit down to walk'.

And so it went on, so that by the time we got back my pupils could, if they were of the with-it variety rather than the glassy-stare-non-communicative type, have mastered a number of skills. And moving in a straight line probably helped with the trotting, as going around corners is always a bit tricky to start with, until you get your balance.

The busy schedule on Saturdays and Sundays meant two extra day staff at the riding school would be needed to boost numbers. Four places, highly coveted and, once gained, rarely given up. Weekend staff not only received a whole pound for their trouble (I know!), but they were also guaranteed a free ride, maybe even two, taking lead reins at the back of a hack or, possibly, leading a small beginner ride. There were three full-time staff working at the riding school at the top of the hill, weekends included, as well as Sylvie, a BHSAI (British Horse Society Assistant Instructor) who worked Monday to Friday, and took charge whenever Rose wasn't there. Landing one of the highly-prized weekend slots was an opportunity for any up-and-coming helper – if she could cut it. You usually elbowed your way in gently.

If one of the weekend staff couldn't work for any reason, they needed to find a suitable replacement in order to cushion the blow when they broke it to Rose. Gradually, we all began to fill in on such occasions. I can remember floating on air the first time I officially worked. It seemed a huge step up. I was, at last, a member of the club from which I had been for so long excluded because Rose didn't just let anyone work. She had the final say and we were all vetted fairly closely. She had to be sure you fitted the bill and were able to work hard all day long.

You started at seven o'clock, had an hour-and-a-half for lunch and left about five in the evening after hours of hard work and pure enjoyment. Now there are laws preventing the employment of children under a certain age and over a certain number of hours. Quite honestly, although mucking out, grooming, tacking up, riding and teaching was physical work, it was a brilliant way to get us all used to a healthy work ethic, and it instilled self-discipline. If you can't work hard when you're a teenager, when can you?

I was fifteen when Rose agreed that I should work every Sunday. By then I knew I had made it.

I was useful.

I no longer felt as though I was on the outside.

I was in.

Levels of competence

JUST AS PONY CLUBBERS work through the grades to win coveted felt discs to display under their badges, demonstrating their knowledge and ability to all and everyone in the know, we who helped at the riding school on the hill had our own, unofficial and progressive, levels of competence.

Novice Level: Rose calls you by your name

Until you were well known by Rose, and because there were so many clients at the riding school at the top of the hill, she usually referred to riders by their mount's name. You might be Bubbles one week, Blossom the next. It made for some amusement as Rose distributed horses prior to lessons. Asking a client whether they were Kentucky-ing today batted no eyelids but the question,

'Are you Blossoming?' took on a different slant. It was no big deal, being referred to by your horse's name – while you were riding. But when you wanted to be a helper, Rose knowing you by name set you apart. It meant she had bothered to find out what you were called – all the better for summoning you, or yelling at you when you did something wrong. You were, in Rose's eyes, useful – which was praise indeed. Before that you'd be Girlie, Lucy or Gladys. Nobody wanted to be Girlie, Lucy or Gladys, and the length of time you stayed Girlie, Lucy or Gladys was directly proportional to your usefulness. Those who failed to pass this particular level tended to progress no further.

A pass is obtained only when the proprietor knows and calls the candidate by her christened name. Using generic names may require this module be re-taken at a later date. Or not.

Novice Level: Grooming Sunshine

Sunshine was a dark brown, virtually black (no, me neither), chunky, eleven-hand-nothing pony with a hogged mane – an old-fashioned sort who, in a previous life, would have looked a picture pulling a governess cart full of the local vicar's children. Word was that she used to be a circus pony and, should Rose be feeling particularly mellow on a summer's day she might be persuaded to stand in front of Sunshine, raise her arms in an animated fashion and shout *HUP*, to which instruction Sunshine would reward with a liberty-pony rear. It was considered prudent to demonstrate Sunshine's USP when no prospective riders were around to witness it.

In her new professional capacity Sunshine was a leading rein pony, only ridden without attachment by competent riders in few and exceptional circumstances. Her best friend was ex-show pony Starlight (same colour as Sunshine – nope, still no idea), who also spent most of her ridden life attached to a leader, pedestrian or equestrian, by means of her lower Pelham rein being lifted over her head, which saved hunting around for a leading rein. Starlight was not only identical to her friend as regards the colour of her coat, but also shared her opinion that going anywhere slowly was for a lower class of pony.

Would-be helpers volunteering their services might be told to groom Sunshine, who lived out and had no stable to call her own, so was usually tied up in the main yard, affording everyone a good view of the inevitable outcome. The newbie always approached confidently, dandy brush in hand, Sunshine's closed eyes and hanging lower lip luring them into a sense of security. The moment the brush made contact, however, Sunshine morphed from sleepy-and-safe to raving bonkers, flinging up her head and squealing like a stuck pig, the shock causing the would-be groomer to drop their dandy and flee. Sometimes, even before the brush touched her, Sunshine would put on a show for the pure hell of it and if Rose was about, the reaction she obtained didn't disappoint.

'Oh now Girlie, you're using that dandy like a paint brush!' she'd boom across the yard, so that everyone who hadn't quite noticed Sunshine's antics was now fully up-to-speed and able to jump up and down, stare and point. It was the worst kind of double whammy – ritual humiliation, and being called *Girlie*, but with no blame attached to the pony, of course.

'You're tickling her! Brush like you mean it…'

The newbie would have another, feeble attempt and Sunshine would squeal with greater zeal for her audience, no doubt remembering her days in the sawdust ring.

There was no real trick to grooming Sunshine, you just had to take no notice of her and brush firmly so as not to tickle: she only did it with the hesitant. But you didn't know that until you'd been made a fool of.

A pass is achieved only when the candidate completes the task with little to no reaction from the pony.

Intermediate Level: Taking Misty for a drink at the trough
In the 1970s, the watering system at the riding school comprised two troughs – one in the main yard, another on the lower yard, with horses being led out of their stables for a drink, and quenching their thirst between hacks. Dappled grey Misty, as you now know, belonged to Heather. About 14.2hh he was, like his owner, a bit of a laid-back and quirky character. Whenever he did anything naughty Heather would dissolve into giggles: behaviour which, everyone knows, does nothing to improve a pony's manners – not that it bothered Heather. Her idea of schooling took the form of placing her hand behind her saddle to get Misty to buck, impressive in

its own way – especially when taking an English exam. But that wasn't the party piece for which Misty was most famous.

Helping out in the winter meant leading horses out to the troughs for a drink, and then walking them around the yard while the staff mucked out their stables. Except that Misty had his own agenda and if you didn't pay attention, or you were incompetent (and that meant whoever gave you Misty to lead was just as guilty) Misty would, as you turned the corner from his stable towards the lower trough, set his neck and tank off to the field. If you didn't let go of the rope in terror he had no compunction about towing you along with him until the closed gate (how you prayed the gate would be closed or that was another happy hour wasted being yelled at as you tried to catch him again) impeded his progress.

The trick was to hold him tightly under the chin, dig your elbow into his neck so he couldn't set it against you and, keeping up by his head, turn Misty rapidly into the trough, threading his lead rope through the rope on the ring and tying it before he could get a hold and do his party trick. Getting him back to his stable was just as tricky. Leading Misty to the trough, without a detour to the field, earned you a big tick on your CV.

A candidate shall be awarded a pass upon showing competence and full control of the horse. Anyone below the standard shall be told to dry their eyes and pull themselves together.

Intermediate Level: Catching Sheri

Most of the riding school ponies were a doddle to catch but Sheri was the exception. If you didn't exude confidence on your approach, he would alternate between refusing to be caught, and pulling a face and lunging at you, teeth bared, determined to do you in – and he wasn't bluffing. You had to have some experience before you could tackle him, and once you could he was fine. It was the Sunshine scenario, only scarier. Sunshine would never have hurt you, but Sheri wasn't so kind. The first time you managed to halter him you hoped everyone was in the yard to see you lead him in, and to acknowledge that you had moved up the ranks. It was a solid pass.

One Sunday, after catching all the ponies, we realised that Sheri was missing. An exhaustive hunt ensued. Girlies, Lucys and Gladyses were dispatched to scour the empty field but they returned, heads shaking, head collars trailing. A search of each and every stable took place before finally, Sheri was discovered at the back of the livery Sabre's stable (which was, thankfully, long and narrow). Trouble was, Russian Thoroughbred Sabre was also in residence. While Sheri stared determinedly at the back wall, Sabre kept his eyes firmly on the yard, each pretending the other wasn't there. Sheri was removed and no more was said about it, demonstrating the 'least said, soonest mended' school of stable management.

Only candidates showing confidence and competence in catching and haltering the pony shall achieve a pass. Any squeaking by the candidate shall result in

*a downgrade, and possibly first aid treatment. For
first aid treatment, see additional syllabus.*

Advanced Level: Taking two lead reins
at the back of the ride

This wasn't an undertaking for the faint-hearted. This was
taking multi-tasking to a new level. Not only might you
be on a horse who considered its place was at the head
of the ride and so jogged the whole way around; not only
did you have a beginner rider on a lead rein on either side
that you had to keep happy as well as teach something,
but Rose expected you to keep everyone else on the ride
going forward, ensuring the riders didn't allow the horses
to eat grass. That she was on Cochise at the front who
not only marched along twice as fast as any of the other
horses, but whose trot had been clocked at 25mph (it was
official, she'd had someone drive their car alongside the
dirt path to record it), didn't help. And also, Rose would be
pushing on and chatting to Carol on Sabre, which meant
that there was no way on God's earth everyone would keep
up without some serious hurrying up.

Throw in the odd rider gazing over at you wide-eyed
as their horse jogged, ate, or ignored them, pleading with
you to help them when you were already effectively riding
three horses; keeping an eye on Punch to make sure he
didn't sit down and roll in any puddles and break his saddle
tree (far more important than keeping the client safe), and
you had yourself a bit of an interesting, multi-tasking time.
You just hoped in these scenarios that your leading reins
were the forward-going Sunshine and Starlight, making a

pass somewhat easier – only Rose usually nabbed them, and you'd most likely be left with Sheri and Smokey, neither famed for their enthusiasm.

Examiners shall take into consideration the complexity of this task and assess accordingly.

Advanced Level: Riding the Chestnut

Every riding school has a Chestnut, the horse only the staff ride. Ours was about 15.2hh, an old-fashioned Thoroughbred, ancient, gentle, well-mannered and well-schooled. The first challenge was actually getting on as you had to be legged up onto the saddle with care because the Chestnut was cold-backed. Even then her knees would buckle and there'd be a moment when you felt that if you didn't sit lightly, you might still both end up on the floor. When you were up and running you still had to be able to sit quietly. The Chestnut wore a Pelham, and as you invariably had a lead rein on either side when you rode her you ended up with a fistful of reins to organise, much like a polo groom.

Riding the Chestnut often came with the responsibility for leading the canters. You'd steer through the ride and hand your lead reins to Rose, who often had two herself (it sounds easy when I write it, but you can imagine the logistics of it all, it was a bit like French knitting with added ponies), and she'd wait at the edge of a field with the walk-and-trot riders while you set off with the ones who wanted to canter, setting a pace strong enough to ensure the horses following you didn't just trot faster because the

Chestnut, after all, could do a wonderful hack-canter at walking pace. Upon your return you had to manoeuvre yourself and the Chestnut to collect your lead reins again, which gave you the incentive to learn lateral aids and rein back.

Until you were asked to ride the Chestnut you couldn't truly call yourself a staff member. It was one of the more difficult passes to achieve.

Examiners may ask candidates to explain the reasons for their approach to this task. Leading rein riders shall be assessed before and after rides to ensure some improvement is shown.

Advanced Level: Smokey on a leading rein
Smokey, all eleven hands nothing with an attitude problem, was no volunteer, and on a hack he'd make you work every step of the way. Generous to a fault – the fault being that he wasn't. He'd lag behind, he'd try to eat, he'd pull back and then, as soon as you took your eye off the ball, he'd perform the speciality for which he became famous: *stopping dead and going into reverse.*

If you were lucky, the lead rein would be stripped out of your burning hand. If you weren't you had a choice between dislocation – as Smokey did his best to rip your arm out of its socket – or being pulled over the back of your horse.

On one such occasion, at the back of a large ride, half-a-mile from home, Smokey slammed on the anchors and dug in his heels. Managing to stop the Chestnut my eye-narrowing, lip-pursing, teeth-grinding smugness was short lived as I turned around to find Smokey's bridle dangling from my hand. Its owner's naked head was already away and passing all the other horses as it led the rest of Smokey towards home at a spanking trot never before witnessed when I had him in my grasp. The force of his braking system had stripped the bridle clean off his head. I watched with a growing sense of dread as his novice rider, clinging grimly to Smokey's saddle and too terrified to utter a sound, overtook Rose and continued through the trees, his mount determined to be first home.

Rose halted the whole ride and turned menacingly in the saddle. Twenty-two pairs of eyes, glinting with Schadenfreude, swung my way as Rose drew breath.

'Ohhhhh Janet', cried my employer, accusingly and loud enough for anyone within ten miles to hear, 'WHY did you do that?'

Like I'd done it on purpose.

It is advised that examiners use their initiative and judgement in passing candidates in this very advanced task. There is no single right way of tackling this module, but losing the pupil shall be deemed a fail.

Horsepower

I CAN NEVER UNDERSTAND how some people get bored on a car journey. For me, there is always so much to see from a car window and, if you are lucky enough to be travelling through the countryside, then the chances are there will be horses to see.

This has always been so. As a child, when family finances finally ran to getting a car, I would scour the view from the back seat, horse spotting. The fact that our first car was an ancient blue van with side indicators that flicked out like pinball flippers, and my view was restricted to the future and the past through front and rear windows, didn't dampen my enthusiasm. Every journey was an adventure, an adventure in which horses would feature. What horses would I see today?

On the well-travelled roads between our house and my grandparents' caravan on the Essex coast where they spent their summers, I knew every field where horses grazed: the palomino that lived just the other side of the flyover, the field where mares and foals played – even the lane where, according to my *Pony* magazines, a posh riding school offered riding lessons, livery and holidays. I noted them all and eagerly looked out for old friends. I could have drawn my own, horse-spotting map of the whole journey.

There is something about a field that betrays its occupants for a field which houses horses has a very different look to those in which sheep or cattle reside. If you know horses, you know this. And if you know this, you know where to look to get your fix so you won't miss paddocks with mares and foals, or fields where horses munch and roll, sleek and shiny in their summer coats, or swathed in rugs to keep them warm and dry during the winter. On well-travelled routes you look forward to catching up with old friends, noticing new additions, missing those horses which may today, at that moment, be in the stable yard or out riding, if they haven't moved on to pastures new. You will see well-maintained areas, topped and dung-free, the horses grazing well-tended grass. But there will also be the poorly attended with the sagging wire fences, neglected nettles, the piles of dung, horses picking at grass around oil barrels and peeling poles over which they'll be asked to jump when their owners tack up and ride.

Even now, as I travel along our highways I may spot riders crossing one of the many bridges over the roads, silhouetted like centaurs as I drive towards the setting sun. Where are these riders going? Are they setting out or returning from their ride? What stories can they tell? And what of the riders galloping in the fields beside me as I snatch a glimpse into their world? Are they in control? Was galloping their idea or that of their mounts? If I am a passenger in the vehicle, I can allow my eyes to linger, my neck to turn watching until trees, a hill or houses restrict my view. If I am driving, I need to contain my interest, my eyes flicking quickly from the horse back to the road ahead. I can't allow my concentration to waver even at the sight of the most noble of beasts. It is difficult, but it must be done.

A while ago, a company hit the headlines by offering coach trips around the M25. The reaction of the press was one of scorn: who would want to pay to travel a road known as one huge car park, as though on a holiday excursion? Well, actually, I might. I often have cause to drive along the M25 and, providing the traffic is moving, I enjoy it. For the most part it cuts through fields, through gentle countryside, ever changing with the seasons, never the same journey twice. There are horses – I know where to look. I recognise individuals grazing with their friends, I notice newcomers. I look out for the unusual. When horses are scarce, I settle for cows, piebald players in their own production, grazing one day, lying down and chewing cud the next, kicking up their heels or walking to or from milking in a single line, one behind the other like bovine pilgrims.

And the scenery, sped past in a mere segment of the frantic traffic snake hurrying to get from A to B, is in a constant state of flux, providing a backdrop to the journey, morphing throughout the seasons if anyone cares to notice: the dark chocolate brown of ploughed fields in winter, trees like skeletal sentinels standing alone, branches like praying hands reaching for the sky. Then the green shoots and white blossoms of spring, stretching tentatively around the thawing landscape with unstoppable determination as the days lengthen. Gradually, shy and reluctant, the verdant fields are transformed by the alchemistic golden crops in summer. The trees swell with leaves which hide their branches, no longer able to stand firm against the warm breeze, swaying like dancers. And suddenly, it is autumn, with its final burst of colour like a desperate finale, the leaves turning crisp and scattering like confetti across the carriageway as the countryside closes down for its winter sleep. The light is ever changing, and so too is the weather as I speed through the counties. Each journey is unique, each journey an adventure.

I never tire of traversing the M25 – and alternating direction breathes new life into the views. The vista opens up before me on the northern side, far-reaching views encouraging me to catch my breath, to look beyond the patchwork that is the earth and upward to the sky. Hurtling along the southern side the Kentish ridge runs parallel in the distance, pointing pilgrims to the holy city of Canterbury.

Even crossing the Queen Elizabeth II Bridge at Dartford affords amazing views of the Thames Estuary – snaking inwards towards the capital on one side, the river narrowing as it flows past the high and ever increasing numbers of towers and skyscrapers in London, shrouded in mists, standing dark against the setting sun or twinkling with lights after dark. On the opposite side of the bridge the river opens and expands as it leads the eye towards the sea, past Tilbury Fort where our first Queen Elizabeth rallied her troops with inspirational words to send the Spanish Armada packing. Even here there are horses, unfortunate ponies on occasional grazing, installed under the maze of flyovers as I speed south, water from downpours rising, shrinking the land around them. A call to the equine charities ensures someone cares enough to prevent them from drowning.

On the Essex side, I emerge from the Dartford Tunnel and continue through deep cuttings formed by the road's construction to the openness of the Roding Valley. Here, before the motorway forged its way through the fields and cut the valley in half, I rode with my friends with only the sound of birdsong and the drone of light aircraft from the nearby airfield interrupting the soft noises of hoof beats on grass, the chink of a bit, the creak of leather. And here, more than anywhere around this roaring, tireless, angry road, horses graze as they have done for centuries.

No, there is no boredom to be had on any car journey. Not if you make it your hobby to seek and to see. Not while there are horses to find.

Being Essex born and bred I got used to the usual jokes. For anyone bothering to explore further into the county beyond the suburbs there are plenty of surprises in store and rich history to discover. There awaits miles of rolling countryside and farms with ever changing fields of crops, giving each season a unique quality missing from less arable counties. The powers that be appear to regard Essex as somehow expendable, of the opinion that building on its historic soil doesn't matter, that there is nothing to spoil. But they are wrong. This county boasts, amongst other treasures, the oldest wooden church in the world, ancient royal woodlands, the highest Tudor tower, the oldest – and probably the smallest – chapel, the country's first recorded town and Roman Capital, as well as providing essential habitats for wildlife and the longest coastline of any English county. Too many old and beautiful houses have been bulldozed to make way for inferior replacements. Too much has been lost already. That matters little to the planners. It's only Essex after all.

Calling to arrange a visit to a Pony Club in Berkshire when I worked at *Pony* magazine, the District Commissioner enquired, in the clipped tones of one born to a large country house, an Aga or two and huge tracts of land either inherited or married into, from whence I would be coming.

'Essex,' I told her, projecting my voice from further back than usual in a pathetic and shameful attempt at mirroring.

'Oh, you poor thing,' came the hasty reply, with great and sincere sympathy.

'Um, it's not that bad,' I replied, somewhat taken aback by her candidness.

'Oh no,' she assured me in honeyed tones, back-peddling like an out-of-balance unicyclist, 'Of course I mean you'll have to traverse the M25…'

That's thinking on your feet for you.

When I first moved to the scenic and more expensive county of Surrey to work for *Pony* everyone assumed (quite rudely, I thought) that I had been desperate to escape the county of my birth.

'Oh,' they would say ever-so smugly, whenever I told them where I had come from, 'you must *love* it *here*.'

They had no idea of the picturesque village which housed the riding school at the top of the hill. No knowledge of the history, the open country, the long and glorious sunsets. Whenever I arranged shoots with equestrian photographers at yards near to the riding school on the hill, where generous riders on their ponies had volunteered to be included within the magazine's pages the photographers – used to taking images all over the country, at the top yards in the land – were dumbfounded by the countryside and the far-reaching views. We came away with the most amazing images of riders against acres of golden crops, green fields and sunflowers, of girls on their ponies skirting the sides of huge areas of yellow stubble, farmland and blue skies filling the frame, nothing in the distance but more fields, more rolling hills, more ripening crops. Show the pictures to anyone and ask them to tell you where they had been taken and Essex would be their last guess. Not for nothing did royalty build their palaces in this county, not by accident did the landed gentry decide that this was a great spot to erect the family pile.

I've nothing against Surrey, I live there now and appreciate its hills and trees, but how you view an area is influenced by where you grow up, the familiar, the imprinting of the contours and beauty of countryside which has been your first home and calls to you to return, no matter to where you may travel. The area where I first moved to in my new county was one of high hills and valleys, of forests and sand tracks. There were no crops to mark the seasons, the land was unbothered by plough, without harvest, just the falling of the leaves to confirm that time wasn't standing still. My inner clock, used to the constant changes outside, of planting and harvesting, of brown, green then golden fields went haywire – months passed and little around me seemed to alter. Time stood still. Even in summer, when the days should have lingered, reluctant to end, once the sun went down behind a hill that was your lot – day over. I felt robbed, short changed. I was used to big skies, to enjoying the warmth and the glow of the sun stretching out the evening before it dipped, crimson and dazzling, behind the horizon. Its summer warmth extended the day, streaks of blazing red and orange held back the dusk until it could stay no longer, slipping away at last to someone else's dawn, surrendering to the darkness, to the bats flying and whistling around the barns as they took over the night.

Even now, as I cross under the Thames in the Dartford Tunnel and drive on to the county of my birth I feel myself taking a deep breath and exhaling with joy. It is as though I can breathe again as the horizon stretches out around me in all directions, the sky seeming to lift higher as I head towards familiar country. At the riding school at the top of the hill we grew blasé about the expanse of fields and the big sky with its cotton wool clouds. It was as though we were on top of the world, where nothing escaped our gaze. Home isn't just where the heart lives, it is where the soul is based, tugging you back when you stray, calling you to return. Home is the familiar, the safe, the keeper of memories.

Essex deserves more than the judgement it gets from the uninitiated. It deserves a look through fresh eyes, from folk open to its charms, its acres of arable land, its gentle contours and its history. It is the county of my birth, and not only do I love it, but you may have concluded correctly that I am proud of it, too.

Sartorial elegance

I BOUGHT SOME RIDING boots recently: long, elegant, leather, fully waterproof and comfortably lined with the addition of – and this really got me – zips all the way up the back. If you think there is nothing remarkable about that you are probably too young to remember struggling with boot pulls, forcing your leg into a boot which, because it had to accommodate your foot traversing the uppers on its way to its final resting place on the inner sole (and back out again on the return journey), was rather bulkier than the amazing, skin-tight, ankle-skimming wonder boots I now own. Boots, like everything else we now wear when riding, have come a long way.

Long leather riding boots were the first purchase made with my full-time wages from the riding school at the top of the hill, for that is where I worked when I first left school in the 1970s, determined to make horses my life. How I had coveted a pair after years of sweating and freezing in the long rubber kind – and they didn't disappoint. Not only did I look the part, I sounded it as the leather soles made a satisfying *clunk, clunk* on the cobbles whenever I was off a horse. This meant that not only did I know I was wearing leather boots, but everyone else did, too. A steal at five weeks wages (fifty quid, no less).

Everyone knows that what you wear says a lot about you. Nowadays you can spot the dressage devotee, the showing rider, the show jumper and eventer – all by what they wear and, perhaps more importantly, how they wear it. Bling for the dressage riders, Diamanté twinkling on their browbands and stirrups; short, bum-freezer jackets sported by female show jumpers and some show riders; less bling more utility for the eventers, out in all weathers.

I don't get the bling. Rose would have hated it and so do I, which no doubt betrays my age. That, and painting ponies like rainbows, pink and purple streaked manes, heart transfers, bloody unicorn horns attached to browbands for goodness sake. I can't help feeling it turns ponies into playthings. Where's the dignity? It isn't, to use an old-fashioned word beloved by Rose, very *workmanlike*.

Talking of colours, when I first started to acquire riding clothes in the early 1970s it was a case of you having any colour you wanted as long as it was brown, navy blue or green. It was accepted that you got dirty around horses, and washing machines weren't the whizzy models we have now – ours didn't even have an integrated spin dryer – and tumble driers were the stuff of legend. Funny then that breeches and jodhpurs came in shades of fawn, putty and biscuit, begging to be sneezed on by your mount, or rubbed by a green-slimed mouth. We were just emerging from the elephant-ear, Bedford cord breeches era, as stretch fabric took the horse world by storm – and *washable* stretch fabric at that! Before then you'd be stuck wearing jodhpurs that gripped your legs from your ankles up to the knees, before expanding into yards of billowy cord between your knees and waist to accommodate saddle-straddling, as though someone had pumped you up like a balloon. Nobody looked like Jill in a Caney illustration, nobody possessed the sartorial elegance seen on the military in World War II films, nothing came close to the dash the be-jodhpured Honor Blackman cut in *Goldfinger*.

Stretch fabric promised no more baggy bottoms, no more fearing that you might get caught in a headwind as you dismounted, and hurled across the yard like a galleon in full sail. Suddenly, riders could wear something almost figure-hugging – there was no hiding place for the larger woman who longed for the nostalgic days of the roomy breeches, when bulky lower regions were hidden by swathes of stout fabric that needed a strong thigh to bend them into shape.

Harry Hall, Caldene and Saddle Master were all big brands, and advertisements showed a whole family riding (or standing next to) their mounts. Man, woman and child were all kitted out like they were off to the local meet in tweed jackets and ties, a bowler hat (he), velvet caps (she and junior – not a chin strap in sight), all immaculate, shiny and glamorous, posing with their similarly immaculate mounts in a cobbled yard complete with clock tower and weathervane. Blurb included the words *stretch* and *washable*. Breeches boasted zipped side pockets, a clean front (whatever that meant, seems like a given to me – who would want a dirty one?), comfortable, elasticated seams and even touch-and-go Velcro. Talk about stir it up – it was little less than a revolution. Riding was suddenly glamorous!

Mrs P was the most elegant woman I have ever seen on a horse. She and her husband kept their hunters at the riding school at the top of the hill, and they even had a pony for their young son, proof that the adverts were no lie, these people really did exist. Mrs P was always exquisitely turned out in the latest equine fashion and was the first (and only, at least in our circle) to buy a radically designed hacking jacket by one of the top brands, boasting a belted waist and two pleats at the back (I told you it was radical). She, of course, modelled it to perfection but no doubt had I tried it I would have resembled something in which the fodder was delivered. It takes not only good bone structure and a slim figure to carry off such a design, it also takes style, something Mrs P had in spades. She was the only person I had ever seen clean tack in yellow rubber gloves. Style yes, but Mrs P was fully prepared to put in the effort – she would no more have dunked her bridle into a bucketful of hot water than have been seen wearing ill-fitting breeches.

When suede knee-strappings on breeches became all the rage I saved up for a pair, wore them twice and threw them into the washing machine without a second thought.

What came out was a pair of breeches with the suede shrunken to half its size, the cloth puckered up around it as if diseased. Ruined. I might have wept – but only until I came up with plan B, snipping off the crisp, Pringle-like strappings, watching them snap into fragments as they hit the floor and replacing them with strappings of my own from off-cuts of something I can't recall.

For those of us without the budget for all these up-to-the-minute innovations of equine fashion there was – da-da-*daaaaaaa* – Jacatex! Full-page advertisements in *Pony* magazine showed an artist's impression of beautifully cut tweed and black jackets, close-fitting jodhpurs, hats and boots on a smiling girl with well-cut hair. *Style and quality at bargain prices!* screamed the headline and on close inspection the prices were, indeed, very reasonable. Everything on offer was, we were assured, *beautifully tailored, superbly cut, washable, drip-dry, superb value by any standard.* The velvet*een* covered riding hat even boasted a *tuck away chin strap for safe jumping.* Confidence to tackle any course restored by a length of black elastic, half-an-inch wide, which stretched like buggery after a month or two so had to be shortened by a knot which dug into your chin and left a mark. Not that I was ever going to stick the elastic where it was designed to go, I always tucked mine under my hair at the back of my head. I knew how I was supposed to look on a horse, the adverts, Mrs P and Jill books being my style guides.

And it was with this attitude that my mother and I rode the train to High Holborn, where Jacatex boasted a showroom. I can't help wondering whether the money we could have saved on the train fare might have made the difference between buying Jacatex and a more upmarket brand but it wasn't just about that, we simply didn't know where else we could go to buy riding clothes. To say availability was limited was a severe understatement and at that time the car with its paddle indicators was but a dream. I mean, we were hardly likely to turn up at Bernard Weatherill and demand I be measured and fitted for a non-existent Wembley debut (because that was where both the Royal International and the Horse of the Year Show were held then, earning them the title of the London Shows). The sole sports shop in our local town had come up trumps with my riding hat, but that was about its limit.

In a frenzy of over-excitement at being in a store filled to the rafters with riding wear we shopped, and I returned with my spoils: one pair of jodhpurs, one tweed jacket and a pair of the essential, yellow string gloves, *à la* Jill. I was kitted out to the nines and from now on I would ride in style.

Only… well, the jacket didn't seem to fit quite as I had imagined it would. My reflection in the mirror seemed a very far cry from the adverts in *Pony* magazine. Instead of giving me a waist in a Caney-illustration-sort-of-way, the sides seemed to drop from the armpits like a smock. I have a sneaking suspicion my mother may have been influenced by her usual thrift policy and allowed for growth when choosing the size, but even so the jacket didn't seem to have much of a shape.

But I wasn't the only one so attired. Jan's Jacatex jacket was black, intended for the show ring, showing off her long, straight, red hair very nicely. But because riding kit was so limited, we didn't have much to fall back on, so jodhpurs and show jackets were often worn on the yard and out on hacks – albeit without the crowning glory of a hat. Jan's jacket, not intended for such rigorous and regular wear but having been tailored (I use the term loosely) for occasional show ring use, seemed to get thinner and thinner as she got her money's worth from it, the black fading, the warp and weft threads emerging as the nap receded, white horse hairs clinging to it, turning it roan.

And what was with the string gloves thing? I only got them because Jill always seemed to have a pair handy. Honestly, have you ever worn a pair? They were tight, they didn't stretch and what with their open weave and lack of warm material, were freezing cold. Waste of time – and in no time they were rein-stained, forcing me to wash them, with my ignorance of household matters, on an ever-hotter wash so that not only did they still show the stains, the heat having fixed them, but their original colour grew fainter and fainter, turning a sort of dirty, off-white colour.

But then innovation stepped up! Husky decided to make quilted jackets in navy and green and everyone had to have one. Well-shaped, with a corduroy collar and welted cuffs they were very smart, inexpensive – but very thin. No lining, no padding, ideal for spring rides but totally inadequate for riding in the cold or rain. So you bulked yourself up with a few jumpers, stretching the jacket and losing your waist. But fear not, for if the skies darkened, or you had to exercise when it was wet, you could wear the essential (according to the adverts) Riding

Mac! Light fawn (again, a practical colour – not, probably the only colour the material came in), with straps attached to the lower end so you could lace your legs into it like some kind of human turnout rug.

A riding mac was one cumbersome, creaky, smelly, dirty item of clothing which nobody in their right mind would wear today. Fashioned from some kind of canvas it was like wearing a tent. Very practical, wearing a tent in the saddle. If your horse shied in a high wind there was a fifty-fifty chance you'd soar off in the other direction like a kite or, indeed, a tent. And yes, Mrs P had one. And no, it didn't seem to get all grubby like everyone else's. And yes, she looked just like they did in the adverts, the only riding mac that ever did. If any of the clothing companies had spotted her Mrs P would have been signed up and splashed across the equine press as the example all readers dreamed of emulating, a marketing manager's dream – or so you would think.

Much later, when working for *Pony* magazine I asked, in a meeting with a top clothing company, why I never saw advertisements for a particular down coat they made, which I thought was rather super. 'Oh no,' their marketing manager told me, inhaling sharply and shaking his head, 'the last time we advertised that particular coat, we sold out.' I still wonder whether I missed something, I mean, God forbid your adverts work and you sell stuff.

When it was cold, the *de rigueur* item of clothing for riders and instructors alike, on or off their horses, was a sheepskin coat *à la* Brian Clough. Without a high collar the wind gleefully whooshed down your neck, between the three football-shaped buttons and whistled up under its hem. I have no idea how I actually survived riding in winter during the early 1970s. By rights I – and all my friends – should have perished in the manner of poor Captain Oates. I lost count of the number of times I sat shivering in the saddle at the back of hacks, a lead rein either side of me, my fingers squeezed by my shrunken string gloves, a headscarf knotted at my chin like I was The Queen (totally the thing then, headscarves, honest to God I kid you not) glancing down every so often to check my feet hadn't dropped off, rising to the trot without stirrups just to get some feeling back into them and hoping my oat-fed, under-exercised mount would keep going in a straight line and stay horizontal, dreaming of the day when someone would invent thermal jodhpurs, thickly quilted clothing, gilets, wicking, Gore-Tex and clothes that might leave no part of the human body exposed to the elements.

While I dreamed, I wondered whether my nose was running or had dropped off, and I offered encouraging smiles to similarly frozen infants on either side of me. Sometimes, upon our return to the yard after a hack they'd be lifted out of the saddle, their bodies frozen in their in-the-saddle shape, thawing out inside the stables, waiting for the moment when their legs would once again meet, their parents booking them in for the same time next week as though instilling resilience and fortitude in their offspring was their duty. Or perhaps they were trying to kill them off. Riding is an outdoor sport – at least it was then, in fact it was an *extra* outdoor sport. But then we wised up a bit and trotted off to C&A to buy ski jackets.

Bliss! Such warmth! Such luxury! They could even be washed – until the lining fell apart and you had to get out the sewing box.

And then, more innovation – the horse world discovered colour. Show jackets which had previously been restricted to black or tweed were now available in brown, blue, grey or – oh the excitement – maroon! And, whoopee-dah, you could get velvet covered hats to match! Jodhpurs sprouted up in similar hues (all dark – no pink or patterned, as yet). What madness was this?

Jan's Jacatex jacket was paired with jodhpurs in a most fashionable shade of what could only be described as *butter*. I bought a maroon jacket and had a hat covered in the same material. Then I went completely barmy and dyed all my jodhpurs different colours (I mean each pair was a different colour, I didn't tie-dye them). The home-made strappings on one pair didn't take the dye, remaining grey while the rest of the material turned black. But they looked okay, as did my green ones and my grey ones. Happy days! Oh, and I eventually bought, second-hand because they weren't cheap, one of those elegant black Harry Hall jackets with the velvet collar and narrow and distinct piping up and down the back, complete with two buttons behind at the waistline. Boy, were they glam. Who did I think I was?

But as we all progressed into our teenage years, we didn't always want to wear riding clothes. If you weren't working for Rose, then jodhpurs were really not so cool. But Levi's were! Levi's – jeans you had to wear for the first time in a hot bath so that they'd shrink to fit you. The only problem was that Levi's in the 1970s were straight legged and this was the age of the flare – or bell-bottoms, as they were called then. So flares they became as we sliced up the outer seam from floor to knee, inserting a triangle of fabric (usually from some old curtains) to form the required swish as we walked. They just needed fraying to complete the look. No problem! We simply cut off the hems and tweezered out the horizontal threads from the raw edge so that the vertical threads formed a fringe. It works even now, I've tried it. Only then were your Levi's bang on-trend and up to being seen in public.

But bell-bottoms had their downside, which became apparent when it rained. They swept along the ground, sucking up the wet like a sponge until your entire lower legs were encased in heavy, flapping, soaking wet denim. We looked like Shire horses after a particularly wet ploughing match. But mainly we thought we looked pretty with-it, except when Rose wanted us to ride out, either to lead out a hack, or to take a lead rein or two.

'Have you got any jodhpurs with you?' she'd shout across the yard over the clients' heads. 'Only you don't 'arf look a bloody mess!' Proving that fashion, like beauty, is in the eye of the beholder.

So, with a free ride in the offing we'd scuttle off to the livery tack room to change into our jodhpurs and boots. Strangely, this seemed to satisfy Rose, who overlooked whatever our upper bodies were draped with, and the lack of riding hats. It was just the jodhpurs and boots she wanted, and so jodhpurs and boots she got. And we got a free ride. It was only fair. The rest of the time we rode out in our Levi's with a collection of upper-body wear more suited to the disco than the yard. Smock tops, t-shirts, billowy-sleeved and big-collared 1970s blouses, tank tops, denim jackets, all personalised with big badges, fashionable at the time, of our favourite pop stars: Alice Cooper, Slade, Wizzard, David Cassidy, Elton John and David Bowie – pinned to our chests and promising to drive a pin into our hearts should we fall off and land on them. So it was just as well we never did.

Funny thing about hats. I mean, they're quite a recent invention. Until the mid-twentieth century they didn't even exist in their present, protective form. When I first started riding they were lined, rather optimistically, with cork, and now they are a technical and necessary item for anyone throwing a leg over a horse. Soooo, hats… because it doesn't matter how good a rider you are, how long you've been doing it, or how quiet and dependable your horse is, there are always the unknown factors of chance and luck. It takes only a second for a bird to fly out under your horse's nose, for him to trip over a tree root, for a driver in a car to swerve and then, instead of being up there all poised and thinking yourself a fine sort of rider, you're flying through the air and hurtling towards the ground, your head about to break your fall. Is it worth the risk? Of course it isn't. In fact, it's a no-brainer and now, of course, riding establishments won't allow you to ride bareheaded as not only do they prefer their clients to stay in one piece, but it invalidates their insurance if you refuse to don the headgear.

As a teenager, the only time I (and my friends) wore a hat was when I was competing, but later, in the 1980s, while teaching and leading hacks, I made sure I was wearing one as I considered it looked much more professional and felt I ought to set an example. Our lack of headgear seems crazy now. Total madness. After all, there are many and varied ways a horse can kill you – you don't even have to get on one to put your life in their hooves. Which is why, of course, safe practices need to be observed, and no guarantees can be issued.

Talking of examples (or not), the only time I ever saw Rose wear a hat was when she once went hunting, even though it was useless. I know this because when I remarked upon it Rose lifted it from her head and squashed it between her hands like an empty grapefruit shell. It was soft, pliable and, as head protection, as much use as, well, an empty grapefruit shell. When questioned about her no-hat policy she would snort and tell us that hats were for people who fell off and she, she assured us, had no intention of doing so. And to be fair, she never did. Early photographs showed a young Rose, her hair swept up in a grip on one side, trailing down in a curl like Vera Lynn. No hat hair for Rose!

'What's up?' she'd ask familiar faces if they turned up to ride, hat in hand. 'Planning to fall off?' That it really wasn't the attitude was a given, but nobody questioned it. And so no wonder my friends and I followed the trend and rode hatless, the wind in our hair, thinking we looked pretty glamorous when actually, let me tell you – not that you need telling – we looked anything but.

Even now the debate rages on: should hats be compulsory at all times? Should riders on the road be compelled by law to wear them – as children up to fourteen years are? Most shows now insist on riders wearing approved and chin-strapped hats, whether in or out of the show ring, but there is still a hardcore section of riders who believe the wearing of hats to be a matter of individual choice, resisting intervention of the 'nanny state'. But surely it is only common sense to insist that nobody rides with such scant regard for their own safety?

Safety is paramount – but then again, there are body protectors. No such thing when I started riding and when, in the *Pony* offices, I was shown how one fitted – around me – I couldn't imagine how anyone could ride in one. I could scarcely breathe. How could riders draw breath enough to jump in them? The inflatable ones seem much better, light, less obtrusive. Now, if they can just incorporate a parachute that activates upon parting with one's horse, we might just be able to say we're as safe as houses – or horses.

Of course, you cannot assure safety on a horse, and you never will. There can be no guarantees, no assurances that you, Madam, or you, Sir, will come back in the same condition as you set out. Horses are not machines – oh, but wait, now they are! You can swap your lesson on that snorting, unpredictable, dangerous beast for one on a horse which isn't made of flesh and blood but of metal, with clever mechanics inside that imitate the movement of a real horse. Unbelievably, a lesson on the mechanical equine can cost you more than the real thing – but there are often taster opportunities at shows.

Jan helped out at a stand at a big show recently and offered me a ride on a robot Dobbin. But… all 'riders' had to wear 'suitable footwear' (in case they fell off and were dragged from there to, um, nowhere, presumably), and – wait for it – a riding hat (in case robot Dobbin bucked, reared or slung his riders off, I supposed). WTF? was my response. I expect it's an insurance thing again.

Robot horse moves like the real thing, it looks a bit like the real thing but, as yet, doesn't go around corners so it's perfect if you want only to ride in straight lines. It's ideal for fine-tuning your position and aids, but not much use if you're looking to fine-tune a relationship with another living being. Whenever I see one, I'm reminded of rides I had as a child on the sixpenny slot-machine pony in our local department store, never missed whenever I went shopping with my mum. Robot horses are more refined and far more expensive, but you can see where the inspiration came from. If you use your imagination, you can even see where horse riding is going…

Falling off

I SUPPOSE A MORE positive chapter heading would have been 'staying on'. Given the almost suffocating insistence on H&S nowadays, and almost total lack of it in the 1970s and 1980s, it seems baffling that we so rarely troubled the health professionals, or even the first aid box. Come to think of it, I don't think Rose actually possessed a first aid box for humans, preferring to treat any slight injuries, such as grazes or cuts, with a dab of gentian violet or iodine from her own equine dispensary, an antique, glass-fronted dresser in her hall behind the kitchen. But such treatment was rarely needed as we rarely fell off, or injured ourselves in any other way (I stress *rarely*, not *never*).

I put it down to Rose's teaching, albeit achieved by trial and error, and by our own sharp sense of self preservation, learning as we did the independent seat so insisted on in all the manuals, terrified of taking up the slightest rein contact as Rose considered it both unnecessary and a hindrance to the horse. The threat of gentian violet may have helped, the bright colour demonstrating to all and sundry that you had been, let's say, careless.

It wasn't as though she wasn't aware of modern advances in horsemanship. Rose had, she often told us in disgust, received some instruction in the *new-fangled, so-called forward seat* when she had gone off for training at a big, modern establishment for which she had little regard. One attempt was enough to convince her it was a bad idea as it had caused her, for one of the few times in her riding life, to feel unsafe to the point of almost falling off. *Perched up on her thighs*, is how she described it, which I am sure wasn't the instructor's intention. Anyway, she abandoned the idea and went back to her old, hunting seat and had, ever since, remained safe in the saddle without further mishap.

Despite her disgust of the forward seat (or rather, her interpretation of it) our instructor never actually taught us to ride her favoured old-fashioned way with our legs stuck out in front of us, but rather to sit tall and straight, shoulders back (we'd sometimes have to thread our whips between our elbows behind us in lessons, which only made our backs ache), knees in, heels firmly down, legs under us. We should only just, Rose insisted, be able to see the tips of our toes. For added security on a tricky mount, we should be able to hold an imaginary penny between our knees and the saddle. As for going with the movement of the horse, good riders, she told us in all seriousness, should be able to carry a glass of water without spilling a drop, just as she had carried a whole jug of cider to working parties in the fields in her youth. Did we think we could do that?

Most people, when they fall off, do so over their horse's shoulder. This is because their centre of gravity is too far forward and, if they are nervous, their human survival instinct tells them to curl up into a foetal position, to protect their vital organs. Unfortunately, this instinct works against them when riding, and actually assists in tipping them onto the ground – the horse only has to stop suddenly for them to overbalance. When I was teaching, it took me a while to realise that the riders who ignored all my advice to 'sit up' were doing so because, in their minds, they *were* sitting up. Leaning forward – albeit ever-so slightly – was their usual position. When asked to lean back, they sat up. But this new position felt uncomfortable, unsafe, they were a long way away from their horse's ears. They had to ride for some time in that new, uncomfortable position before it felt normal, before it became their default position. Sitting tall, shoulders back, weight in the heels, that's the safest position in which to ride, and will help keep you in the saddle when your horse misbehaves. And, of course, the more your hands creep up the reins, the more likely you will lean forward, which is interesting when you take into account Rose's view on reins, and how they related to riders.

The main thing Rose impressed upon us all, many, many times, was to *leave the horse's head alone*. In other words, she wanted to see us ride with our reins in loops – contact was not simply frowned upon, it was positively a crime. The aim was that A. we shouldn't interrupt the horse's natural way of going, and B. we should learn to ride without hanging on by the reins. The independent seat, so favoured by all the books, was to be achieved by treating the reins as though surplus to requirements. It sounded like this plan was for our benefit, although everyone knew that Rose was thinking only of her horses. We were not to interfere with our mounts' mouths in any way. Not to stop. Or steer. We also had to figure out how to do these, some might say essential aids, ourselves. Riding with the handbrake on was a crime most terrible. Only later, when we had developed balance, when we had figured out the safest position in which to sit, were we allowed to take up a contact.

These may not be the approved methods of teaching today but it is as well to remember that at the riding school at the top of the hill in those days, lessons were rare – hacking was the norm and the horses might be employed on up to four or five rides a day at weekends. But hacking is different from working in an arena, and walking, trotting and cantering in straight lines in a relaxed manner doesn't demand the same gymnastic effort as schooling. Being ridden on a contact and up to the bit is hard work for everyone, whereas enjoying a social ride out in the countryside is much easier on horse and man, with a single hand on the reins and people to chat with.

No wonder most riding schools now restrict the number of hours their horses work every day for if they work on lessons, in a school, it is harder on their joints as well as their mental state. Our school hacks, with riders of mostly limited ability, were little more demanding for the horses than a social wander around the countryside with their chums, with the opportunity to snatch a few tasty snacks on the way (frowned upon by Rose), not to mention the fun of ignoring the occasional and ineffectual suggestions from whomever frequented their saddles.

Dressage, the wildly popular activity of today's riding scene, was something the Germans did, or that viewed occasionally on the telly whenever Badminton was on – the boring preliminaries to the exciting bits. As for schooling (sorry, what?), the indoor school was where you rode when it rained (the school had replaced the outdoor school with an indoor one in the late 1960s), or for when you wanted to pop over a few jumps or, when Rose was out riding, for mucking about sitting sideways on your mount, chatting with your mates. If anyone did attempt some schooling they were branded as either agoraphobic, or scared of riding in the great outdoors, aka *proper* riding. I know… I *know!*

Of course, we did have lessons, but these mainly took the form of drill riding, and on these we were encouraged to think and act quickly. Rose would think nothing of ordering us to quit our stirrups (not for us the faff of folding them over the front of the saddles as we were expected to be able to find them again at a moment's notice, which is good practice for if you lose them out riding), to trot around briskly and then, on her command, to '…whole ride…*DISMOUNT!*' Anyone stopping their mount before throwing themselves out of the saddle risked a dressing down or, more usually, ridicule. The idea, she told us, was to fling ourselves off while the horse was actually trotting. What you gained by not being told off you lost in the possibility of doing yourself a mischief, if not actually *getting yourself killed*. I'm not sure what we were supposed to learn from this exercise apart from confidence, and abandonment of any regard for personal safety. Of course, it was always carried out on the left rein so we had an inkling of when we might be asked to do it and could psych ourselves up accordingly.

While trotting around we'd be instructed to carry out a few exercises with a free hand – touching our horses' polls and tails, and as well as our own toes; standing up in our stirrups, sitting down without our stirrups – the sort of thing folk do on the lunge nowadays. And then, at the end of a lesson this torture-with-a-purpose would continue. We'd be expected to join in the usual stationary exercises: scissors, half-scissors, around-the-world, folding our arms and lying back on our horses' backs (try doing that today with the high cantles on modern saddles) and more I've forgotten – all without anyone at our horses' heads. With Rose in front of them, they didn't dare put a foot out of line anyway.

Anyone falling off, either in the school or out hacking, found sympathy in short supply. You had dismounted without permission! What were you doing down there? Get up – you weren't hurt! Stop messing about! Letting go of the reins as you fell was a worse crime than actually hitting the deck because nobody wanted the bother of catching your horse. A fall prompted much eye-rolling or might be the cause for amusement – providing you weren't hurt, of course. If you were hurt, it was your own fault for not staying on and you'd know better next time.

If your horse happened to misbehave – maybe nap or throw in a buck or two – you were loudly accused of upsetting it, or teaching it bad manners. The fault was always and entirely considered to be yours. No matter how many days the horse in question had been confined to its stable in winter, eating buckets of oats, wound up like an eight-day-clock and standing on its head, you were supposed to let out surplus energy in stages by sitting lightly and riding with elastic reins.

Rose had little sympathy for riders who made a habit of falling off. One livery owner seemed unable to defy gravity for any length of time, and although always nursing a bruise or two from falls maintained an admirably positive spirit. When spring finally arrived one year, she boldly headed her ungenerous mount out of the yard, trilling, 'Isn't it lovely, Rose, being able to ride out and look at all this wonderful scenery?'

'Well', Rose replied, laconically, 'I suppose it makes a change from sitting on it.'

On another spring day, Rose led a large hack back into the yard sporting a *thank goodness we're back* look on her face. Rose's relief was nothing compared to the child who had ridden Bubbles. A small spotted pony, round and popular, Bubbles had an eye for the spring grass and had twice during the hour caused his rider to tumble down his neck as he dived for a snack. Uncomplaining, the child had gamely remounted each time, and Rose decided to take a route home which meant the last five hundred yards to the riding school would be along a quiet road. At least this way, she reasoned, there would be no grass to tempt Bubbles, and the child had a good chance of ending on a high note.

Nothing wrong with the plan...

With the riding school within their sights Rose allowed herself to breathe a sigh of relief – but she had relaxed too early. At precisely that second, a pedestrian on the pavement finished the last bite of their apple and, with the timing of a circus juggler, threw away the core, watching it tumble into the gutter at the exact moment a small spotted pony passed by. Down went Bubbles' nose, closely followed by his rider. After that, Bubbles was condemned to a life in grass reins.

It wasn't only clients who suffered. Diminutive Doublet arrived one day as a new livery. He belonged to two small children whose mother thought, as the pony was always being ridden on the leading rein, and not very often at that, someone else might like to exercise him – which was how Julie got the gig. Small, round and dappled grey, Doublet was totally up for haring around the countryside with his more competent rider, her chums and their ponies. The trouble was his saddle was of the flat, felt variety, without a tree. As Doublet traversed corners at speed with his new friends, his saddle – topped by Julie – tended to continue in its original direction and our rides were punctured with cries of: 'Hold on, Julie's off again,' or 'Hang about, Julie's hit the deck!' It always seemed to happen at a place we called the Windy Canter, so called because not only was it very windy (it wound around the trees, I don't mean it was breezy) but also, we always cantered along it. We possessed a rare talent for original path-naming. It was Nicky who christened the small field near the riding school the Furry Field, as the grass was long and wafted in the breeze. It caught on. Nowadays it is actually so named on the map, which proves how these things work. Wonder no more when you come across Falling Off Lane, or Swearing At Your Horse Road.

Years later, Doublet found a new career at the riding school and alternated between proceeding snail-like and at a mile-a-week in the school so I was continually telling his riders to cut the corner and catch up, and overtaking me on canters on hacks, his riders wondering how their slow, seemingly almost-dead pony had managed to morph into a raging lunatic whose life appeared to depend on being at the front of the ride. Doublet was reliving his glory days! Luckily, he had inherited a proper saddle by then, so casualties were few.

Twice a week there were scheduled late night rides for adults, and on the light summer evenings these took the form of hacks. You had to be made of stern stuff to go on these rides. Rose led them herself, and the Rose who led rides in the week, when all the riders were more experienced and therefore up for something a bit faster than the norm, was nothing like the Rose who led the more sedate hacks with lead reins at the weekend. On these mid-week rides Rose was a bit of a lunatic. Actually, her lunacy was total. Whereas we, as hack leaders, were always instructed to ease into a canter gently, not to go too fast, to make sure we kept everyone happy so that they all stayed on, Rose abandoned all her own advice in the evenings astride her own skewbald Cochise, launching without warning from a standstill into a gallop, insisting that nobody overtook her as her horse didn't like it. Which he didn't. She had got him, after all, from someone who was terrified of riding him, and Rose was his last chance. I've lost count of the number of horses she acquired this way. Oh, no, wait a minute… ALL of them (the ones she herself owned and rode, you understand, not the school horses – they were much more dependable).

You ignored these instructions on pain of death – or at the very least a dressing down in front of everyone. Rose always told us a good rider would never be seen jogging sideways but would rather be able to get their horse to walk calmly. She never seemed to take her own advice, and when questioned it was a case of, *do what I say, not what I do*. Oh and of course *her* horse, she reminded us, giving it an affectionate pat as it jogged sideways, was *very highly strung*. Ours, it was implied, were not.

And so, on one such evening ride with the sun red and low in the sky, the birds singing, the stubble fields beckoning, we all set off behind Rose at what was supposed to be a canter. The stubble had a rather hysterical effect on the horses, particularly as we were riding on fields previously out of bounds, for obvious reasons. At the end of this particular long stretch, Rose pulled up inches from the fence in her usual late, abrupt manner, and we all piled up behind her like train carriages whose engine had hit the buffers at speed. We relaxed, loosening the reins and patting our mounts, turning their heads to the breeze.

A few riders engaged in small talk.

Somebody lit a cigarette.

What a lovely way to spend a summer evening…

Suddenly, someone let out a cry and pointed, and all eyes turned to Chalky. Standing about 13.2hh, grey, willing, cute as a button, Chalky stood apart from the other horses, flanks heaving, ears flicking back and forth in a self-conscious, wide-eyed, bordering-on-bewildered fashion. Something about him was different. Whereas Kate, all five-feet-nothing of her, had been sitting astride Chalky when we had hit the ground at canter, there was now just a saddle.

Chalky was empty.

A quick scan across the field yielded nothing. There was no sign of Kate, prone or upright. She had, quite simply, disappeared. Somebody leant over and grasped Chalky's reins and we retraced our steps, calling her name. Kate's husband was, understandably, concerned. Rose frowned. Everyone was puzzled. It didn't seem likely that Kate would have got fed up, dismounted and let Chalky continue without her – but where on earth was she? Were we witness to the first alien abduction in the area?

'Down here!' cried a small voice and, as one, all heads turned to the direction from where the sound had originated. Suddenly, like a target on a fairground rifle range, a head popped up out of the ditch – from which all the horses promptly snorted, shied away and tore off up the field again, putting as much distance between themselves and the talking-ditch-with-a-head-in-it.

This didn't help.

It took a while to persuade our mounts to return but, eventually, we managed to extract Kate from the ditch into which she had fallen, dust her down and check she had two arms, two legs and that nothing else was missing. Then we hoisted her up on board the disconcerted Chalky, and continued our ride, making up for lost time.

The main thing was, of course, that Kate didn't make a fuss. The incident was the subject of much hilarity and re-telling. Falling off could be acceptable – providing you took it all in good part, Rose could get a good story out of it and you didn't make a habit of it. Making a fuss was possibly the worst thing you could do in Rose's eyes. So nobody did – at least, nobody who wanted to continue riding at the riding school at the top of the hill.

But we rarely fell off. Why? Did we stay on because of the way we were taught? We all learned to ride on hacks, bouncing around on leading reins, desperate to learn rising trot because, as soon as we could, we would be set free, masters of our own mounts (or so we kidded ourselves). Sunshine was the perfect pony on which to learn – the only time she broke out of trot was when she was led up the big hill, where she broke into a canter instead. So, on Sunshine it was possible to learn to canter before you had even mastered rising trot, which saved time later. We were all anxious to fly solo and excited when, for the last half-mile of a ride, our leader unclipped the rein anchoring our pony to their hand, leaving us proud to be riding into the yard alone. At last, we were riders!

At the riding school at the top of the hill we were introduced to the great outdoors from an early age, from the moment we started to ride. We were used to hauling up our ponies' heads from enticing grass, used to riding both sides of our mounts instead of just the side away from the arena wall, familiar with riding surrounded by acres of nothingness. And we took risks. At the end of summer weekends, we all elbowed each other out of the way to grab our favourite pony after the last hack, legging each other up onto bare, sweaty backs and riding down the lane to the field, a glorious, snatched, free five minutes of riding. In the early days the route even included a deep dip, down which the ponies would canter. Nobody was vetted – it was assumed that if you volunteered for this, you accepted the consequences and hung on.

Rose went ahead on the tractor, a large water container on the back, a plank of wood floating on the top to prevent the contents from splashing out as the tractor bounced down the lane and into the field to fill the trough. With the horses all turned out and the gate fastened everyone was invited to clamber aboard for a lift back up the hill, Rose steering around the ruts in the tarmac to squeals and laughter as we all gripped tightly to each other and whatever else we could find to avoid hurtling off into space.

Out hacking we felt more in partnership with our mounts. Today, most pupils are introduced to riding within the confines of an arena where riding school horses – especially beginner's horses, bored by repetition – tend to switch off. It can be a struggle to get them going, to steer them into the corners, to get them to even acknowledge beginner aids given by ineffectual and complaining muscles. Riding becomes more of a battle than a shared experience; how can you get this horse onside, to do what you want when you are just starting out? And, of course, you are under constant scrutiny. It is more hard work than pleasure. Hacking out – even on a leading rein – is more how you imagined riding might be. Your horse is more forward-going, helping you with your momentum, especially at trot. You have time to experiment as you steer around the trees, you can exchange ideas and suggestions with fellow riders. You feel more at one with your mount as you share this freedom and excitement of the great outdoors. This is riding!

Later, we were instructed by Rose to let go, to be confident, to get comfortable in all situations. We learned how to deal with horses and ponies fed on oats, who weren't push button but who challenged not only our riding ability but also our resolve. If we wanted to be riders we had to put in the effort, to do it ourselves. I've lost count of the number of times I'd defied gravity simply through sheer bloody willpower.

Or maybe Rose just weeded out the feeble riders, the ones who wanted their riding homogenised, safe and slow. Those likely to make a fuss, those who were never going to volunteer to ride the tricky horses, horses that improved your techniques, turning you from passengers into riders. Perhaps those riders sought out riding schools where their sensitive nature was nurtured and went on to make riders all the same. Different to the ones Rose made, but riders, nevertheless. Diversity is no bad thing. As a teenager I gave it little thought at the time, considering it to be – as we all did – natural selection.

But riding isn't all about the expected – it's the unexpected that teaches you how to stay on. Or not. Not being exposed to problems means you never get to learn how to cope when they crop up. But if you do, you can progress from just coping to recognising the signs so you can take steps to prevent the problems from happening in the first place. It is as well for someone else to tell you what to do, what not to do, but sometimes you just don't get it until you overcome it yourself. You don't want to just cope, you want to be in control – as much as you can be in control with horses.

Happy hackers is how we describe horse owners without ambition, but whose horses are not just their hobby, but also their lives. 'I'm just a happy hacker!' they tell everyone, using the same apologetic prefix as the housewife asking us to excuse her lack of employment, as though being paid a wage is the definition of a life well spent, qualities valued enough by others to receive a salary. The *just* word warns others to lower their expectations, to set their sights low. They *just* hack, they explain, they and their horses, exploring the countryside without the drive to raise their game. Do they organise clandestine, *Happy Hackers Anonymous* meetings? 'Hello, my name's Gladys and I'm a… a… (gulp, deep breath) … a *happy hacker.*' Clap, cheer, clap, you go girl!

But maybe hacking is the biggest challenge of all. Maybe riding your horse in the great outdoors, where there are no walls to confine you, no roof to keep you dry, no psychological safety net, this is where daring-do is practised, where the real riding occurs. Just being at one with your horse, confident you can cope with the odd swerve as you canter, sharing the experience of getting out there rather than confining yourself and your horse to a life within four walls. You don't learn everything in an indoor school, you can't practise all things in the manège. That's for introduction, for refinement, for experimentation, for honing skills. Schooling sessions are for improvement, rather than condemning you and your horse to a riding career in an artificial environment, just riding around and around.

At the riding school at the top of the hill we hacked from the first time we threw a leg over the saddle, Rose determined that we shouldn't be afraid of the great outdoors. It was real riding, she always said, getting out there, not tip-tupping around in the school in ever-decreasing circles, boring your horse to death so that if you did venture outside he was so excited and hyped up, the whole experience put you off for life. And hacking is perfect for young horses, stepping out and forward, learning confidence, inducing the right mindset and discovering their courage.

Outside is where challenges are thrown at you. Outside is where you learn to steer around the trees so you don't have your kneecaps taken off, to use lateral aids to prevent your horse's hindquarters from swinging into another horse, to adjust your speed as you canter in a group, teaching your horse to go first, last, upsides. It is where you learn to sit quietly and breathe regularly as your mount jogs for home, to get him to walk straight instead of sideways, encouraging him to relax. The great outdoors is where the wind whistles and blows up ghosts and terrors, teaching you to anticipate problems and deal with them, teaching your horse to expect – and accept – the unknown.

Outside is where a long stretch of grass on a cold winter's day teaches you to sit quietly, to regulate your breathing, to play out the reins rather than bottle up energy that may result in a buck. It is where the bogeymen live, where it's your job to give your mount confidence, to let him know you're there for him, and that you won't let anything bad happen. Outside is where you learn to trust each other.

Perhaps we need to change our perspective of our so-called happy hackers. They're the brave ones, learning from their horses who are the best teachers of all. Riders shouldn't always be measured by their perceived successes, by how much they achieve, perpetuating the myth that the ones who compete and win are somehow more valued. They work hard, their knowledge is enviable but, like all athletes, they succeed for themselves. Success isn't always measured by rosettes or medals, or is something tabled, drawn up on a chart or documented by certificates. Success is personal and it takes many forms – humble and elite – and that is one of the strengths of our shared passion for riding.

Happy are our hackers – for they are the real riders. They need a re-boot, a re-brand, no more *just* happy hackers. Why not the *great* happy hackers, the *dedicated* happy hackers, the *brave* happy hackers, doing it for themselves and their horses? Maybe the happy hackers are the *real* riders, the ones who ride not for glory but for love, love of their sport, love of their horses, love of the never-ending challenge of riding.

Equality

IF YOU ARE LOOKING for a sport where there is total equality between the sexes, then look no further for horse riding is the game for you! When I rode at the riding school at the top of the hill in the 1970s and 1980s women were the majority, by a long chalk. Rose was in charge (and how), and most of those working and helping there were female. But there were plenty of male riders, too and, thinking back, more than you usually find in many establishments today. Maybe because everyone hacked out – maybe that was a reason the school had a higher-than-average female/male ratio, the men enjoying the freedom riding offered them rather than being restricted to taking lessons in the confines of a school – from a woman. A lot of men owned their own horses, too, proving their keenness wasn't a passing phase. And then there was Dick, who came up in his half-timbered Morris Minor Traveller every weekday from his cottage half-way down the back lane, who drove the tractor, rolled the oats and did all the general maintenance and odd jobs, including mending the tack. Indispensable, was Dick, with a repertoire of one-liners and wry and succinct observations collected along the years.

For centuries, riding horses was what the men did, in much the same way as, when I was a child, it was always the male of the species who drove the family car, relegating the little woman to that of passenger. All those funny gears and pedals – far too much for *the wife!* If women did have to travel anywhere before the invention of the combustion engine, they had to do it aside their horses, not astride – or better still, go by carriage. There had been exceptions, of course, but riding astride was not considered seemly. It just wasn't done. Sitting sideways behind a man was allowed, or you might be led along like a beginner, both legs on one side, unable to control your own horse from such a precarious position.

Besides, it wouldn't do for a woman to become in any way independent, for a woman to go where she might please, for a woman to do anything other than the bidding of men. Women were not supposed to get astride anything they weren't married to and, of course, a weak and feeble woman could hardly be expected to control a powerful horse. Fed up with all this gender-restrictive nonsense, Catherine de Medici is credited with having added a pommel to the front of her saddle which enabled her to keep her femininity intact by sitting sideways yet take some control of her horse – and all this in the 16th century. It wasn't until the 1830s that anyone thought to add a second pommel, and riders locked their left leg below this, secure between it and the stirrup, their right leg wrapped around the upper pommel.

Without pommels, there could been no way a rider could do anything but sit quietly aside a saddle without sliding off. There was no purchase to be had, nothing to resist against, no way of holding the rider on board. Your horse only had to turn sharply, and they found themselves on the ground. Now, with pommels around which they could entwine and anchor their legs a rider was secure and could hold the reins with an independent seat. By gaining control of her horse a rider took charge of *herself*. Women were off the leash!

You could say that the side saddle kicked off feminism, levelling the playing field between the sexes. Equestriennes – at last – threw of their shackles and went a bit bonkers. Imagine how liberating it must have been. No more wafting your silken, laboriously self-embroidered handkerchief to the menfolk as they trotted off the front lawn to follow hounds. Instead, you got yourself a becoming, all-covering habit, hid your modesty behind a close-fitting veil twirled around your top hat, stuck two pommels up to society and galloped alongside the boys, matching them stride-for-stride. Weaker sex their arse! So this was what it was like to be a man, this freedom, this excitement, this sport!

It was the beginning of the end – if only for the upper classes. But it has always been within the upper classes where girls have dipped their toes into independence.

Unrestricted by poverty, not weighed down by the necessity of earning a crust, unencumbered by childbirth – at least until they had done their duty with an heir and a spare and could leave them with Nanny. Without the freedom enjoyed by the upper classes, with time on their hands for sport, experimentation and causes such as women's suffrage, with the luxury of education, their questioning of the status quo and pushing of boundaries (and, of course, the money to do all these), would the rights of women ever have been ignited?

It wasn't until the early 20th century that the idea of women riding astride became more commonplace – astride was the new liberation, women's suffrage viewing sideways riding as a further evidence of male dominance over the female rider, rather than recognising the liberation it had once offered. And so the side saddle, which had been instrumental in offering women a way to escape the bounds of male expectancy, was now abandoned. At least, that was, until 1974, when Valerie Francis and Janet Macdonald formed the Ladies' Side Saddle Association (now the Side Saddle Association), and lady riders once more took the veil by choice rather than necessity.

To the uninitiated, riding side saddle looks precarious, as though the rider defies gravity. But with the left leg between stirrup and lower pommel, the right leg hooked over the upper one, the rider is very securely placed – providing she sits centrally. From behind, it should look as though the rider is sitting astride – minus her right leg – and not only does it *feel* secure, but it is. Providing the rider keeps her right shoulder back and her body central, she will stay in the saddle till the cows come home. I have heard that horse trainers used to saddle up persistent buckers with a side saddle to teach them that their behaviour wouldn't necessarily dislodge their rider. It is not the saddle to put on a horse prone to rearing, though – you want to be able to slip off a rearer if there is any danger of them going over backwards, a terrifying idea made worse by the thought of being entangled in one's saddle.

Ladies' hacks were intentionally trained to be one sided – because striking off on right canter lead is more comfortable aside – and to suppress any inclination to trot altogether. A whip replaces the missing leg, and the rider needs to stay central because side saddles are still liable to slip to the nearside, hence the balance strap. Why do riders always sit with their legs on the nearside? Presumably because that is the side one mounts and dismounts, and a leg-up can see the rider elegantly in the plate, even with all the yards of skirt ladies wore in times gone by. Now, of course, a side saddle habit has an apron, darted to fit neatly over both legs, wrapping around the back when dismounted to save the rider's modestly. It could also save her life should a dismount be unplanned. Before such attire (a buttoned seamed safety skirt first made an appearance in 1875) ladies courted danger by riding in their huge skirts, yards of material which could, and often did, cause them to be dragged by their horses in the rare event of a fall.

The rules for modern attire to wear aside are long and complicated – and in times gone by some items of riding fashion advertised the riders' marital status, so handy for the men, useful for avoiding embarrassing advances. (Even recently, I met a man who tried to convince me that the title *Ms* was invented for, and to be used only by, divorced women. I know. Will it ever end?) If you wish to ride aside you will be expected to conform to tradition – silk hats must be of a certain height and only worn after midday, bowler hats must tone with the habit, hair is to be worn in a bun. Not enough hair? No matter, falsies are acceptable, but must be the size of a doughnut and be worn directly below the brim of the hat. Make-up should be worn under the veil (otherwise your features will disappear), which must be stretched tightly, no creases or wrinkles – making the wafts of flowing and unrestrained netting one sees in period dramas a joke. If only the faux pas stopped there – it detracts from authenticity when knee rolls, rubber stirrup treads, padded nosebands and stainless-steel bits and stirrups glare out at us from the screen in period dramas, obvious to anyone in the know.

Interestingly, it hasn't always been the ladies who have ridden aside. Male riders found the absence of a right leg useful when laying cable for field telephones, leaning over the offside of their galloping horses to lay lines in haste. Returning veterans from World War I, men longing to return to the hunting field and deciding to treat a lost leg a mere inconvenience, stopped at nothing to get their fix of following hounds after the horrors of the battlefield. A leg which went no further than the knee could still enable its owner to hunt on a side saddle – and if the missing leg was the wrong one for a conventional side saddle, another could be made which accommodated the rider on the offside.

And so it was on the backs of horses, both legs on one side of their saddles, that feminism was born, nurtured and grown. On the backs of horses, countless girls questioned whether deferring to boys was natural or necessary. On the backs of horses, women were truly equal in ability and talent. On the backs of horses, women and girls were free. Free to be that which they wanted to be, to be the best they could be with no self-doubt, no deferring to second place. They could even challenge the menfolk in sport.

At the riding school at the top of the hill there was true equality for I can remember no occasion when the men demonstrated – or even attempted to demonstrate – male superiority over the girls because, of course, they couldn't. Even with a high percentage of male riders there was a distinct lack of chauvinism: everyone just got on with their riding, equality a given. It wasn't as though I was conscious of it, it just seeped into my bones, into my being, and I only became aware of how unbalanced the rest of the world appeared when injustices and inequalities loomed large in other spheres of my life.

Girls were expected to smile, be pleasant, interested – but never pushy or, heaven forbid, do anything better than the boys. Being 'bubbly' was a personal trait greatly admired (for 'bubbly' read 'annoying airhead'). Hearing it attributed to girls today still makes me gag. Grown men would shout a cheery *'Oi'* at you in the street before ordering you to, *'Cheer up, darlin', it might never 'appen,'* or, *'Blimey love, a smile wouldn't hurcha!'* I never heard them offer such advice to a man (fat-lip territory) but it was given quite freely to the fair sex because a girl or woman's purpose appeared to be to make life more decorative for the men.

As a tomboy, and in sharp contrast to my girlie-girl sister, I was always being told I needed to be more ladylike. If I came back with a retort to any man's comment, either to an uncle or perhaps a man serving in a shop who thought himself amusing or tried the 'Cheer up love' routine, my mother would tell me, in hushed and embarrassed tones, not to be cheeky, mortified by my bravado (she continued to do so even when I was in my forties). I thought it grossly unfair – men were allowed to be cheeky. Why should I defer to men, most of whose comments were anything but amusing anyway? They were not, I refused to acknowledge even at a very early age, my superiors, and every utterance was not worth laughing at – or even clever. Why encourage them? Most of them were pretty boring and boorish. This wasn't the 1920s, I'm talking the 1970s, here.

I wasn't allowed to take woodwork or metalwork at school, for example, merely on the basis of gender. The Sexual Equality Act was passed after I had escaped full-time education, so I had no basis on which to challenge my school regarding the injustice of it all. So I trotted off to school in my skirt (or summer frock), grudgingly played hockey and netball – wondering why my PE teacher was allowed to swan around in her fur-lined tracksuit while I shivered in my navy gym knickers – and despaired of the sexist world in which I found myself, the sexist world which I left behind at the riding school at the top of the hill.

Today there is much talk about female empowerment. I have never had an empowering moment simply because with horses, it was a given: I've never felt *un*empowered. Empowerment was mine since I first threw a leg over a saddle. Confidence in oneself, in one's gender, in one's ability to be oneself without conforming to the social stereotypes of the day – of any day – was not only nurtured by equestrianism, it was insisted upon. We were all empowered – there was no need to label it. There was no room for sexism in the stable, in the saddle, in the yard. Empowerment was a by-product of the environment.

A very long time after our teenage years at the riding school at the top of the hill, Jan and I met for dinner at a pub in the middle of nowhere for a catch-up. Who should be sitting at the next table but one of our contemporaries, a fellow alumna from the riding school at the top of the hill, enjoying a quiet drink with her boyfriend.

Well, not any more!

After a gap of over twenty years or so there was, of course, a noisy reunion. In an odd coincidence we three shared not only our teenage experiences around horses, but also our Christian name, Janet being popular in the late 1950s, early 1960s – common, even. And so a happy evening of the three Janets doubling up with laughter between excited cries of: 'Do you remember…?' and 'What about when…?' and 'I'll never forget when Rose…' ensued, while the third Janet's boyfriend looked on and smiled indulgently at our shocking manners, waving away our apologies with a martyred hand.

Naturally, careers cropped up, and the third Janet informed us, somewhat modestly, that she was now a pilot for a busy airline.

'I'm responsible for settling the hotel bills for the crew's accommodation,' she told us, 'and more often than not, if the hotel receptionist is male they smile indulgently at my request for the bill and tell me they need to present it to the Captain to sign off. To which I smile back,' she continued, 'and tell them, yes, I know, I *am* the Captain.'

Now that's empowerment!

Talk about give us an inch... it started with a couple of seemingly innocuous pommels on a saddle, and the next thing you know, the sky's the limit!

In a telephone conversation with the third Janet a few days later, I asked how her boyfriend had taken the evening, and told her we hoped he had recovered from being surrounded by horsy-jawing-nostalgic Janets.

'Actually, it was our first date,' the third Janet confessed. 'I haven't heard from him since.'

Oh.

Oh, who cares – she's the Captain!

First dates can be enlightening. Sylvie once told me of a first date she had at a pub with a promising potential boyfriend. When his reaction to the news that she had a pony was to stare deep into her eyes before telling her, in total seriousness, 'I hope you don't think I'm going to play second-fiddle to a *horse,*' Sylvie had nothing to say. She just got up and left him there.

Look, let me be clear, lest you imagine me to be one of those femi-terrorists so cross with their lot that they turn into man-haters. Equality, of course, isn't just about the girls, and I rally equally against women I hear complaining and dishing out sweeping generalisations such as *all men are the same,* or that *they would say that because they're a man!* Women who boast to their friends how well they've *trained* their husbands, and how it has taken them years to get them to *do as they are told* make me shudder. He's your partner, for goodness sake, not a bloody collie, show some respect. Equality means equality, it doesn't mean more so. I am against positive discrimination for this reason, as well as women-only awards, competitions and clubs, it cuts both ways. If we have to try harder to get the same jobs then so be it – but we should, of course, get the same pay.

When I was at *Pony* magazine I would receive letters from parents of boys bemoaning the fact that the models in the magazine were mostly female. I wrote back, encouraging their sons to contribute, to send photographs, to write their real-life dramas, to do their bit to remind the girls that the boys were out there, too. I was desperate to improve the balance. Whenever I arranged a photo shoot at riding schools and livery yards, I would always make a plea for any available boy riders to help us. But if there were any boys on the yard, only a few were up for it. Invariably they declined. They were reluctant to pose for our photo stories, they hesitated to take part in any of the instructional images needed. It was the classic catch-22: we longed for the boys to give our magazine balance, the boys saw our magazine as being for the girls, reluctant to accept that it might be within their power to change it.

One visit to a Pony Club camp illustrated perfectly that there is, indeed, a difference between the sexes: five groups made up of girl riders, the boys all grouped together in a sixth – possibly for their protection. There were female groups practising their dressage, diligently schooling in the corner of the field, jumping orderly grids, grooming and cleaning tack. And then there was the solitary male group, whizzing from A to B, back to A, over to C, on to D – all at the gallop, their ponies reduced to four-legged bikes, rarely slowing down, wide-eyed and panting, sacrificing themselves in order to nurture the next generation of gung-ho polo players, jockeys and three-day-eventers. The mums were just grateful their sons had an interest, grateful enough to look after their ponies – grooming, cleaning tack, washing riding clothes – for when the boys dismounted most of them lost interest, reducing their parent to the role of groom as they threw them the reins. No wonder so many boys expect the girls to do all the work for they've been trained from birth – and by their *mothers!*

Not so at the riding school at the top of the hill. At first glance, you might have mistaken the Housewives' Ride in the 1970s for a sign of the times, a nod to encouraging the little women to get a hobby, but there was more to it than that. The school advertised riding lessons, twice a week, specifically for housewives (imagine that now). These were special classes to get you out of the house, ladies, away from the kitchen sink and out into the fresh air. And the housewives came! Nervous, but still up for it, learning to stop and steer and trot around the school on their patient and gallant steeds before braving the great outdoors, hacking behind Rose, bonding together as their confidence soared – for

Rose always displayed a softer and sympathetic side with nervous riders, young and old, believing everyone was entitled to enjoy riding.

The local press, intrigued by the concept, came to report, to take pictures. The reports (for they came twice, a couple of years between each visit) were full of clichés about sore bottoms, of spending the housekeeping money, of the drudgery of housework escaped from for an hour on the back of a horse. The photographs that accompanied the copy showed the riders in the saddle, their hair coiffured, Rose mounted beside them and about to head out with her charges for a hack into the unknown.

All very patronising, all of its time but the message was clear: riding was for everyone, young and old, male and female, experienced and beginner. It was an adventure in which everyone could take part, even if you had to put up with a sore backside to do it, or return to the drudgery of housework afterwards, cheeks flushed, a taste of freedom dangerously luring you to stretch yourself beyond the importance of getting your whites right. It was the forerunner of me-time, of mixing it with the girls, of doing something for yourself around all the doing you did for others – a concept with which we are now so familiar, we forget that it has not always been so. The horses had done it again, lighting the fires of rebellion and stirring the hearts of females whose role had previously been restricted to supporting the needs of their families. The message was that there was more to life than vacuuming, ladies. You could still have a life of your own.

And this message, of course, had been Rose's intention.

In the 1970s, all around me women were burning bras and battling for equality, but in the horse world equality was a given and bra-burning is never to be recommended for anyone in the saddle. In the horse world, the girls were already doing it for themselves – Marion Coakes and Stroller, Ann Moore and Psalm, Alison Westwood and The Maverick. All competed against the men in show jumping, their dark coats signalling that here was the fairer sex, willing and not just able, but sometimes more so when it came to winning. And so it was in the demanding sport of three-day-eventing – Princess Anne was even getting in on the act, for goodness sake, winning the European Championship on another, very different, Doublet. I doubt she would have come to grief around the Windy Canter.

But then there was a glitch. With so many girls competing in eventing it was inevitable that falls would include a number of women riders. People began to grumble. The falls were spectacular and sometimes fatal, for frangible pins, now fitted to cross-country jumps as a matter of course to ensure previously unforgiving rails fall when the horse hits them, were unheard of back then. And then, the crazy, unimaginable, ridiculous question someone felt they had to ask: should girls be *allowed* to compete in what was clearly a tough game? Should eventing, that dangerous sport which had begun in the military, should it perhaps be restricted to *men*?

The women fought back. They may have looked like they were mere slips of girls, but they had grit, and they weren't going to give up their fun, thank you very much!

With the likes of Ginny Holgate and Lucinda Prior-Palmer racking up win after win the critics backed off. Women have been competing with, and against, men ever since. Now equestrianism – and therefore equality in sport – faces another threat from those who question whether a sport with a non-human partner has a place at the Olympic Games. We wait to see how that pans out.

We never ask for the concept of equine sport to be changed in our favour. We never expect the authorities to give us an easy ride or clamour for the sexes to be divided so there are more medals and trophies up for grabs, as is the case in other sports. Riding does not rely on strength. It relies on ability, on talent, on feeling, determination, skill and the building of a partnership. We women expect to be able to compete on equal terms with the men, for that is part of what makes horse riding and sport so wonderful and unique. We're all in it together, men and women and, frankly, I don't know why more sports which are based on skill, rather than strength – shooting and archery spring to mind – don't adopt the same rules and amalgamate their gender-separated competitions. Equestriennes are an example to everyone – housewives included!

The customer is always wrong

LEARNING TO RIDE WITH Rose was an education – in more than horsemanship. 'This business,' she would tell us, gravely, 'is the only one where the customer is *always wrong*.' With this philosophy spelled out, we knew where we stood when it came to our riding lessons with Rose.

During the 1970s and 1980s when I rode and worked there, the riding school at the top of the hill was more than busy. Five hacks every Saturday and Sunday, between two and four rides every day in the week, including evening lessons on Tuesdays and Thursdays – the first for juniors after school at half-past five, and another at seven-thirty for the grown-ups. It often catered for over a hundred riders each Saturday, the same number on Sundays, and between rides we'd all be frantically swapping over riders and horses as Rose stood in the yard or in the school, or sat on Cochise, taking the money and allocating horses to riders, or the other way around. People who rode one week invariably rode the next, but if anyone telephoned to see whether they could book for a hack Rose's advice was to come along and she would do her best to accommodate. This way, anyone who had dropped out would have their place filled. If the weather was fine, however, we might be faced with a crowd bigger than we had expected.

'Who do you want tacked up, Rose?' we'd ask. To which the reply was invariably, 'Everything. *I want everything that can walk!*' As we scuttled off to saddle up and bring out every horse and pony on the place she would call after us, 'And listen…' her tone changing from one that told us she was serious, to one that warned us she was bordering on losing it, '…*don't make a career out of it!*'

Taking more than two minutes to appear with a fully tacked-up horse was considered far too long and if that happened, Rose would launch into one of her favourite lectures, informing everyone within earshot how it used to take a team of four men a total of two minutes to harness and put-to four horses to a stagecoach, and we were taking all day twittering about to get a single horse ready (for twittering, read faffing in Rose-speak. This was, obviously, before Twitter in its present tense).

'D'you know,' she would mutter, shaking her head, 'I don't understand why it takes three men and a boy to tack up one horse.' To anyone who might be looking a bit vacant she'd cry, 'Come on people, hop about, don't just stand there like this has got nothing to do with you!'

Of course, we did have shortcuts: saddles were often left on between rides, bridles put on in advance to ease our burden – although we soon learned not to dress up Smokey and leave him unattended. He would immediately, almost before we were out of sight, rub his bridle on the wall until it surrendered and the sight of Smokey, forelock in disarray, the remains of what used to be a bridle dangling by his knees, meant a guilt-ridden confession and a lecture so terrible, the guilty would wake in the middle of the night in a nightmare-induced sweat.

Prior to every ride, young riders would cluster around Rose, arms up, jostling and elbowing out the competition as they pleaded for their favourite ponies.

'Can I ride Bubbles?'

'Can I ride Amber?'

'Please, *pleeeeese can I ride Simon?*'

Dark chestnut and 13.2hh, Simon was a saint in equine form – even if he did fail to teach his young riders a single thing. He went at a steady pace, never tried to pull the reins out of his riders' hands to snatch grass, looked neither right nor left – he even volunteered to weave in and out of the bending cones in the school, long past any expectation of instructions from the saddle. He popped over jumps at a steadiest of trots, cantered if you wanted to, trotted if you didn't – this accommodating pony didn't even breathe heavily. Everyone wanted to ride Simon. You could imagine the patter of a horse dealer, selling you this perfection-made-equine, assuring you that were you to place a child – no, a *baby*, a *blind* baby, a blind baby with no arms or legs – in his saddle, then the paragon that was

Simon would look after them, make no mistake. Never mind Dolly – cloning Simon was where the real money was.

And so, one summer day, as was usual to Rose's question, 'Who do you want to ride, little one?' the answer came back breathlessly: 'Can I ride Simon?'

'No,' explained Rose, kindly, 'Simon has a poorly leg so he can't be ridden today. Pick another pony.'

Rose selected another child, breathless with anticipation. 'So, Gladys,' she said, 'who's it to be?'

'Simon,' came the earnest and practised reply. 'I'd like to ride Simon.'

Rose took a deep breath, her voice rising dangerously. 'Now you've just heard me tell that little girl that *she* can't ride Simon because he's *lame*. If she can't ride him, neither can you. Go and ride that Cracker pony over there.'

Rose sent a few adults here and there to ride various horses before giving another young rider, who had been standing there all the time, sucking the end of her whip, her face warningly and dangerously vacant, the benefit of her attention.

'Okay, Lucy, who's it to be?'

The hitherto dreaming child woke up with a start. 'Can I ride Simon?'

There was an audible, collective gasp as the rest the waiting riders took a step back and everyone held their breath in anticipation of the inevitable explosion. Rose drew breath and didn't disappoint.

'Oh now listen up people, pay attention! Use your grey matter! I'm not standing here talking for the benefit of my health. I've already said it twice – Simon can't be ridden today. NOBODY can ride Simon because SIMON IS LAME!'

There was a pause while nobody dared to speak. The dust settled. Everyone braved a step forward to be considered. Rose put her hands on another small child's shoulders and asked her who she would like to ride.

'Can I ride Simon?' came the clear reply.

I am not making this up. I am not exaggerating for effect. You can guess the rest by now.

Even now the words, *Simon is lame!* resound in my head whenever anyone repeats a question I have already answered. It seems some people exist in a world of their own or think that something said to someone else can't possibly relate to them – or hope by repeating the question they will get a different answer, the one they are seeking. And so it was with riding Simon. Bagging Simon to ride was all that mattered, nothing else, the rider zoning out everything around them until it was their turn to ask their urgent question.

Rose possessed an uncanny ability to match rider to horse. It was instinctive and she never got it wrong. Pupils were dispatched to mount horses and ponies that would be just right for their abilities, perfect to build their confidence. If she ran out of ponies, she'd look around and locate a confident child to ask whether they'd mind going up in the world, putting them up on Kentucky or Polly or Jester, generous horses who would look after their young riders, the child bursting with pride at being singled out, determined to do Rose proud.

For a small rider who was particularly determined to ride a 'white' pony, Rose led her over to Penny, very obviously chestnut since birth, a tiny star between her eyes the only non-chestnut part about her.

'You ride this one,' she said. 'It was white once, only it got a bit dirty.'

To an adult novice, she would get them to ride the gentle and generous Polly, a large skewbald with hooves like dinner plates, but without a mean bone in her body.

'Ride this Polly horse,' Rose would say. 'I know it looks big, but it's a gentle creature, a real Christian.' Not much of a selling point when you consider the crusades.

During the summer, and whenever casual riders might occasionally turn up to join a hack and we were pushed for horses Rose would, rather than disappoint, take three lead reins – Sunshine on one side, Starlight on the other and a third, a pony who might keep up and happily stare at nothing but Cochise's chestnut tail for sixty minutes, tucked in behind. Only Rose could do this – it would have been madness for anyone else, but she never had a mishap and neither, more to the point, did the riders.

'Are you going riding?' she'd ask livery owners who, if they answered yes, would be press-ganged into accompanying a busy ride, helping out with the riders, leading the canters, few horses left for the official staff to ride. It may sound quite haphazard now but it was all quite jolly, nobody minded, and everyone enjoyed their ride. It was very much a case of the more the merrier.

Those of us who helped at the riding school at the top of the hill grew used to living in a perpetual state of anticipation of being told off or taking the blame for something. It was always our fault and, furthermore, that we had done whatever it was on purpose was taken for granted. Credit was rarely given.

The world-weary, 'Why am I the only one who can see it?' was a regular Rose soundtrack, as was the well-practised, 'What did you do that for?' (guaranteed to draw attention to anything you had hoped to have got away with). A popular variation on this theme was a long, drawn out, 'Oh *wwwwhy* did you do that?' said in tones of such utter despair as to suggest that whatever you had done meant we might as well all just give up and go home. When Julie got her own beautiful pony Mecca, Rose's reaction was to look her over and agree that yes, indeed, it was, right now, a very nice creature – then adding the caveat, 'Before you ruin it.'

When the vet made too many visits one winter, Rose observed that he was in and out of the yard like he had his braces caught on the gatepost, an interesting image. 'Hello there, we thought you'd died,' was a cheery greeting reserved for those clients who might have missed a few lessons, or for old chums who turned up on a yearly basis. How this was received depended largely on the age and health of the person involved.

Turn up when all the work was done and you'd be greeted with, 'Where've you been?' Or a sardonic, 'You're just in time to be too late!' On particularly trying days, when our efforts in the saddle fell short, Rose might shake her head and mutter, 'D'you know, it makes you weep to watch it,' which did nothing to raise moral. But even Rose acknowledged that sometimes the odds seemed stacked against us all, and when they were, she would give a rueful smile, telling us that, 'It's one of those days when everything *for* you is *against* you.' You know the sort of days she meant.

Combined, all these little reminders kept us on our toes and ensured we didn't fall prey to getting ideas above our station. As you might have gathered by now, there was not much chance of that happening…

Galloping across the page

EQUESTRIAN MAGAZINES COME AND go. Now, of course, the biggest threat to print is the internet, free information, however dubious, at the touch of a button. When I was a child, *Pony* magazine was my source of all things equestrian outside my miniscule sphere of influence (the library). Printed monthly, I duly put in a regular order at my local newsagent where I would collect it as soon as it arrived, scanning the magazines behind the counter every day around publication date, almost breathless with excitement when I saw its green masthead nestling amongst *Woman's Weekly* and *Princess Tina*.

To say *Pony* magazine then was a bit different to how it appears today would be pushing it. For a start, there were no coverlines, no screaming attention-grabbers to entice you to buy, just a big picture. It was printed entirely in black and white – even the cover – and sandwiched between the masses of tiny classified advertisements front and back were pages and pages of copy with very few photographs. Readers were expected to be just that, to *read* rather than just glance at the pictures. The attention-span of a child in the 1970s was far higher than it is now – or rather, it was expected to be. There was always a fictional story every month for light entertainment, and this gave me an idea. Aged fourteen, having scribbled plenty of pony stories in notebooks and stared into the distance imagining equine scenarios where I might be the heroine, I wrote a very short story called *The Scrapdealer's Mare* – about a neglected working horse – and, chancing my arm, submitted it. The then editor, Michael Williams, sent me back a nice letter telling me he liked it and that he intended to publish it in a future edition.

Now this was a Big Thing to me. A Very Big Thing. And when it was published, I received a cheque for six-pounds-fifty and that, I thought, was that. But it turned out that it wasn't, quite. For the following issue contained a letter from a reader who made no bones about how much she had hated my story, urging *Pony* to never print anything like it again. I had committed the error of writing a story where the horse died at the end. All the stories I had read up until then had ended happily, with any ill-treated horse finding a good home, and its tormentor receiving his or her come-uppance. I had, in an attempt at originality, decided that a happy ending wasn't for me, causing the reader who wrote in (who today would be labelled a snowflake) to condemn it as being 'vile and cruel', and demand the ending be re-written as she had cried her eyes out and been inconsolable for days.

Oh dear. What a horrible person I must be, I thought. Except that other readers then wrote in to disagree with 'vile and cruel' of wherever she was, and to defend my more – as they saw it – realistic storyline. Nowadays I would have no doubt been trolled, Twitter would have erupted and I would have silently thought that 'vile and cruel' ought to get over herself. In 1972 it all took several months for snail mail to go back and forth and be published, which rather took the sting out of the tail, although still I swung from the depths of despair to feelings of elation.

Thus began my writing career.

There were other equestrian magazines – principally *Horse and Hound* (of course), and *Riding* (sadly, no more), both for grown-ups. There was also a magazine available only by subscription, published bi-monthly. The format was unique in that each issue was dedicated to a single, highly rated commercial yard, showcasing how the yard was run and accompanied by a photograph of the proprietor at the front of the feature either thoughtfully seated in their study surrounded by horsy dogs, or teaching a class of tweed-clad and earnest-looking students on strapping ex-eventers. Occasionally, a copy would turn up at the riding school at the top of the hill and Rose was never very impressed – mainly because of the photographic guide included in each issue. Six pages filled with dozens of photographs in a how-to format. The reason Rose wasn't impressed was due to the how-to subject matter, which was usually something fairly basic.

'Six pages on putting on a tail bandage!' she would scoff, throwing us the magazine in disgust. 'Next month they're promising a six-page guide to putting on a rug!'

Rose was never impressed by anyone who took half-an-hour to do something she considered ought to be done in five minutes. And in the busy commercial yard that was the riding school at the top of the hill, she had a point. This theme was revisited on a regular basis as during the 1970s and 1980s any training for would-be instructors or grooms would take place at a commercial yard where they learned their trade at speed, realistically equipping them for the workplace. You could gain a BHSAI (British Horse Society Assistant Instructor) qualification in six months if you were a paying student – three in the very top establishments (which would only take you if you were of a suitable standard). Working pupils usually had to sweat it out for a year. Jan passed hers after training at a school near London, but now there are so many separate exams making up the qualification, it seems you almost have to *make* a career out of *getting* a career. When NVQs were introduced, and equine colleges sprang up, we couldn't understand why it would take a whole year for someone to achieve a billy-basic NVQ I, when it used to take three to six months for a student at a top yard to become an assistant instructor.

At least a decade after Jan gained her assistant instructor qualification, another helper took the same course at the same establishment. Only when she returned to teach at the riding school at the top of the hill, she had gained not only a new qualification, but a shiny new teaching voice.

No noticeable change in conversation, but the moment she stood in the school and started her lessons she morphed into a sort of English, female Loyd Grossman. Everything she said was elongated, stretched beyond comprehension.

'*Whoooooole riiiiiiiiiiiiiiiide waaaaaaaaaaaaalk oooooooon. Whoooooole ride terrrrrroooooot oooooooon… aaaaaaaaaaaaaaaaaaand waaaaaaaaaaaaaaaalk.*'

The horses, used to the usual commands, ignored her and carried on regardless and the riders, used to the horses obeying their instructor, had to work doubly hard: firstly translating what their instructor was saying, and then actually, for a change, transmitting those commands to their mounts. It was all very confusing – especially for the riders who hadn't realised their instructor was riding their horses for them. Maybe that was the point.

Meanwhile, back in another life, I wrote more stories and features for *Pony*. I watched the magazine evolve as it embraced colour, as the copy/picture ratio turned on its head, as free gifts started to appear. Later, I also wrote a couple of equestrian soap operas and a horsy whodunnit for grown-ups in *Pony*'s sister publication, *Horse&Rider*. When *Pony*'s editor left in the mid-1990s I was invited to work at the offices while they interviewed likely replacements – a chance at which I leapt. I never left, chaining myself to the editor's desk for the next twenty years.

I had a lot to learn and the curve wasn't just steep, it was practically vertical. Your idea of an editor may be of a person making leisurely decisions about the cover, commissioning features, attending boozy lunches and getting staff to write about this and that between attending photo shoots and interviewing famous riders – and there were a fair number of those jobs to it. However, on a small team I was writing most of the copy and taking a lot of the pictures and, in the early days, assisting with *Horse&Rider*, too. It was mostly writing, writing, writing. But I love writing, so that was all right.

My philosophy regarding the content in *Pony* magazine was always threefold: the information had to be *correct*. It had to be *safe*. Above all, it had to be *fun*. After all, if it's not fun then what's the point? Rose taught me that. But there is fun and there is fun – fun is subjective. I can't be the only one left wondering whenever I see a formidable Pony Club mother having her arm wrenched out of its socket by a powerful and snorting 17-hander at the starting gate at an event, and hear her parting words of encouragement to her ashen-faced daughter as the pair hurtle towards the first of what seems like a hundred or so intimidating cross-country fences, '*Remember Annabel, we do it for fun!*'

What's all this '*we*' nonsense?

Instructional features in *Pony* comprised riding and stable management, and I was always conscious that many readers didn't have their own ponies. Indeed, the most frequent letters we received were from readers demanding to know how they could make their parents buy them a pony – one even added that she considered her parents to be totally selfish, as they were always buying things for themselves – a can of worms on which I felt unable to comment. As I had never managed to persuade my own parents to fulfil my dreams, I could hardly advise readers with any confidence but I could, at least, sympathise with them, especially as by this time, with the creep of health and safety measures, and hardly any riding schools allowing riders to help out after their lessons, opportunities for horse-mad youngsters to spend time around horses and ponies were shrinking. No riding school at the top of the hill for them.

This has far-reaching consequences for the industry for if fewer young riders are encouraged to take their riding further than a once-weekly lesson, it stands to reason that their interest will die, and there will be fewer horse owners in years to come.

Luckily, those young riders who were determined to learn as much about horses as they could eagerly soaked up all the information we threw at them – and we made sure *Pony's* features were aimed at owners and non-owners alike, including features tailored to the riding school rider, and different types of riding school ponies. We even devised a postal achievement scheme, rewarded with certificates, for readers who might not have the opportunity to take tests with a pony in a more conventional setting.

Occasionally, the odd letter from a parent would arrive, complaining if we increased the cover price. This was understandable, but I always took the trouble to explain how the magazine was put together. It took two or three editorial staff to research, write and take photographs for each feature. A dedicated designer put the magazine together and, of course, this all had to be checked through. But a magazine doesn't rely on just editorial staff: there is an advertising department (without which the cover price would be much higher), accounts, reception, marketing, the website, subscriptions and event and merchandising departments. All this is overseen by management, paper needs to be sourced, delivery to outlets organised, and various other, boring yet necessary jobs crossed off the list every month. When you consider the price of some greetings cards, displayed on the window ledge for a week before being slung into the recycling, and compare these to a magazine into which so much effort has been made, and with so much information within its pages, the term 'value for money' springs to mind.

This is why I get so cross when I see people standing by the magazine racks in WHSmith reading a magazine from cover-to-cover, before replacing it and picking up another to read with no intention of taking it to the checkout. I hope you don't do it. What else can you call it but stealing?

Writing for young readers is never a case of dumbing-down. It was important that as *Pony* writers all bases in a feature were covered, without making readers feel stupid or patronised. We simply wrote as we would write for the grown-ups, without embellishment. We always joked that a subject that appeared as a six-page feature in *Horse&Rider* would, the next month, be covered in *Pony* via a double-page spread. It was the ultimate exercise in précis. Eight-hundred to a thousand words a feature concentrates the mind.

There were other features in *Pony*, of course: quizzes, puzzles, real-life experiences, stories, celebrity interviews, breed profiles, news, competitions and giveaways, pull-out posters – essential for adorning pony-mad teenagers' bedrooms – and the photo story, written and photographed in-house. These were fun to write and photograph – although we were unable to use the one written by an enthusiastic student on work-experience, due to her liberal inclusion of a police chase, a fire engine, and a celebrity cameo. Our fault, of course, we should have briefed her more fully and explained that our budget – not to mention our props department – was rather smaller than the BBC's.

When arranging a photoshoot at different riding schools and livery yards you never really knew what was going to greet you. At one riding school, having been assured most emphatically by the proprietor that she upheld the highest standards and that we would, should we wish, be able to eat our lunch from her spotless ponies' backs, I spent a good hour before picking up a camera, scrubbing them all up. Other yards were fabulous: gleaming ponies, tidy and competent riders and good humour all day long – but we still took along our equine make-up bag full of brushes, sponges and saddle soap just in case, as well as a brush and hair bands for any girls with Veronica Lake tendencies.

When I first worked for *Pony*, cameras needed film – rolls of it. And you never knew what images you had until the films were developed. And what you did have, invariably, were images and images of teenage girls with missing hands. Gloves for teenagers were, apparently, uncool, and in the winter all our models would draw up their hands into their sleeves, like a tortoise draws its neck into its shell, leaving us with photo stories littered with what looked like amputees. A solemn briefing before each shoot became the norm.

Winter shoots were always dreaded for not only were we at the mercy of the weather, but good light is essential for photographs. Winter sunshine casts long shadows, and images are never as good as when the sun is overhead. That is why most of our poster images were taken abroad, by professional photographers, where the weather and the light are more reliable.

Pony, and publishing, underwent a complete metamorphosis during the time I worked there. At the start of my editorship we published twelve issues a year, checked outsourced film of the pages prior to publication and used film cameras. By the time I left there were thirteen issues a year and we had re-launched the *Pony* Annual – all conceived and written in-house. Desk-top publishing had taken over film, and digital cameras had revolutionised our photoshoots. In addition, the magazine had its own website, a range of merchandise and even published books. Twenty years is a long time in publishing.

The trickiest – and most important – page of any magazine is the cover. It is the magazine's identity, its brand, and must be instantly recognisable amidst the sea of other magazines on the rack in a newsagent or supermarket. The masthead, including the logo at the top, must stand out and call to readers. We occasionally tweaked the *Pony* logo, ever mindful that evolution, rather than revolution, was the name of the game. You can find social media posts from past readers till coping with personal trauma following *Pony* changing its masthead from green to blue, its logo from italics to fully-blocked in the 1970s. These things matter more than you might think.

There are many rules for cover design and *Pony*'s designers followed them faithfully, replacing laid-back ears on the pony for those pointing forward to make the pony smile, ensuring the barcode was easy to scan and never obscured by a covermount (supermarkets impose hefty fines when barcodes are wrong or unreadable), and placing coverlines in appropriate positions where the most important can easily be seen on the bookstands, all the while ensuring the new cover was as different as it could be from the last in terms of colour. Once designed, management and several key staff members would be invited to view and offer suggestions prior to sign-off. Coverlines might be moved, fonts tweaked, positions altered, everyone standing back to assess the changes. Then, nine times out of ten, everything would be changed back to how it had been before. Designers know their stuff. There is no accident to good design but everyone – as one *Pony* designer used to say with a resigned sigh – thinks they're a designer.

One thing you learn on a magazine: you. Cannot. Please. Everyone. Whereas some people will love the pony on the cover, others will consider it ugly. If there is a girl model included, opinions again will be divided regarding her suitability (the absolute rule, however, is that she must be the right age – very young models put readers off for they will consider the magazine is for tiny kids). Someone will hate a blue background; another will have a thing against a certain font. Personal opinions must be sieved from professional ones. If you are not careful, and if you try to please everyone, you risk your cover becoming a camel. Getting the cover signed-off was cause for celebration.

If you want to live in the now, working on a monthly magazine is not for you. We wrote about what to do in the summer holidays as April showers pounded the office windows; clipping and rugs were planned as we sweated through July. A feeling of déjà vu and festive fatigue was experienced when Christmas arrived, as the season of goodwill been put to bed during September. Always there were relentless, unforgiving deadlines which could not be missed. In publishing, time waits for no-one.

For anyone who is horse mad, working on an equestrian magazine has to be a dream job. The next best thing to working with horses is writing about them. Actually, when the weather is foul, and old age starts to creep up on you, it might even be better.

Wish you were here... part two

ONE OF THE WONDERFUL perks of a job on an equestrian magazine was when various riding establishments offered journalists a holiday in return for a write-up in *Horse&Rider* magazine. We were happy to oblige – it would have seemed rude to refuse. So we rarely did. One such offer came from an establishment in Spain: three days' riding, followed by three days at the *Feria del Caballo* in *Jerez de la Frontera*. Well, that wasn't to be sniffed at, so I set off on the plane for Malaga, notebook and camera packed, primed and ready to go. These excursions had to be paid for by copious note-taking (it being easy to forget things when so much can be crammed into just a few days), considering what to include and what not to, and hauling the camera everywhere I went (even when riding, and the camera in question was large, heavy and took endless rolls of film, not the tiny digital jobs around now). Then, upon my return there was a much-laboured-over feature to be written. So not a total jolly – oh who am I kidding...

I was no stranger to Spain, and I had seen Spanish riders on their beautiful horses riding along the dual carriageway which runs from the airport in Malaga to Marbella, a terrifying, frantic road you would hesitate to walk alongside, let along ride a horse on. I can only compare it to hacking along the North Circular during Friday evening's rush hour, with bells on. But the Spanish seemed to think little of it. When I went on my riding holiday, I learned why.

Our base for the first three days was situated on the Atlantic coast. It was windy. It was windy in the way the Sahara might be described as a bit dry. I mean it was really, really, windy, the sort of wind you could lean in to, arms outstretched, just to see at how many degrees you could angle yourself before falling flat on your face. All this relentless blowing had formed huge sand dunes, high as mountains, pine trees anchoring the sands in place beside long beaches just begging to be galloped on. But these were no tourist beaches, tame and serene; rather the Atlantic foamed and grasped at the horses' fetlocks as we galloped along them, crashing and splashing onto rocks before being sucked back into the ocean mass. They were brutes of beaches, angry and relentless.

My mount was a small, black mare called Bruja, Spanish for witch. This little Pure Spanish Horse was the perfect ambassador for the breed that used to be known as the Andalusian and I appreciated that, as a journalist, I was lucky enough to be offered a quality horse to ride. Together with the other suitably mounted guests, we galloped along the beaches and rode amongst the pine forests, the branches swishing against our thighs as we pushed our way along the paths. We climbed the hills of Andalucía, griffon vultures dipping and soaring above us, the smell of crushed mint beneath our horses' hooves filling our nostrils. We marvelled as vast vistas opened up before us, and we held our breath in admiration of our mounts' surefootedness, each horse seeming to place its hooves in the imaginary prints of those in front as we climbed paths filled with loose and scattering rocks. At the summit we caught our breath as the greens and blues, the viridian and azure hues of the landscape spread out before us like a canvas, meeting more blues as it lifted towards the sky, cloudless, empty, stretching up and over our heads.

Away from the frantic activity and ever demanding deadlines of the office I had left behind, Spain worked its magic. Irritation when things took a while to get going was replaced by a more mellow feeling, of a sense of all being well with the world. The *mañana* philosophy gradually slipped into place, seeping into my bones. So what if dinner was at ten instead of nine? Who cared if breakfast came in dribs and drabs, or that the water in the bath was brown and brackish? What did it matter if it took everyone an hour to tack up, mount and adjust their girths? (Rose would have had apoplexy.) The mountains weren't going anywhere, the sea still lapped at the shore as it had since time began and the sun beamed down, with us for this day, and every day.

Bruja was a delight and we got on just fine. She went where she was pointed, she slowed when asked. She couldn't have been more perfect, but then, on the third day, somebody's mount got kicked and we were a horse down. The rider of the lame horse would have to return to base in the Land Rover which had brought our lunch. I felt guilty – here I was, essentially a freeloader on the beautiful Bruja while a paying customer was missing out. I heard somebody offering the paying guest their horse. They didn't really mind, they said, they could take photographs on the way back. Honest. It was my voice, I had said it – I had even meant it. But when I watched my little Spanish horse being ridden away by someone else, I minded. I minded so much it hurt.

Horses, they get right under your skin, and they don't take long to do it. Bruja, the witch, had me under her spell. I wished I could deflate my mount like a plastic unicorn, put her in my suitcase and take her home with me. Spanish horses are not only beautiful: they are kind and gentle, horses that want to please, horses that have been bred over the centuries to be the perfect horse – and Bruja fulfilled the brief spectacularly.

Some years later I learned that my perfect Spanish horse had been stolen, untied from outside a tavern, sneaked away by a stranger, leaving her distraught owner to wonder about her fate, to hope the thief was someone knowledgeable, someone who would appreciate her. How passionately I wished it, too. For only three days Bruja had been my horse but if I close my eyes as I sit in the sun I can still feel how she moved beneath me, responding to the merest suggestion of my weight in the saddle, feel her gather her energy into a willing canter, up for anything, my Spanish partner in another world.

It had been our last day in the saddle and everyone said their tearful goodbyes to their mounts for it was onward to the *Feria* for us all. Bags packed and bundled into the minibus, we were driven through the rolling hills of Andalucía, where fighting bulls grazed in ignorance of their destiny, and storks soared over fields of barley washed gold by the sun. Away from the tourist hotspots, Spain delights and amazes.

Jerez reverberates to the sound of scooters, trains, lorries and, during a week in May when it stages the *Feria del Caballo*, horses! Sherry *bodegas* at every corner of Jerez welcome visitors for a tour and a snifter or two. Then it's on to the bar-lined avenues at the *Feria*, where you can sip sherry in the sun or the shade, and watch the world go by. It was one big party, and everyone had dug out their best bib and tucker. Flamenco dresses were everywhere – the different styles, colours and combinations were bewildering – frocks which fitted, or once had. The women danced at every opportunity, showcasing their talent, their training, their passion for the traditional dance of Andalucía.

For three days I and my fellow holiday makers roamed the streets watching the parading horses, the flamenco dancing, the fairground and the most amazing horse shows – driving, dressage, showing, you name it, it was there, and I was lucky enough to be there to watch it. I hadn't really known what to expect but was blown away by the sheer scale of it all. Riders, mostly men in traditional Spanish dress, paraded their horses along the lanes made up of bars and eateries, essentially showing off. There was no end to the number of high-stepping horses with their tasselled fly fringes which had been fashioned by nuns, girls in frilled and spotted dresses sitting up behind the men, carriages of two, four and six horses – and sometimes mules – trotting along, the bells on their bridles announcing their arrival.

This was the *Feria*, a celebration of the *Caballo*, horses in Spanish bridles and saddles, riders in Spanish riding attire, the short jackets, the chaps, the low-crown hats. This is a chauvinistic society where the manes and tails of the dressage-trained mares and geldings are hogged and docked, where only stallions are allowed the vanity of flowing manes and tails. *Vaqueros* back their horses into line with the one-handed ease of a boy racer parking his Golf GTI. Poles used to control cattle are slung nonchalantly over the shoulders of the riders. Mares are led five in a line, linked by rope from their neck collars and handled by one man, the foals galloping and bucking around them, taking advantage of their freedom, unaware that once they are broken in, no such exuberance will be tolerated.

It was impossible to ignore the questions which formed in my mind: so many horses, all so well behaved, not a hoof out of line, obedient to a fault, no display of character tolerated, permitted or expected. Was this a result of training or of temperament? How much could be attributed to the mentality of the riders, their expectation of good manners? How much could be attributed to the spur at the heel, or obedience to the *serreta*, the spiked noseband worn low on the nose? I saw horses with scars running from below the eyes all the way down to the nostrils, shameful evidence of the *serreta* having been moved to fresh skin when too much damage had been done, disfiguring tell-tale marks that could only have been made by the metal teeth on a tender, thin-skinned skull.

It seems that the Spanish do not play at riding – their horses behave and do as they are told – there is no dialogue, no argument. This then, is how they can ride along the dual carriageways, knowing there will be no difference of opinion, no occasion when their mount ignores their leg and puts them under a lorry.

We like our horses to be our friends – but if we are pleasure riders then we can afford for them to have personality: we encourage it. Although good manners and obedience are necessary, there is still margin for character. Perhaps it is the Spanish horse's breeding, his long ancestry that has blessed him with his obedient nature. After all, when one is fighting the bull from his back there can be no committee, no discussion about the best way to dodge the horns. There is only one way: the horse must obey the rider, for a second's hesitation invites injury and death to both. Extreme, yes, but horses for us are a hobby. Horses to these riders are a way of life, and many are a means of transport. You expect your car to go where you steer it; the Spanish expect nothing less from their horses.

It was a strange trip, the juxtaposition between the first three days and my experience riding Bruja and the spectacle of the *Feria*, the obvious obedience of the horses under their Spanish riders. The thoughts and memories from those six days still linger, still suggest debate in my mind. It is not enough to be judgemental about another's culture, one has to see it operational and in situ, drawing conclusions only when all factors are taken into account. There is no definite line to be drawn, but rather each question invites yet another. We are supposed to walk a week in another's shoes before judging – maybe the same should be said for riding another's horse.

Seasons to be cheerful

FUNNY THING, MEMORY. WHEN I think back to helping at the riding school at the top of the hill, it is mostly the long summer days of the holidays that spring to mind, when we could ride all day, and all evening too, if we wanted; when it always seemed to be warm and sunny, and the living, as the song says, was easy.

As we rode down the back lane in late summer, we would see the combines in the fields relentlessly cutting through the crops, dust kicked up from the wheels and the blades. Transforming the landscape, the huge machines shaved the fields as they gobbled up the dry oceans of waving wheat and barley, spitting out the waste straw behind to lie in wavy lines on the fields. From afar, the harvested fields took on the semblance of huge squares of yellow knitting before the balers and trailers followed, compressing the straw, transporting the bales to the safety of the barns, bedding for the whole area's horses safely gathered in.

If we were lucky we could ride the stubble fields for a week or two, but eventually they were torched and burnt, as was then the custom. Great clouds of smoke billowed up towards the sky like tornados as the flames crackled and stretched across the ground like greedy, scarlet vandals, scorching off the stalks left behind, leaving the ground black and smouldering, the dragon threatening to flare up again as we rode past, our nostrils filled with the smell of smoke. The landscape turned dark with the promise of autumn, awaiting the cut of the plough and the sowing of next year's crop.

Summer was when we could take the ponies on a two-hour ride to the other side of the Roding Valley, paddling in the river, desperately keeping our mounts moving so they hadn't a chance to get down and roll, yet sneakily hoping someone else wouldn't, and that their ponies would. During the summer holidays we all got to the riding school early and stayed until the sun went down. For six weeks my parents saw me first thing in the morning and last thing at night. Sometimes, we didn't go home at all.

If there was an event – the annual gymkhana for example – Rose would let us stay in the loft. Running the whole length of one side of the stable yard, above the stalls, the loft was accessed via stairs hidden behind a door in the feed room. Originally, it was probably designed for storage of fodder and before our time it had been used as a clubhouse (and would be again in the 1980s). In the early

1970s it was full of rubbish – old furniture, magazines, stuffed animals, old gymkhana schedules – even a kayak and paddle – and we knew this because we'd sneaked up and had a poke around while Rose was out riding. But then the loft was cleared out, leaving only a few armchairs, and some of us who helped at the school, gluttons for punishment, thought it would be a fine idea to stay in the loft overnight.

Why do teenagers have such bad ideas? But Rose agreed to it – strings attached – we had to behave, be quiet, etc, etc. And so, our parents' permission granted (again, why? How?), a number of us, armed with provisions from the village shop, settled down for uncomfortable and sleep-depraved nights on smelly old chairs. We thought it was great fun, and I suppose it was at the time, but I can't imagine why we thought so. It was just another adventure.

During the famously hot summer of 1976, when I was in my late teens and working full-time at the riding school at the top of the hill, it took all my energy just to get through the day. How well I remember feeling like a piece of chewed string at the end of each and every sweat-filled shift. Hacks out were slow, the ground baked hard like concrete, the clay which, in winter, sucked off horseshoes and stuck to our horse's legs like glue shrivelled and shrank, cracking and crazing like a jigsaw, the gaps growing wider, a measure of the days without rain. The grass turned yellow, then brown, the landscape needing only the bones of a perished cow, its skull and horns bleached by the relentless sun, to compete with scenes from the deserts of Australia and Texas.

The horses, who began the day with sweat under their tack, on their necks and their flanks, were sponged down between rides, hosed over at the end of the day, turned out to roll in the saffron grass and pick at the precious hay we'd put out to replace it. Cantering was out of the question and riders grew bored, but understood the need to save legs and joints. We feared for the hay crop – that was the year the price for a single bale trebled in price to a pound.

Of course, the sun didn't always shine, even when I was helping out at weekends and after school. When we brought the ponies in soaking wet, rain still falling and seeping through our thin Husky jackets, we needed to improvise when it came to scrapers as no official ones were included in essential equipment.

'Here, use these,' Rose would say, bending down outside the kitchen door and gathering up a few shallow tins. 'These' were already on their second life. In the first they had held Fray Bentos steak-and-kidney pies before being re-imagined as plates for the cats' food. Their third reincarnation was to make excellent water scrapers, even if the ponies did leave the yard with globules of Whiskas clinging to their coats like pink ticks.

Recycling was one of Rose's obsessions. Take baler twine. There were not many repairs that couldn't be accomplished with the versatility of the humble twine, otherwise redundant after a bale had been used. In Rose's hands, baler twine became the stuff of legend, morphing into nails, screws, wire, fastenings of all kinds. It gained magical properties, injecting a new lease of life into practically anything – even a belt for Rose's mac when it rained. If you could baler-twine it, it was sorted! If you couldn't, well, it was probably dead and beyond revival.

When we were all about fifteen years old, boys arrived on the scene. On the far side of the nearby park was a farm where two brothers lived. They had friends – you know how it is. In the time-honoured way we rode our owned or borrowed ponies over there with the sole purpose of honing our flirting skills, such as they were.

Attending the weekly discos at the school at the bottom of the hill we danced in a line, ready to be snapped up by any scouts seeking replacements for *Pan's People*, and the parties – getting progressively wilder – began. We sang along to Sweet, The Carpenters, Slade and Alice, we all sported hair like Suzi Quatro and Dora from *Follyfoot*, and wore our Ben Sherman shirts on the outside of our Levi's. The Glenn Miller revival saw 1940s-style dresses and huge, golf-ball-like necklaces which banged against our necks as we danced, bruising our bones. Platform shoes made us taller, Crombie coats smartened up the boys, hiding hideous 1970s tank tops, but not quite masking the smell of Brut. Managing quite successfully to mix our interests we had become the older girls we used to look up to, the ones with the transistor radios, who could ride out alone and were helpful to Rose. Mindful of the example up to which we needed to live we embraced a pursuit new and exciting to us.

The guys would head to the handy breaker's yard nearby and exchange a couple of quid for a clapped-out old banger that was no longer roadworthy, but still had a few miles left in it. Once filled with fuel from the farm pump several of us would squeeze inside – the brothers' smelly and panting Labrador amongst us – and two guys would climb up onto the roof. The object of the game was to drive the car around the field and see how long it took for the outside passengers to come to grief. The inside passengers would all be bouncing around, screaming whenever the car went up on two wheels as the driver threw it around, banging their heads on the sides as it swerved, and shouting encouragement when an arm, leg or the occasional head dangled teasingly down from above. The game concluded when the two outside riders had been thrown from the roof, or when the car upended into a ditch, wheels spinning, having reached its absolute final resting place – whichever came first. Cue another trip to the breaker's yard. I seem to remember the dog being the most enthusiastic of us all. Oh, and in case you're wondering, nobody got killed. Or even hurt. How or why? I have no idea. It wasn't through lack of trying.

One freezing winter's day, after a hack and on the way home through the park's official bridle path, a few of us detoured into the farm just before the sun went down, and passed the time of day with brother M. After a few minutes standing still, Trina's pony Babycham started to shiver. No worries! Brother M dived into the house and reappeared with a blanket, throwing it over Cham's newly clipped back so that conversation could resume. A few moments later, an upstairs window was flung open, through which a furious brother T stuck his head shouting, 'Oi, M you stupid (insert worst insult you can think of here), that blanket's off my (and again, this time ending in *ing*) bed!'

Unfortunately, this action caused all the horses to spook and scatter in terror, the blanket sliding off Cham's back into the mud where it gradually sank, like some beast left for dead by its own herd, to be fossilised for future generations to ponder over and name.

Siblings, eh? Nicky shared her pony with her elder sister, Chris, but they got on really well when, sometimes, siblings don't. With six years between us, my elder sister and I enjoyed a good relationship with unshared interests. A colleague at *Pony* magazine told me that when she was a child, she thought nothing of obeying her older brother's instruction to hold balloons while he attempted to pop them by hurling darts in her direction. She was just so enamoured of him, and possibly had her eye on a future career in the circus – although whether she'd still have any left to see the missiles coming by then is debatable. People's reaction to this non-horsy story is one of either wide-eyed horror or a loud guffaw, take your pick. Another colleague remembered her older brother pushing her over on to their gravel drive, following through by shoving her face along the stones for good luck. The overriding lesson seems to be that if you must have a brother, best to ensure he is younger than you to give yourself a fighting chance of making it to adulthood in one piece.

Some of us had bicycles by the time brother T's blanket sank into the mud, and would freewheel down the hill at great speed after a day at the yard, at least nine of us gamely clinging on to three or four bikes rather than wait for the bus. Rose used to do the same when she was a girl, telling us about her friend who would work the handlebars with her feet while she combed her hair on the way down. I couldn't see this working as our hair streamed out behind us like horses' tails, we went so fast. It took all of five minutes to get home, instead of half-an hour. It was, of course, a totally different story getting to the riding school in the morning as we had to walk the bikes up the hill, the gradient getting the better of us. Once, one summer, three of us decided we'd ring the changes and take a different route. Instead of the road, why not walk up across the fields? A short cut, surely? Turned out to be anything but and we finally arrived, wheezing and red in the face, a furious Rose tapping her foot and looking·at her watch.

'You're supposed to be coming to work,' she told us crossly, throwing the head collars at us and storming off to the field to catch the horses, 'not going for a Round Britain Tour.' We stuck to the road after that.

On a slow day, some of us would catch the bus to Epping, to the magical place that was Mr Batchelor's saddlery, where the beautiful glass-fronted, wooden drawers held strange and wondrous things: bits, gloves and pieces of saddlery, the uses for which we could only imagine. There were racks of jodhpurs and jackets, beautiful saddles, bridles and rugs – although nothing like the bewildering choice of rugs on offer now. You could have jute, a canvas New Zealand (which is what a turnout rug was called then) or, if you had money to burn, a glamorous woollen day rug edged in a contrasting colour, like the one worn by Mrs P's beautiful mare, topped with its fancy, anti-cast roller.

Decades later, when I was at *Pony* magazine, every season I'd be shown the new rug collection from each of the famous rug brands, spending several hours perusing racks of equine coats in a bewildering array of colours, patterns and weights for all eventualities, the marketing manager for the company enthusiastically explaining each rug in turn. Turnout, heavy turnout, *extra*-heavy turnout, sub-zero turnout, light turnout, slightly lighter turnout, heavy rain turnout, downpour turnout, drizzle turnout, turnout with hood (interchangeable light and heavyweight). Stable rug, winter stable rug, summer stable rug, stable rug for low temperatures, stable rug for even lower temperatures, stable rug for sub-zero temperatures, stable rug with lightweight hood, stable rug with heavyweight hood. Fly rug, sweet-itch rug, travel rug, summer travel rug, winter travel rug, winter travel rug for sub-zero temperatures. Wicking rug, super-wicking rug, extra-super-duper-wicking rug, dust sheet, exercise sheet, sub-zero exercise sheet... on and on and on and on...

All these rugs came in an amazing selection of colours, in all the sizes... the listings continued until I could feel my brain shutting down in turmoil, my eyelids going from light to heavy, to super-heavy, as one with the rugs. I mean, if you got fed up with reading that exhaustive list, imagine having to not only look at each one intently, but be enthusiastic about them, too. But it had its upside for even now, when I can't sleep, I try to list all the rugs I've ever been shown, in all the weights, in all the colours and before lo... *zzzzzzzzzzzzzz*.

When did rug buying become such an ordeal? It is now thought that over-rugging contributes to equine weight gain. Traditionally, horses put on weight over the summer and shivered some of it off over the winter. Not now. Now, horses have bigger wardrobes than their owners and are turned out practically all year round without ever feeling the sun or the rain on their backs. Stables have rope lines full of rugs around the walls, and it is more unusual now to see a horse without a rug in the field than with one.

Whenever we pass a field of horses in turnout rugs my husband gleefully declares there they are, all wearing their jackets. Horsy folk often call rugs their horses' coats, but *jackets* – the term just doesn't sit right, does it? It suggests they're all out there in the mud in satin paisley, smoking cigarettes jammed in holders and sipping whisky from cut glass like a herd of equine Noël Cowards. Or is that just me?

Of course, rugs are for our benefit. Apart from rugs to compensate for clipped coats, and fly or sweet-itch rugs, most are unnecessary for the horses. They keep horses clean, they flatten their coats, hoods protect manes. Horses are designed to combat the elements without help – their wet coats form points from which water can drip, the crazy arrangement of hair at the stifle ensures water runs away from their nether regions, keeping their bellies dry. An unpulled tail prevents rain from running down between the hind legs. A good hedge and band of trees will be utilised more by horses than any man-made shelter, and only a combination of wind and freezing rain will see them shivering and wanting to come in out of the weather.

Back when rug selection was limited to indoor, outdoor and possibly exercise (no wicking, if your horse got wet you 'thatched' it, piling straw onto its back and covering this with an inside-out jute rug until it dried off – and very effective it was, too), our purchases at Mr Batchelor's were confined to a new hoof pick or dandy brush, which we would squirrel away in our personal tack boxes kept in the school horses' tack room. They were for the school horses' benefit after all, because we used our own brushes to groom them. Despite this, when we got back after our three-hour trip Rose would berate us for having gone AWOL, even when we weren't officially working.

'Where have you all been?' she'd ask, 'I could have done with you all here! Come on girls, hop about, we've got a lot to get through today!'

Mr Batchelor's emporium is, sadly, no more and sorely missed.

Winter meant freezing taps, icy cobbles, the horses living in and almost fifty stables to muck out. The smelly jute rugs were held on with surcingles with a square of foam underneath, which held rugs on with only limited success, especially if a horse's back wasn't clipped. In the morning you often found horses sporting their rugs like aprons, having slipped around in the night. Cross-over straps are a brilliant invention – not only for keeping a rug in place, but for keeping pressure off the wearers' backs.

We had green or blue canvas turnout rugs, with only a thin under-blanket sewn inside. No tail flaps. No shoulder-hugging neckline. No hoods or neck covers. The Essex clay had to be picked off by hand from the tender legs and bellies of horses who were still hacking out at the weekend. Washing boxes were a future luxury, equine solariums the stuff of science fiction. We brushed, and brushed, and brushed. As we brushed, the clay came off in clouds and settled on us. I must have swallowed pounds of the stuff. Rose considered washing horses to be the devil's work and only to be undertaken on grey horses in the summer – and even then only if an event was in the offing. Dark horses or tails were never to see a bucket and sponge. The most exotic potion we could buy to help us win the battle of dirt was a squeezy bottle of Gallop shampoo. That was it. Oh stable workers today, how I envy you – although I can still dry-scrub a stable stain to oblivion.

Opening the door from the yard to the stalls on a winter morning you would be greeted with the body heat from six horses, the Victorian-designed high ceiling ensuring such good air flow that I can't remember any of them getting a cough, as the *Manual of Horsemanship* promised lest top stable doors be shut. The wooden walls which had converted stalls into loose boxes proved a mixed blessing for one day one of the cats, having explored a plastic carrier bag which held someone's lunch, emerged wearing said bag around its neck like a feline superhero's cloak, and leapt up onto the wall before anyone could grab it. Desperate to escape the monster following it, the cat scampered along the top of the wall in panic, the bag filling out like a parachute and causing a domino effect of horses scrabbling about on the tiles, snorting and crashing into the partitions as the cat-bag combo skipped past on high.

Instead of a muck heap we had a huge skip, changed weekly. A new skip made life easy – we just wheeled our barrow along a plank and dumped its contents at the far end. But it soon filled up. When it did, the doors were shut and muck then had to be forked up over the side, a particularly unpleasant task when it was windy. It always got too high before it was due to be collected, so several of us would be tasked with climbing up into it, jumping up and down to make room for more. Lamenting holes in your boots cut no ice – you were simply handed a couple of plastic carrier bags and told to get on with it. It was a horrible, smelly, steaming job which meant that you were never bothered on your journey home on the bus by the nutter – because, of course, you *were* the nutter.

You might understand then, why we didn't cut much sartorial ice as we went about our work. Things got dirty, smelly, wet. We did have cause to re-think this strategy when one well-meaning rider brought us a huge bag of her cast-off clothes, from which she invited us to take our pick. Clearly, she thought we couldn't afford anything but the clothes in which we stood. Kind of her, but a bit, well, you know – especially as it wasn't even horsy apparel. We decided we might possibly need a bit of a make-over and to up our game.

We may have learned our lesson regarding walking to the riding school at the top of the hill across country in the mornings, but that didn't mean we couldn't experiment when it came to going home. One freezing, starry, moonlit night, caught up with the romance of the oncoming festive season and the falling snow, several of us set off for home across the fields, our boots making unfamiliar human tracks in the whiteness, the twinkling lights from the housing estate beckoning us home. It took *ages*, so that was a one-off.

Snow brought its own problems. We cleared paths so the horses wouldn't slip, and all rides took place in the school, Rose telling everyone to get their horses moving as they hunched their backs up against the cold and threatened to buck, the riders' backs copying the horses as they froze in the saddles. Instructing in the freezing cold, even in the indoor school, meant you'd be shivering minutes into the lesson. I used to trot around on foot behind the ride every ten minutes or so, just to convince my body that I hadn't died.

Growing cold meant your reflexes slowed down. If one of the fond parents watching from the gallery decided to leave, they somehow always managed to time it just as Caramac, a pony who was a martyr to his nerves, was passing below. This would prompt Caramac, convinced the parent was about to leap onto his back and tear his throat out, to spin from the wall in terror, at speed, and hurtle across the school, his rider spitting sawdust on the floor behind him and you, if you happened to have been in his path, spinning like a top. He was no volunteer, was Caramac, his ambition being to do as little work as possible, whether in the school or out on a hack, mainly because he was always on the lookout for something to be scared of.

I sympathise with nervous horses and ponies: the ones who drive you bonkers by shying at a falling leaf, who tremble at the sight of something out hacking that was there yesterday, the day before *and* the day before that, who leave you gasping as they shoot sideways when a terrifying puddle blocks their path. You can't wipe out fifty-five million years of evolution in a blink of a mere few millennia, and the most nervous are no doubt descended from a long line of horses possessing high personal survival skills, living on to breed by dint of their reflexes.

Or perhaps they just need glasses.

As an example of learned behaviour, rather than inherited, my mother was always jumpy around loud noises – but then she lived through the blitz. She and my grandmother preferred the War-Office-approved air-raid response of sitting under the kitchen table when the doodlebugs hit, rather than repairing to the spider-ridden Anderson shelter in the garden. Bombs or spiders… bombs or spiders…? Mmmmm, tough call.

My relationship with Caramac changed dramatically one summer's day. A pleasant afternoon's hack was continually held up by Caramac's reluctance to break from his usual holiday, aided and abetted by a particularly ineffectual child in his saddle. The pair displayed less urgency than a French duke on his way to the guillotine, both oblivious to my frequent requests for them to keep up. By the time we reached the yard I had had enough. The child I could do little about, but the same couldn't be said of one lazy palomino pony, creeping along as though his legs were tied together with lead weights.

'Who are you taking the next ride out on, Janet?' Rose asked me, expecting the usual reply – Mo. It was a small ride with some gung-ho youngsters who could all canter.

'That bloody Caramac!' I told her, letting down the nearside stirrup and hopping up into the plate. 'I'm fed up with him faffing about and doing half the work of the other ponies!'

Rose's eyebrows shot up into her forehead in surprise, a reaction shared by the paying clients – not to mention Caramac, as I headed him, wide-eyed, towards the gate. He was having none of it.

'Come on,' I told him, 'you're going in front.'

'I can't!' he replied, his eyes out on stalks, as if I had told him to take off and fly.

We argued like Keith and Orville for a few minutes…

'You can!'

'I can't!'

'You can.'

'I *can't*!'

'You *can*!'

He could.

He went.

I had the best ride! True, we wobbled about a bit, zooming from side-to-side from one imaginary scary thing to another, particularly when we cantered, but given a firm hand – or more accurately, leg – Caramac morphed from reluctant to racehorse, and went like a rocket. By the time we got home, any previous behaviour had been forgiven. I was smitten.

'How did you get on?' asked Rose, bracing herself for a negative reaction.

'Fabulous!' I grinned. 'I'll take the fast ride out on him tomorrow.'

And I did. And when the riders looked down and saw who I was riding they laughed and told me not to worry, they'd wait for me to catch them up. But they didn't need to as my new, improved mount led all the way. I expect Caramac rued the day he crept along on that ride with the child on another planet, because I rode him quite often after that.

I even entered my new favourite pony in a club dressage competition one evening. Unfortunately, the outdoor school, usually quiet and still, reverberated to the sound of an enthusiastic wedding party in the village hall, which was adjacent to one side of the school, causing Caramac to suffer an attack of the vapours every time we passed. The word *erratic* cropped up quite a lot on my score sheet. It is a word I have avoided when teaching, ever since I advised a gentleman rider that his trot was erotic. Still don't know where my head was that day, don't like to think about it too much. Freud would have had something to say about it, but we all know his mind rarely lifted from the gutter anyway.

In bad winter weather there might be only a few riders in the week so by the time it got to Friday, Rose would moan that the horses hadn't had enough exercise and were all standing on their heads. We'd be ordered to saddle the worst, mount up and take them down the back lane to get the tickle out of their toes in an effort to keep the weekend's body count as low as possible. The only reason *we* stayed on was because we weren't allowed to fall off.

Creeping along the back lane, aware of equine backs beneath us like camel humps just itching to buck, we'd play out the reins so to let some energy out the front end, trotting on the level parts, gingerly turning our mounts around when we got to the farm and praying it wouldn't excite them – because even idiots know that turning and retracing one's steps when hacking can be tantamount to suicide. Then we'd clatter up the hill again, rising gently to the trot, breathing regularly, keeping our knees in and our heels down, trying to hide how relieved we were when we all reached the safety of the yard, only to find that Rose had another group all saddled up, waiting, snorting and all too raring to go.

If things got too bad, one or two of the most lethal creatures might be let into the indoor school to do their worst without a rider. They were rarely turned out in winter – that Essex clay would take too many man hours to get off.

Christmas Day meant getting to the school before dawn if you wanted to finish early. The jolly and festive atmosphere meant there were plenty of extra hands to help, and with no rides and all the tools and wheelbarrows working flat out all morning the stables were finished well before lunchtime, the staff enjoying some rare time off with their families. Families who, when informed you were intending to go and help on Christmas Day sighed, shook their heads and asked, seriously, whether you couldn't give horses a rest for just *one* day of the year. Some people still don't understand how animals don't take a day off, or stop eating and expelling, just because it's Christmas.

Rose would welcome old friends for Christmas lunch in her big room next to the kitchen, the fire crackling in the grate in fine Dickensian style, the wood-panelled walls covered in photographs of horses, past and present, owned or bred. In the afternoon not only would Rose and her friends water and feed all the school horses and liveries at the riding school, but they would then go on to the two livery yards Rose managed to do all the same jobs there. When I was much older, I helped in this way and there was something about caring for the horses when nobody else was about during the festive season that was quite magical. It beat sitting at home watching *The Great Escape*, anyway.

Victoria

WHEN I WAS FIFTEEN, it seemed I was always short of money for rides and so I decided to do something about it. I advertised, by way of a postcard, in the window of the village shop.

Odd jobs undertaken. Janet. Phone number.

I sat back and waited for the offers to flood in, and in they flooded, to the tune of one. But one, it turned out, was all I needed.

Did I, the female voice on the other end of our landline asked, happen to know anything about horses?

What were the chances? Pretty high when you think about it, as even today the village boasts that it has more equine inhabitants than human. Because, the voice continued as I held my breath, she and her husband had a horse stabled at the farm at the end of the back lane, and they were unable to get there twice a day to dress a wound it had sustained.

Well I'm your girl, I assured them, arranging to meet them at the farm. The mare was dark bay, about fifteen hands and, sure enough, sported a wound on her side which I dutifully cleaned and redressed twice a day, every day, for about a fortnight. Nice mare, no trouble, job done. Only, as is the way of these things, it turned out it wasn't. Because the couple were re-locating to a neighbouring county where they were having stables built. They had enough room to take the bay mare right away, but their other horse would be staying at the farm for a while. Would I, they enquired, be willing to look after her for them throughout the coming winter months? They'd pay all the bills and I could ride her – she'd be my total responsibility and, to all intents and purposes, mine.

Well, paint my legs blue and call me Charlie, I wasn't about to say no. A horse of my own, all expenses paid? Yes please, bring it on. For years I, and my friends, had all dreamed of being offered a horse or pony to ride and now that we were seen by Rose as valued helpers and therefore fairly competent, it was beginning to happen. Many of the livery owners – at the riding school at the top of the hill and the two yards close by – asked us to exercise their horses for them on a regular basis, and we appreciated the privilege. But we had our rules, unwritten yet strictly observed by all except one of our gang, which were that we didn't tread on each other's toes, and that offers were to be made without obvious touting. As a result of some serious sucking-up (which was obvious to us, if not to the owners) by this one exception within our ranks, there were few horses around which she hadn't exercised at one time or another. But while most of us had our fair share of rides, this offer was on another level, this horse was to be totally mine for *months.*

It turned out the owners ran a carriage hire business, the two horses taking it in turns to pull said carriage and tow brides to their nuptials in style. The horse-that-was-to-be-mine was called Victoria. About 15.2hh, dappled grey, just an ordinary, nice, honest mare with no hang-ups, used to the unusual, unfazed by practically anything. Talk about a dream come true – I had a horse!

Of course it was a huge responsibility. I had to go there every night after school to muck her out, feed, water and exercise her (no problem), as well as every weekend. Luckily, the farmer fed her every morning and checked she had water. But this was winter, so it wasn't quite as easy as it would have been during the long, warm days of summer. But hey-ho, I wasn't complaining. Only now, as I write this, does it occur to me that they should perhaps have paid me.

Walking down that lonely back lane after school wasn't nice. If my mother had known what I was up to, she'd have had a blue fit – quite rightly. It was like I was just begging to become a statistic. I was always grateful whenever any of the horse owners, driving down on the way to their own horses, stopped and offered me a lift, clearly horrified to see me alone, and wondering whether I was totally mad. When nobody drove by I'd walk briskly past the woods, not daring to run in case I lapsed into panic, for certainly there was the potential to go a bit mad.

There were always all sorts of ghost stories bandied about at the riding school, and we'd mucked about a bit with an Ouija board that summer, turning livery owner Mrs T's tack box upside down and writing the letters on the bottom so she wouldn't know. She must have wondered why, when she had left her tack box in good order, the sight that beheld her when she opened it up again was that of total disarray. Maybe Mrs T believed in ghosts – with our help. We'd scared ourselves witless on more than one occasion, convinced we'd conjured up some horrible spirit, and these memories always seemed to surface and whirl around my head as I walked to Victoria in the dark, listening for anything unusual, counting the footsteps to ensure those I heard were mine and mine alone. Getting to the yard with its friendly lights and other people was always a relief – and I tried not to think about the return walk back.

Strangely, the one thing that never seemed to bother any of us was the church graveyard, slap bang next to the riding school. It was just there, and we never gave it any thought at all, even on the darkest of nights. Whenever I watch those moving-to-the-country shows on the telly I'm always amazed when people refuse, point blank, to consider living in a converted church with a graveyard still attached. Creepy, they protest. Oh no, never, *ever* could they live in such an environment. Are they mad? Dead people must be the most perfect neighbours in the (under) world! No balls kicked about, no noisy kids screaming all summer long, no car doors slamming. You wouldn't have to ask me twice.

With the only indoor school belonging to the riding school, and no outdoor one at any of the livery yards, exercising in the week meant you had to hack. If you've never ridden in the dark let me tell you it can be rather fun – much better than walking in it, anyway. Away from the street lights you can see remarkably well. Throw in a full moon and you even get shadows. Oh, hang on, I probably need to add a disclaimer at this point. I am in no way endorsing the idea of hacking in the dark. Don't hack out in the dark. No really. Don't. It was all right in the 1970s, though. But as with so many pastimes deemed acceptable during that decade, you can't consider it a reliable barometer in today's world.

I would meet up with my friends on their horses – borrowed or their own – and we'd all charge about the countryside for a happy hour, trusting our horses' eyesight when our own failed. It's a wonder we didn't all come to a sticky end, but we didn't, and the horses weren't fazed at all. Open spaces were a doddle, even though the woods were a bit spooky on a windy, moonless night, but it was just something we did. The horses had to be exercised, and we wanted to ride. So ride we did, peeling off and returning to our respective yards after we'd dashed about a bit: Jan and Moo to the park yard, Jill with Tina and Julie with her own Mecca to the pub yard (she'd outgrown Doublet by this time), Trina and Babycham and Nicky and Carousel to the riding school and me, on Victoria, to the farm.

But then, Jan and I devised a plan which worked for both of us. We would meet up after school at the bus stop and, alighting from the 4.30pm bus at the village green, walk down to the park yard and brush over and tack up Moo. Moo belonged to Pam, a member of the group of cool girls who had preceded us. At this time Pam was at work or had progressed to boys, something anyway that occupied most of her time, so Jan had Moo as her own. Her real name was Harlequin (Moo's not Jan's) and it was easy to see why. She was mainly white, with a black head and neck, and another black splodge across one flank. Nobody, not even Rose, ever called her anything but Moo.

Anyway, with Jan riding Moo (Harlequin, *whatever*), and me walking alongside, we'd make our way along the not very busy road, an ineffective stirrup light on Jan's outside stirrup (a candle would have thrown more light but stirrup lights were all we had available, no reflective clothing being on offer in the 1970s, even with the three-day-weeks and blackouts – which were a barrel of laughs at the yards – I am not recommending this, remember), before heading past the riding school and down the back lane towards the farm, hearing Rose's dulcet tones in the indoor school as we crept past – as much as you can creep with a fully shod horse in the party. Only then would Jan quit her nearside stirrup and I'd struggle up behind her. With Moo being what breeders like to call a roomy mare, she might have been designed for two.

At the farm, Jan would then wait for me to flick a brush over and tack up Victoria, and we'd head off around the countryside for our ride, ending up back at the park yard where Jan put Moo to bed. We'd then retrace our steps back to the farm, with Jan now up behind me. The next day, we'd do the whole thing in reverse. We didn't dare let Rose see us – she'd have had a fit – but surely all those cowboy films I'd watched as a child couldn't be wrong. Plus, we were only teenagers and very lightweight. We'd get back home at about nine at night, if we were lucky. And that, as I explained to you at the time, Mr S, is why I didn't get much homework done.

One evening, with us both up on Moo and heading down to the farm, Moo stopped dead parallel to the woods and refused to go on. We didn't know why, and we didn't want to think too much about it but we couldn't just stay there forever. Even the frantic kicking of two sets of legs couldn't persuade our previously willing piebald to change her mind so in the end I had to slither off and lead her, the hairs at the back of my neck standing on end, my eyes firmly looking ahead, unwilling to discover what, if anything, Moo might have seen or sensed. I was aware that should anything nasty burst out of the trees and come for us, Jan was perfectly poised to make a break for it on her trusty steed, whereas I would be left to take the hit. But nothing did. Maybe Moo had just wanted to make a point. She never did it again so it remained a mystery.

Opposite the park yard was, surprise, surprise, a rather nice park – the park adjacent to the farm where we enjoyed fun times in terminally ill cars. Not a park with swings and children's paraphernalia but a nature park, with ancient trees of note, views towards London and a huge deer enclosure full of, well, huge deer. Its country house had been occupied by the fire service and the military during the war, and you could still see some of the posts which had supported wires for the field telephones. After the war it had fallen into disrepair so was torn down and eventually replaced by a typically 1960s café. It used to do a rather good egg and chips, but even the café has now been replaced by a modern visitor and wildlife centre, from where you can catch glimpses of the O2 Arena, formerly known as The Dome.

We weren't allowed to ride around the park. *Horse riders must keep to the path,* commanded the sign. Well that was boring – the path just went straight through, plus it was tarmac so you could only trot, and even then it was only open during daylight hours. But the rest of the park was full of open spaces, lovely flat areas of grass just begging to be ridden on. Besides, it wasn't as though anyone went in there after dark – the gates were shut and the park was closed to the public, which included us. Only you could still slip in through the trees if you knew where to go. And we did. So in we slipped. It was perfect going – all our usual bridle paths of sucking, squelching Essex clay around the permitted routes around the riding school and the farm resembled something like the war-torn Somme in winter, and the park offered us virgin turf. Except we didn't know the lie of the land and, as Victoria couldn't see the rise in the ground one evening, we both hit it.

'Your head's bleeding,' Jan told me.

Of course it was – I wasn't wearing a hat. Even small head wounds bleed a lot so it looked worse than it was. I hoped. I checked Victoria's knees as best I could by the pathetic gloom of Jan's stirrup light and, after making sure she was unblemished and sound, (anyone who's read *Black Beauty* knows the shame of broken knees), got back on, riding beside Jan as we headed for the break in the trees.

'You're going to have to get something on it,' said Jan, making like my mother.

I knew that.

'Not iodine,' I replied, thinking of Rose's dispensary in the hallway. 'Not that horrible yellow stuff. It stings.'

'What are you doing?' said Jan, in alarm, leaning over to take one of Vicky's reins as I rolled my head around in circles. 'Are you all right?'

'My neck aches,' I told her. She'd thought I'd gone a bit doolally. I couldn't rule it out.

It was Rose who went doolally, dabbing the tiny cut with iodine, just as I was afraid she would. At least it wasn't gentian violet – imagine the mess. Of course, we never told her *where* I had hit the deck, only that I had. I still have a small scar. It could have been worse. Maybe it was and I just didn't – and still don't – know it.

Some of us braved riding in the park during daylight hours, at least during the summer as the sun was going down and the park was almost empty. If you hugged the tree line around the first field you could crash into the woods through the bits of Victorian park railings that were broken, past the KEEP OUT and PRIVATE LAND signs painted on the trees (so you weren't, technically in the park any more – I am aware of the irony and suitably ashamed of our cavalier attitude to trespass), and enjoy a great ride through the undergrowth – providing you didn't fall into the ice house.

The ice house had been in the woods for at least a century, installed by the minted folk who had owned the big house down the hill (there was no shortage of big houses in the area and this one still stands). The ice house, however, hadn't fared so well and had collapsed, allowing us to lean over and gaze into the huge, cavernous, brick-built, gaping hole that was no longer fit for purpose. Honestly, if you fell in it, and nobody knew, you could easily have died there, held captive by its sheer brick walls. This, of course, may have explained the notices on the trees. It was for our own good but we, like all teenagers, knew best.

It was quite a creepy place, quiet and dark, and I always imagined it would be the perfect place in which to dump a body, which is why I included an ice house in my *Pony Whisperer* books. I could still find it if I wanted to, and I suspect I am not alone. If you're unfamiliar with the concept of an ice house (you probably know more about them than I do) it was where ice cut in winter from a nearby frozen lake was stored, so the landed gentry could use it in the summer – a huge, deep, brick-built fridge, buried deep into the ground for insulation. The lake from which ice was cut to fill this particular one was at the bottom of the hill so I imagine it wasn't a favourite job of the poor servants who had to cut the ice, haul it up the hill and pack it into the ice house. The dark shade of the woods, of course, was the perfect location for it.

The lake was next to a field Rose used for summer turnout for her mares and foals (she bred up to four foals a year), and we were all roped in to lead them down the steep hill from the park yard to turn them out for the summer, returning after a couple of months to catch and lead them back again. You can imagine how death-defying those trips were. The one on the way down wasn't too bad, the foals being young and fairly amenable and the gradient in your favour. The return ascent, however, when the foals had filled out and grown a couple of hands into delinquent bruisers who had spent three months flexing their muscles by beating each other up, was altogether more interesting.

Rose had a variety of mares through the years and, later, her own Arab stallion. When I was a teenager her mares comprised Harmony, a large, golden-coloured Russian Thoroughbred; Vanity, a bright chestnut Anglo Arab, and Serenity, an English Thoroughbred who, due to an accident long prior to Rose's ownership, was unable to hold her head straight but looked at you sideways, a bit like a budgie does in its mirror. Not that anyone ever called her Serenity (I'm surprised I even remember her proper name, frankly), for she was always known as Wonky.

When I first knew Rose, the mares were covered either by a local Arab stallion, or one of the big, Hunter Improvement Society sires, resulting in some interesting progeny. Harmony's were always big boned, useful hunter sorts, with a lovely sheen to their coats. Vanity and Wonky's were lighter in build, as they were often put to the Arab. Every year, everyone was excited to not only see the foals, but also hear what they would be called, Rose favouring nouns and other words ending in the sound of *eee*. She soon exhausted the obvious ones: Fantasy, Rhapsody, Royalty, Gaiety, Charity, Tenacity, Reality, Finality, Audacity…

you get the picture. Endless fun was had whenever Rose asked for suggestions – lavatory, hysterectomy, vasectomy, lobotomy and sexuality being some of the favourites. Rose didn't share the joke.

Naming new horses is always an exciting thing to do. At the riding school at the top of the hill names, like saddles, tended to be recycled. There had been several Beautys, a couple of Williams, two Cheyennes. Royal names seem to suit horses – at least the male ones do – Henry, William, James and George, for example. The female names don't quite cut it – Elizabeth, Charlotte, Anne – although we did have a Mary, a huge, bay livery with a white blaze, but it never really sat well, and there was Victoria, of course. Ponies are easier, and their names are often inspired by their colour: Amber, Flame, Caramac, Jet, Smokey, Jester, Zorro and Tammy (who, during one gymkhana, gamely mounted and trotted along the 'stones' in the stepping stone race behind his rider).

One livery answered to the odd name of Nice Girl – but actually, she was, and one of our gang, Frances, owned a lovely-natured cremello with the customary blue eyes who, despite possessing a perfectly good name I can't recall, was always known as Wally-wall-eye. We had Snowy, Rocky, Dunhill, Tanglewood, Copper, Merlin, Folly – all the usual suspects. A name needs to be chosen with care for it may last that horse for its lifetime but with repetition, any odd meaning no longer registers. Sometimes, despite having a perfectly good name it is never used – such as with Harlequin and Serenity. The riding school horse Shadow was only ever known as the Big Grey – despite there being no corresponding small one.

Having returned from holiday one year I was bringing up the rear of the 2.30pm ride, straddled on both sides by leading reins, when a girl on a new black livery pony asked me whether she would be allowed through the jumping lane on the way back. The jumping lane was just a few fallen logs in the woods some of the more competent riders were allowed to negotiate. Having been told by my – let's call them *friends* – that the new livery's name was Sidney I called up to Rose to enquire whether Sidney could jump. (We had a thing about the name Sidney at the time, I can't remember why. Rose was getting a bit fed up with our constant references to it. I do remember thinking it a bit of a wheeze somebody had actually called their pony Sidney…) Rose's reaction seemed to me extreme. Pulling up Cochise so that the whole ride stopped, she turned in the saddle and screamed at me, '*Aaaaaay*?' (She was always telling us that it wasn't *what* but *pardon*, but she never took her own advice.)

Oblivious to the warning signs, and the bewildered look on the face of the child who was riding Sidney, I obligingly repeated my question. Could this Sidney pony, I asked in all innocence, jump?

'Don't call it that!' Rose shouted. 'It's name's *not Sidney!*' (Or something similar, only far less polite.)

I had, as the expression goes, been done up like a kipper.

One livery owner by the name of Jackie owned a large, dark brown mare called Pride. Only there were two Jackies so to clarify, everyone would refer to her as 'Jackie-with-Pride', which I always thought sounded like the title of a

1950s book about a daring woman in special ops during the war, or a land girl keeping things going on the home front. Anyway, enough of ice houses and trespass, of mares and foals, of equine names… My park accident didn't stop us riding in the dark. It was ride in the dark or not at all so there was no contest. I don't think I'd fancy it now. Just as I wouldn't walk down that back lane in the dark. Because, you know, with some things, you really do get older and wiser.

Lessons

IN SUMMER, PRIOR TO the junior five-thirty lesson in the evening, Rose would spend a couple of hours in the school, hosepipe in hand, radio playing, spraying water – well dribbling, really – around the outside track in an effort to lay the dust. If we weren't careful, she'd ask one of us to do it. I hated the job. It was such a waste of time and water, although saving water wasn't really a thing back in the day. Sometimes, if the weather was hot, I would stand behind the school and wash my hair with the hose and some horse shampoo, drying it afterwards in the sun. In winter, Rose almost froze as she took lessons, her body seizing up in the damp air. As is the peculiar way with some structures, the temperature inside the indoor school seemed lower, and the atmosphere damper, than on the outside.

Drill riding on our lessons was, as I have said, the thing. As pupils we'd be sent around at a brisk trot before being ordered to ride up the centre line and split alternately between left and right at C, slotting ourselves in again at A and repeating the process, only this time we would form pairs and later, when we could handle it, fours. We would thread the needle across the diagonals, adjusting our horses' pace to avoid collisions or gaps. We were instructed to turn across the school in rides of three or four, making sure we were level. All the time Rose would be urging us to push on, or steady the pace, to get level with our partners, and to hurry up at the back, as well as her biggest concern, which was to use the corners, people!

Using the corners. It was important. Underrated but vital, and not only because the school wasn't the biggest and we needed all the room we could get, but also because if you can't steer your horse into the corners, if he starts to turn before you've asked him to (because he's not stupid and he knows a shortcut when he sees it) then you were, Rose informed us loudly, *out of control.*

'You may not think it matters,' Rose would begin, having halted everyone in order to get their full attention after corners had been cut, and also to afford her horses a break, 'but if you let your horse cut the corners, people, and if you owned that horse for a week, it would gradually do smaller and smaller circles before coming to a grinding halt in the middle, going nowhere.' And she was right, of course.

There were plenty of other ways you could be out of control, but they all seemed to be related. You would be berated when your horse was going too slowly because this, in turn, would lead him to cut the corners.

'The rider,' Rose told us as we shivered in the cold, our horses taking some time out again and dozing beneath us, 'must always choose the pace. When their horse goes too fast, everyone knows they're out of control, but what people don't realise is that they are just as much out of control WHEN THEIR HORSE GOES TOO SLOWLY!'

There would be a short pause to allow this to sink in. Your horse might shift his weight from one resting hind leg to another and you'd pull up your collar, particularly if you were unlucky enough to be beside the open side of the school. After all, the horses had heard it all before and for them, providing the inspiration for this particular lecture was an ongoing concern.

'Your horse is testing you,' Rose would continue. 'Before he cuts the corner, people, he slows down a fraction – and if you don't feel it he knows he's in charge and he can do what he likes. When your horse is going too slowly then he's CHOOSING THE PACE, and listen, because this is important…'

You'd wake up a bit at this point and look interested – I mean, it was all good stuff, and it was all perfectly valid, but you had probably heard it many times before. If only that new person on the ride hadn't cut the corner!

'… if your horse can go too slowly then he knows he can just as easily… (pause for dramatic effect)… *GO TOO FAST*.'

There it was. If you wanted control then you had to have it all the time. You couldn't ride, as Rose put it, now and again, or in bits. Control had to be constant. It was up to you to choose the pace. The decisions had to come from you, the rider – and they had to come from you *all the time*. 'Otherwise,' Rose would tell us, 'the tail is wagging the dog.'

'Now!' Rose would say, injecting energy into her voice in order to galvanise us into action, the horses lifting their heads at her change of tone, 'Let's try again – and this time people, use the corners!'

There seems little emphasis on drill riding nowadays, it being regarded as a military tool, archaic and of not much use to the modern rider but it taught us to ride our own horse or pony, to be aware of the pace, of where the other riders were and adjust our riding accordingly, without thinking about it too much. It was also enjoyable – not to mention being enjoyable to watch. I would happily spend half-an-hour on a winter's evening watching Rose's lessons from the gallery.

Especially if Kentucky was on the lesson.

Kentucky was born at the riding school, bred from a school horse and a Welsh Cob stallion. Maybe it was a love-match, perhaps that's the reason why Kentucky was such a merry soul. Bright chestnut with a snowy blaze and white socks, he was certainly the happiest and most confident horse you could ever hope to meet.

When it was time for Kentucky to be broken in, Rose tasked full-time staff member Barbara with making the 15hh chestnut her project. And when Barbara approached Kentucky's stable for the first time with his saddle, he could hardly contain his excitement.

'At last!' he seemed to say, his head nodding in glee, eager to get out of his stable and get to it. 'I've been dying to get out with the others and join in the party!'

I'm convinced Barbara's sensitive handling of Kentucky's early education had a lot to do with his outlook on life. She never scolded him, never dampened his enthusiasm. She was always quiet, encouraging his *joie-de-vivre*, appreciating her pupil's love of life and happy to go along with him for the ride, more partners than trainer and pupil. When she made Barbara responsible for the little chestnut's early lessons Rose knew what she was doing. But of course she did. She always did.

Kentucky retained his enthusiasm for life and his job throughout his career and was a complete joy to work with. He was the perfect riding school horse because he just loved his job. You could put anyone up on him – he'd happily look after a small, confident child or be up for high jinks with a game adult, although he was no push-button horse – you had to ride him. Whatever he was asked to do, Kentucky always threw his heart and soul into it.

But Kentucky possessed another admirable quality: a sense of humour. So whenever Rose halted the whole ride in the school and started one of her lectures – maybe the one about cutting the corners, or a good rider not needing the reins – Kentucky would get bored. Whereas the other horses would take five and doze off, the little chestnut horse was having none of it, determined never to waste an opportunity. While Rose warmed to her subject and continued her soliloquy, almost absent-mindedly, as if he wasn't really conscious he was doing it, Kentucky would take a miniscule, baby-step forward. Then – and this was the genius part – he'd stop and give it a few moments before taking another step, followed by another. The little chestnut horse had invented his own game of *Kentucky's Hoofprints* and success was measured by how far he could progress before Rose clocked him doing it. This usually proved to be when Kentucky had gone just far enough to be able to stretch out in front of him and nibble Libby's tail, prompting a squeal, or maybe he might sidle up to the side of the school and tap a front hoof on it, as though drawing attention to how far he had progressed because, obviously, if nobody noticed, he was wasting his time.

And then Rose suddenly would notice and let rip – although not at the horse.

'Make that horse stand still!' she'd bellow, waking up the rider who would gather up the reins in a panic, noticing for the first time how close he was to the horse in front, or that his leg was being ever-so-slightly crushed against the wall.

'Why can't you people tell when your horse is moving? Would you notice if it crept towards a motorway? D'you know, if you owned that horse for a week…'

As Rose ranted Kentucky's eyes would sparkle and he'd nod his head at a job well done. He loved this game and never tired of playing it, probably because he was never the one who got told off. And I never tired of watching it. I'd giggle in a happy and juvenile way in the gallery – Kentucky never let me down. I only hope the riders didn't think I was laughing at them because I never would. I'd been there.

Kentucky embraced his career and was a shining example of how a positive attitude can influence one's working environment. I also wonder whether his personality stemmed from the fact that he had only ever had one home. He was secure in himself, and with his friends all around he'd had no surprises to shake his confidence.

Some people think school horses have a hard life, but I disagree. At the riding school at the top of the hill the horses had a home for life. They had routine, were well fed, well shod and well looked after. They lived and worked with horses they knew, who became their herd. They knew what to expect. When retirement beckoned, one of the regular riders would invariably offer the horse with which they had shared their first, happy lessons, a home as a companion to their own horses, or even as a light hack.

Of course, it doesn't suit every horse. There is always the odd one or two who fail to adapt to the irregularity of their riders, who worry off their weight, unable to come to terms with the hustle-and-bustle of a riding school, but these are the exception rather than the rule if they have been purchased with the work in mind. The majority find their lives in good riding schools comfortable and routine-led. Horses like routine. All the manuals say so.

When Rose taught a lesson with riders of mixed ability (whenever it rained a hack would go in the school – and it wasn't a large school so whoever's turn it was to stand in the middle and make the best of it had to be fairly creative), she gave a brilliant demonstration of loose-schooling her horses – with added riders. Moving to the head of a fast pony to slow it down, taking a step or two towards a slow pony to encourage it to go faster and catch up, adjusting her tone in order to encourage the horses to wake up and go up a gear, or to slow down. Most instructors do this, particularly with novice riders. It is safer for novices to ride in closed order; it presents fewer opportunities for the horses to take matters into their own hands and put in a quick spurt which could catch out the novice, too intent on keeping their position and worrying about the reins to notice whether their horse was going at the pace they had asked for, if indeed they had requested a pace at all.

When I learned to ride I was *instructed*. Later, instructors seemed to turn into *teachers*. Now, it seems we are *coached*. It's all moving towards a softer, more caring and inclusive image but the message remains the same. Perhaps in the future our teachers, coaches, whatever, will just make suggestions. But really, it is better now. We've gone from the customer always being wrong to working *with* riders, giving them a much more inclusive experience, the emphasis on helping and progression, of learning feel rather than barking out orders and hurling insults.

Riding in a lesson recently at a decent riding school, everything was so positive I found it impossible to decipher exactly what I ought to be working on. I knew I needed to work on something – lots of somethings – but the main purpose of my instructor seemed to be to keep me happy and coming back for more. But more what? Why would I return when I wasn't learning anything? Rose, on the other hand, did like to get her point across in her own way, but that way was never taken personally at the time. We all recognised that she had only our best interests at heart, and when she could inject humour into the situation, she did. After all no-one was exempt: we all experienced Rose insults throughout our riding careers.

We'd be told that, *as horse riders, we'd make good piano players.* We'd be instructed to use our legs before being told that we wouldn't be able to *ride a good-sized hamster*, that we *couldn't knock the skin off a rice pudding*, or *ride even one side of the horse.* The horses, Rose sighed, were *making fools of us.* When we lined up at the end of a lesson we were berated for the line being *about as straight as a dog's hind leg.* We were, she said, shaking her head, *riding wonderful bad.* We were *teaching her horses bad habits.* Did we know, she'd enquire, that was a *valuable animal we were messing about with*? When our mounts misbehaved, we were accused of upsetting them. If she was really exasperated by our efforts, Rose would declare that we *might as well give up horse riding and take up knitting*, which was encouraging. Her *pièce de résistance* was to insist that *if brains were a disease, we would all be in the best of health.* Well, that told us. No swollen heads at the riding school at the top of the hill!

In the late 1970s I spent some time at a big riding school in Kent where my riding was well and truly polished up. At this training and examination centre you always knew when Christine was teaching as her lessons were punctuated by flocks of terrified birds taking flight from the surrounding trees, and the local wildlife bolting for cover. That her pupils (and anyone else within earshot) received the benefit of her wisdom in amplified form meant there was no excuse for instructions not to be obeyed on the premise that pupils had failed to hear them. Christine *screamed* at her pupils and, surprisingly, they kept coming back for more.

Nobody today would put up with being shouted at as though on a parade ground – who needs it? We're not victims. Although, thinking back, I seem to remember that a high percentage of Christine's pupils were men, so maybe there was something in that. Could be we're missing an opportunity for an equestrian dominatrix. Forget standing over a paying client as he scrubs your floor, just stick him on a horse and slap your whip against your boot as you scream insults at him for half-an-hour. It could be a winner – a lucrative winner at that, an alternative for dads who usually sit and watch in the gallery as their little darlings bounce around vacantly on Simon.

Come to think of it, one *Pony* magazine advertiser, during a lull when recession hit, took a punt on taking the whips he manufactured to an erotica show in London in an effort to drum up trade. Instant hit! From then on he never missed a show, extending his range to sell even more to the leather-bound, scantily-clad customers who couldn't get enough of his goods, demand outstripping supply every time. Thinking outside the box certainly paid off.

Far from putting all responsibility to learn firmly onto your pupils' shoulders, as was the charming custom in the late 1970s, it is now the teacher's or coach's duty to find a key to each pupil, to understand that riders are ignoring

Maybe my first mount was a donkey – which would explain a lot. Here I am with my sister Margaret (left) at Clacton in the early 1960s, and I look pretty much in charge of my mount - although I think my donkey may be calling for help. Judging by the length of my stirrups, I seem to have missed a vocation on the racetrack.

Riding Texas at Bournemouth, with my dad at the pony's head. My legs are still not long enough for the stirrup irons, but using the leathers was quite a common thing in those days. Cute pony!

If there were no pony rides on offer, I'd get my fix with any obliging horse in a field.

Riding on Canvey Island with my cousin, probably aged about eleven. I'm on the right on a pony called Danny Boy – and, wonder of wonders, I'm wearing a hat (it must have been new)! We were just allowed to ride around the field for an hour, doing our own thing, which was quite a novelty for a non-pony owner like me.

Rose on Mo, mid 1970s. I'd like to say he was attempting piaffe, but he just hated standing still. This was taken at the hunter trial and Rose was stewarding. The martingale looks more like an American tie-down, but it was removed from his tack shortly after this was taken, never to be put back on.

Me on Victoria. The drop noseband never fitted properly, and she didn't need it so I don't know why I didn't just take it off! I know what you're thinking – cool 1970s outfit!

*Nicky on Carousel, me on Victoria and Trina on Babycham, just prior to our bareback ride.
We were obviously full of misplaced confidence to the extent that having no saddles seemed a
little tame and we thought side-saddle (side-no-saddle) might spice things up a bit. The legs
rapidly returned to either side of the horses as soon as we set off. You can just see Nicky's
Alice Cooper badge on her lapel.*

*Pickwick. I always think this looks like a
Hollywood Studio portrait. It just needs his
signature for an adoring fan.*

Pickwick (left) and Rose's donkey, Donk. Honestly, as soon as you get something different, everyone wants one…

Me on Caramac, awaiting our turn in the riding school's summer evening dressage competition, hence the plaits.

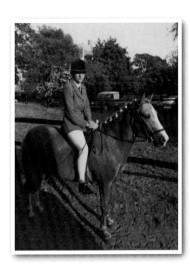

On Mo, outside the yard. It must be spring because Mo is still clipped, but I'm dressed for summer. It must be the mid 1970s.

Twoy the day he arrived at the donkey stud, aged just six months.

Twoy in his winter coat, and it looks like he needs it.

Towy, show mule! Photo: Mike Shinners

Twoy making like a racehorse; me making like Tina Turner, circa mid-1980s.

their requests not because of some kind of power-struggle or spite, but rather because everyone learns at a different pace, responds to different stimuli and forms of encouragement, and that some riders may just be, well, terrified. No use shouting, better to change what you are saying until you hit the button because whatever you're telling them now, if your pupils are not getting it, then telling it louder won't help.

On the other hand, there is rarely any excuse for pupils not to make an effort. 'Don't just sit there, people,' Rose would tell novice riders. 'Don't think, well, I'll wait until I'm a better rider before giving some instructions to this horse. If you do that, *you'll never be a better rider.* Take charge now!'

Riding isn't about strength, and sometimes, it isn't even about experience or technique. A determined novice will transfer their attitude to their horse, which will respect them and attempt to do as they ask. You can ride every day for a year but if you just sit there hoping for inspiration to strike, waiting for time to evolve into experience you'll be disappointed – for this strategy will fail. Your horse will take little more notice of you after day three-hundred-and-sixty-five than he did on day one, however much prettier you sit. Nobody wants to be an *ineffective rider.* Whoever it was who observed that most riders do not *ride* but are merely *conveyed*, had a point.

Riding is never about just sitting there – no matter how much the top riders might make it look as though it is. It isn't fair, novice riders sigh, if only they could find a horse that goes at a regular pace all the time, who never argues, just like the one the experienced rider has. They don't realise that a good rider is constantly correcting their horse. Novice riders ignore the clues, the subtle tests their horses throw out, and only notice any changes in speed when they are magnified. It's a bit late to only realise your horse is out of control when you are hurtling towards the edge of a cliff. Small corrections mean that big corrections won't be necessary because you will have headed them off at the pass. The ground rules have been set – and riding can't be a democracy because there can only be one person in charge.

'Teamwork', Rose would delight in telling us, 'is a lot of people doing what I tell them'.

The same is true of riding. It may sound new wave, progressive and animal-friendly, but letting your horse take charge now and again, to choose where to go, at what speed, due to some misplaced sense of equality is just asking for trouble – and I have heard owners declare this to be their policy. What if your horse decides it is his turn to be in charge at a road junction when a car is approaching, and his ideas don't quite match your own? Yes, you are partners, but there can only be one person making the decisions – and that person needs to be the rider. Remember, you can't ride in *fits and starts*. The Spanish know this, and so do their – very obedient – horses.

Rose taught us all this. We progressed from the slow horses, from the dependable, insensitive horses to the fizzy ones who taught us to sit still, to sit quietly. We got the lazy ones to go faster, we learned how to get the fast ones to walk when they didn't want to, learning how to let some energy through the reins so we didn't store up trouble, keeping hooves on the ground instead of flying high in a dance only the horse would think amusing. The horses taught us. Every horse can teach a rider something, but only if the rider is open to it. You have to learn to ride the slow ones before you can graduate to the fast ones. You have to be able to ride them all.

So we would have great lessons with Rose – providing it wasn't on Thursday nights. Thursday nights was when the church next to the riding school held bell ringing practice. Oh boy, did they practise. For. Bloody. *Hours*. And not even lovely peals you might hear after a wedding or at Christmas, just repetitive *ding-donging* as though, Rose often suggested angrily, they were doing it *just to annoy*. She took it personally. Now and again the peals would pause and hope would soar. But no, the bell ringers were toying with us, starting up again just as we began to relax, the torturer's tried-and-tested method of breaking you. It was one of those noises that went on for so long, you might just get used to it and fail to notice so much. But not Rose.

I think the bells certainly contributed to our instructor's own brand of constructive criticism. Nowadays managers and instructors alike know to sandwich criticism between something more palatable: good, bad, good again, off you go, happily concentrating on the good bits, accepting (or ignoring) the bad. Rose did not subscribe to this particular school of thought. Bugger that! You'd be riding around, thinking to yourself what a fine rider you were, and Rose would be telling you to push, push, push, or maybe to use the corners or something.

But then, out of nowhere she would suddenly raise the octaves and shout: 'WHOLE RIDE *HALT!*'

This would be immediately followed by, 'VERY BAD. VERY, *VERY* BAD!'

Break it to us gently, why don't you?

Nobody would dare look at anyone else. You'd slump down in the saddle, trying to appear much smaller than you really were and offering up a prayer that Rose didn't mean *you*. (*It wasn't me, God, swearing about the bells, I like them, honest I do.*) Surely she couldn't mean you. Please, *please* don't let it be you.

It was usually someone hauling a horse around by the reins. It was the worst of crimes, failing to use your legs, pulling on the reins. Relying on your reins would, in Rose's perfect world, have been a hanging offence – preferably with one of those bloody bell ropes.

I'd hate you to think our instructor's teachings were all based on fear. Rose had a wicked sense of humour, even if she did always side with the horse if there was a difference of opinion between pupil and mount. Once you were one of the team then minor discrepancies might be overlooked – providing the bells weren't doing their worst. We had a lot of laughs. That these would be at our expense was a given. Riding, Rose always knew, was supposed to be enjoyable, and so she did her best to make it so.

Merry Christmas

IN 1972 THE LATE, great Raymond Brookes-Ward organised an international horse show at the Grand Hall, Olympia. It wasn't the first time horses had competed there, for the venue had hosted horse shows in the early years of the last century, where horses and riders competed in leaping competitions, which then evolved into modern show jumping. But there were no more after World War II, until Mr Brookes-Ward and his accomplice Reginald Heaton decided it was time for a revival. Here was a brand new show! All glittering and Christmassy, with circus ponies, dog agility and top-class show jumping. Horses and riders from Europe travelled over the water to see that the home riders didn't get things all their own way.

The show was billed as unmissable so my riding chums and I decided we'd better go, buying tickets and boarding the train. Compared to the Christmas show at Olympia today with its enormous shopping village, its hospitality boxes, and the whole grandeur of the splendid occasion, it was quite tame, but even so the first one set the tone for the spectacle we all now know and love.

But, of course, we weren't content to sit in our seats and watch from there. We wanted more and because the only barrier behind the seating, between the public and the horses and riders in the stables were some large, black, curtains, we got more. Slipping behind them revealed the stables, the grooms, the collecting ring and the display horses. We could wander around unchallenged and wave to the big stars of the day – Alwin Schockemöhle, Hartwig Steenken, Malcolm Pyrah, Ted and Elizabeth Edgar *et al.* It was all very jolly, all very casual.

It isn't like that now – security is, understandably, tight. You need to practically offer up your first born to get a backstage pass these days, and it got progressively more difficult every year when I was with the horsy press. *Win the chance to go backstage at Olympia* screamed our competition page in *Pony* magazine. It was always a winner. Who wouldn't want to see behind the scenes, to get up close and personal to their favourite show jumpers? Who wouldn't want to see the Shetland Pony Grand National entrants residing in their decorated stables, crammed to the gunnels with tinsel and bulging stockings? Not to mention the other displays – Cossacks, police horses, agility dogs – there is always a fair selection. Plus, there is the exclusivity element with which to arouse envy in the breasts of your friends.

But these backstage tours are popular and all the magazines battle for them. Someone from the press office, walkie-talkie in hand, has to accompany you and numbers are limited to two or three at a time. Not only do you tour designated areas well away from the foreign riders, but you could be asked to leave at any moment. It is not the thrill you might imagine it to be, but it still excites the young and their parents, for whom a glimpse of life behind the scenes is a novelty.

I've been lucky enough to watch the action at Olympia from the glitz, glamour and comfort of the hospitality boxes, again because of competitions in *Pony*, courtesy of generous equine companies whose employees enjoy the experience as much as the young winners, munching sandwiches and cake while famous riders and their talented horses leap impossible heights below. And not forgetting dinner in the press box, my husband unfamiliar in a dinner jacket, with me reminding him in a confidential hiss that he's the only one who thinks calling dressage *pissage* is faintly amusing. Once you've viewed the show from a box it spoils you for the hard, plastic seats (even the press seats are hard, plastic and very, very high up from all the action). I'm not trying to rub it in, honest. I know how this must read.

Sorry.

It is always a gamble to visit a horse show or event with someone with no interest in horses and one such person is my husband. We once sat through an amazing liberty act, one woman guiding and directing a dozen horses in different directions, making equine patterns like a Spirograph all – and this was the impressive part – with no tack on the horses *whatsoever*. I was enthralled, on the edge of my seat, watching for her visual and body cues, listening for her vocal cues, marvelling at the trust and training demonstrated. When I asked my husband what he had thought of the performance his reply of, 'Well, it was just a load of horses milling about', made me think. Because essentially, I couldn't argue. Ignorance prompted his reaction but to the uninitiated, 'milling about' described exactly what those horses were doing. It can be educational to see your passion through someone else's eyes. I have learned, too, never to rush in because, with his love of running marathons and competing in triathlons, when my husband tells me he intends to show me a good time it doesn't necessarily mean we're going to a party – more likely a cross-country run.

It was the same when we went to Vienna. Naturally, the Spanish Riding School was on top of my wish-list, a total no-brainer. We sat in the gallery in the Winter Riding School, watching breathlessly (well, I did) as the young horses were led out by the grooms for the *Bereiters* to school. To the soothing strains of classical music we, together with countless other spectators, watched entranced as the horses were schooled below us, a masterclass to end all masterclasses. For two hours my husband sat with me, bored out of his mind. To his eyes it was more horses milling about – this time with riders. And he wasn't the only one. As we tried to find the Riding School that morning we had asked directions from a young man dressed in powdered wig, frock coat and buckled shoes, drumming up trade for the opera.

'You don't vant to see zee Riding School,' the young man scoffed, unaware of his sacrilege. 'It's a freak show!'

'You're the one in the wig!' I retorted, scandalised by his irreverence. To my uncultured mind, opera is just a load of people in fancy dress shouting in a foreign language, proving that perception and interpretation works for everyone, for everything.

Later, I was privileged to visit the Spanish Riding School of Vienna once more, in connection with the magazines. Again, I and my colleagues watched as the horses demonstrated their craft – only this time we could ask questions, visit the stables, pat the snowy necks of stallions prized and revered like no others. If we thought we were honoured guests then the appearance of a world-renowned philanthropist and his family soon put us in our place; we were relegated to the back seats while the would-be benefactor was shown to the best seats in the house, still warm from our excited and unimportant little bums. Fair enough. And talking of seats, as you sit in the aforementioned, hard, plastic seats of the indoor horse shows, are you privileged to hear an armchair expert in full flow – or am I the only lucky one? For whenever I've been part of the audience there is always someone (usually female) offering a running commentary in order to give everyone around the benefit of their 'experience' – and not in a quiet way.

'Oh, I could tell he was going to have that pole down!'

'Took off far, far too soon. Very silly.'

'Needed another stride there!'

'Oh he didn't give that horse a chance!'

And – the best one – 'Oh, exactly the same thing happened to me at my last show.'

If you can't keep your remarks to yourself then please can you talk very, very softly so as not to annoy the other paying customers who have their own opinions. Ta ever so.

The Christmas show at Olympia was always on the magazines' agenda as far as having a stand in the shopping village. In the early days, all the stands were sited around the main arena, and you could hear all the excitement and action going on behind the black drapes so you felt very much part of the atmosphere. Then the trade stands became more popular and everyone was shunted into the area next door. More stands were added upstairs. Hours were increased. People were invited to attend the show *just to shop*. The show added more days and nights. Two days of dressage were tagged onto the front end. This meant that working the stand was, far from the jolly everyone believed it to be, very hard work, for long hours, on your feet, your back aching. We were used to sitting at our computers all day. Not only would you be stuck inside for days, watching day turn to night through the glass roof, but everyone dreaded catching what became known as the *Olympia bug*, which could see you flat on your back all Christmas.

What made up for all the work was meeting the readers. There is a buzz about Olympia, a real party atmosphere, and of course this is helped by its being held so close to Christmas. Everyone is excited and in a good mood – even the long-suffering parents, some of whom are not horsy at all. Everyone comes to the shopping village to stock up on Christmas presents and to catch a glimpse of their heroes. Competitors wander by in riding kit, agility dogs pant their way around with their owners and, in the evening, we'd be selling magazines to people in evening dress, on their way to the hospitality boxes, all sequins, jewellery, clipped vowels and James Bond dinner jackets.

Young girls (our readers were mostly girls, of course) would rock up clutching one of those huge furry horses you could win, if you were lucky, at several of the stands, and tell us they were going home on the train. At least they would have somewhere to sit, their highly valued prize being strong enough to take the weight of a small person. I was always very envious, and tried several times to win a snow-blanket Appaloosa but without success, my disappointment tinged with relief – I mean, what does one do with a two-foot-six Appaloosa once the novelty has worn off? Just when will I move on from my nine-year-old, model-pony-collecting self? At exactly what age do horsy folk stop coveting horses that aren't real?

Goody bags were a big part of *Pony* magazine's USP at Olympia, but these were never delivered to the show complete. Instead, when stocks got low two of us would be dispatched to the stock room we had hired (up the stairs, out the back, freezing cold) where we would spend an hour or so stuffing bags with a magazine and various goodies from a collection of boxes, ensuring each one was identical. Then, just as we were about to lock up, we would discover a box of key rings or fridge magnets and have to grapple about adding these to all the bags lest little Grace returned to the stand in tears because her friend Emily had got a unicorn eraser with her magazine this morning, whereas she, with her bag this afternoon, did not. Finally, we would each haul one of those big, plastic tubs some people use for water buckets, brim-full of bags, out of the stock room and down the stairs, trying not to get in the paying customers' way, nursing a few new paper cuts and ignoring the niggle in our backs which we knew could only get worse. Yes, my job as editor was glamorous in the extreme.

One year we thought it would be brilliant to include a lucky-dip on the stand. Big tub, woodchips, what a draw! It was. Only after the fourth 'dip' there seemed to be more woodchips littering the surrounding area than in the tub. Management wasn't best pleased. Our stand looked like it was coming apart. A broom was hastily purchased from one of the other stands and somebody spent the whole time sweeping up, when they should have been interacting with the customers.

Another time, arriving at the venue, I overheard a distinguished gentleman registering at the entrance desk, exchanging his coat for a VIP badge. He was, he told them in lowered tones when asked, Mr Something-someone of the FBI. My ears pricked up and I went into *Secret Squirrel* mode. Whatever were the feds doing at Olympia? What was going down? Was this a scoop in the offing? Later, the same man presented a prize in the arena – which I thought was weird. I listened to the announcer informing everyone that this was the well-known Mr Something-someone, a big noise in the *FEI (Fédération Equestre Internationale)*. Sometimes, I think other people would have to work very hard to be as dim as me but, if pushed, and in my defence, I can only maintain that he looked dead shifty as he handed over his coat.

The Christmas show at Olympia nowadays also means dressage, and not so long ago I went along with my colleague Andrea one evening to enjoy the spectacle. Deciding to treat ourselves – after many years of working on the company stand, standing up all day, eating nothing but a jacket potato or some soup, wondering whether our feet were bleeding because the shopping village nowadays, as I may have mentioned, is open ALL DAY AND HALF THE NIGHT FOR CHRISSAKE – we booked a table in the posh restaurant on the first floor. Oh how very civilised, this was more like it, sigh. And then it was time to take our seats – those hard, plastic jobs from where we would no doubt receive wisdom from our fellow spectators, whether we wanted to or not. Feeling trapped and not a little panicky, I took a peep around at the hospitality boxes – all empty, poised for business in two days' time.

'Come on,' I said, heading along behind them all, putting distance between the busy restaurant where officials tended to lurk, where people with clipboards and lanyards were on the lookout for anyone who might be getting away with something – anything. Half-way along we slipped quietly through a box door and sat down. Some habits are hard to break. I hope this doesn't prompt a rush during future shows – we can't all get away with it.

Andrea's phone went – it was a freelance photographer we knew, sitting opposite and below us in one of the hard, plastic seats, having his ear bent by those around him.

'He wants to know whether he can join us,' said Andrea, giving him a cheeky wave.

I shook my head, knowing he'd only draw attention to us – and who knew who he might want to bring with him. 'Fraid not, no offence. First rule of clandestine activity: limit the numbers. Two very quiet women in a box is one thing; a whole party of people, all laughing, joking and drawing attention to themselves, is quite another.

Heroes

WE ALL HAVE OUR heroes – those riders who inspire, horse folk who provide role models, who make us laugh, make us think, make us want to do what they do, if we could only do it half as well. Riders who make our difficult and dangerous sport look deceptively easy and attainable, when not only is it impossibly tricky and achieved through a lifetime of hard work and dedication, but relies on a heavy dose of talent and not a little dash of luck.

You no doubt have your own list – but horse riders and horse folk have local heroes, too. Not the A-listers with their medals and caches of international trophies, but people closer to home who inspire for different reasons, many and varied. Some are like Rose, imparting knowledge, nurturing and fostering your interest, encouraging you to try harder, achieve more and to enjoy what you do. Others may just make an impression, and make you laugh.

Will was the sort of bloke useful to have on your side – you certainly didn't want him off it. He kept a hammer in the footwell of his car, *just in case*. You never knew when someone might need *persuading*, he would say, the word said in a slightly menacing tone, a smile which should have softened, but instead highlighted, the implied menace. You always knew when Will had little respect for someone for he would address them all the more quietly and politely, raising hairs on the back of your neck. If you exchanged banter with Will then you knew you were on the same wavelength and there was nothing he wouldn't do to help you. However, there was the underlying feeling that you either laughed along with Will, or you didn't laugh at all.

Will was a man who knew horses, who owned horses – an old-fashioned horse person who had forgotten more than most people would ever learn. He was a driver, not a rider, and passionate about everything that happened between the shafts or on either side of a pole – which sounds dodgy, but you horsy people will know what I mean. But he wasn't above diversifying. He once told me a story of how he used to load a few ponies up in his lorry and drive to somewhere every weekend, earning a few bob giving pony rides. Every week, he said, they'd pass an old donkey tethered by the side of the road.

One day, with a pony down through lameness, instead of rattling past the donkey as usual Will drew up in a cloud of dust, lowered the ramp and bundled it, wide-eyed and stiff-legged into the back of the lorry to make up for the shortfall. It was replaced on its customary tether at the end of the day with equal swiftness, and Will and his lorry sped off up the road, content that equilibrium had been restored, even if the donkey must have been pretty traumatised. I never knew whether this story was true, but it didn't really matter as it was a pretty good one.

He wouldn't suffer fools, but Will had a lot of patience with his horses. Once, with a youngster harnessed up and heading through the gate for only its third or fourth drive out, the pony came to a sudden and determined halt between the gateposts.

'Get on, son!' urged Will gently, clucking encouragement. The pony refused, standing its ground. Will tried again and then, when that instruction too was ignored, gave it a touch of the whip with a growling, 'Get on yer lazy little bugger!'

The pony obliged, leaping forward and taking the gatepost with it, the harness having caught around the gate fixing on passing. Even Will could make mistakes. Perhaps that was what made him such a hero.

And then there was Jean. When the riding school at the top of the hill opened its doors to disabled riders in the late 1970s, Rose was determined that they would ride as well as possible. As the riders' disabilities were of the cerebral rather than the physical kind, and they were mostly adults who were strong and capable of riding unaided, and able to respond and converse with Jean, their teacher, this was not only possible but also encouraged.

The horses took this new challenge in their stride – even if things didn't always go according to plan. For a start, the time it took to get everyone mounted up and in the school equalled at least the duration of their eventual lesson. One rider's decision to ride swung from positive to negative in the time it took for him to reach the top of the mounting block. As his right leg lifted to stretch over Bracken's saddle it would hover, trembling with indecision, before being pulled back once more to the top step, where it would proceed to lead the other leg back down in a retreat to terra firma.

'Oh now come on R,' Jean would say in a jolly, encouraging way. 'I thought you said you wanted to ride today.'

R would pause, remember that he had said that, and mount the block in renewed determination until he again stood level with Bracken who, used to the ritual, remained rock like, staring into the distance throughout, wondering whether today might be the day he would be led back into his stable for some downtime, rather than join his fellow workers in the school. The leg would once again rise, slither over the saddle… only to be recalled once more. This up-and-down exercise would be repeated at least half-a-dozen times until R finally made it onto Bracken's back and into the school, where his fellow riders gave him a hard time, and he told them all to eff-off.

The riders would be in good spirits throughout their lessons, shouting and daring each other on to greater achievements. One day, however, one poor rider slid off Sinbad and rolled over in the school, suffering an epileptic episode. Sinbad, unused to his riders displaying such behaviour, lowered his head to gaze intently at what was happening on the ground before turning to his friend Shane behind him, his expression clearly protesting his innocence as if to say, *It wasn't me. I didn't do anything!*

When HRH Princess Anne visited (I don't mean she just popped in when passing, but rather she turned up as part of a big, official visit) she was most impressed as she was treated to a spectacle she would not have expected. The riders rode independently, without leaders – they even gave a musical riding display and tackled a small show jumping course. The whole event was a testament not only to the riders themselves, but to the riding school's wonderful horses, and the whole attitude of the management and staff in believing all its riders should be encouraged to ride to the best of their ability – to say nothing of their instructor Jean's patience and teaching prowess. Make no mistake, it was a challenging job but she is on record as having been reduced to tears on only one occasion – when a pupil came up behind her, put his arms around her and grabbed both of her breasts. This gave us all reason to wonder about vulnerability, duty of care and who exactly needed protection from whom. I mean we wondered, but not in those words because they hadn't been thought up yet.

Jean was one of those people whose entry into one's life counts as a blessing. Down-to-earth, knowledgeable, a hard worker and possessing a well-developed sense of humour, Jean was one of Rose's favourite people – and she still is mine. She had two ponies: Kelly, a bay New Forest mare (at least that was what Jean assured the judges whenever she entered Kelly for native pony classes at the local shows), and Spot, a small cob about 13.2hh, grey and chunky. To keep them, Jean worked not only at the riding school at the top of the hill, but also for Rose at the park yard. One day, a man drove into the park yard and told Jean that he thought somebody ought to know that a horse – a magnificent white horse – was loose on the village cricket pitch, sited opposite the yard entrance.

Jean and her friend Chris were enthralled. This was news! The man reiterated that it was, indeed, a *magnificent* white horse, wearing a *bridle*. If he'd had a drum on him, he would have given it a roll. This description matched no horse kept at the park yard or even the surrounding area, so Jean and Chris hurried out to the cricket pitch, breathlessly prepared for whatever amazing apparition might greet their eager eyes. A Lipizzaner? A Spanish horse with bejewelled headwear? Some valuable creature for which they would be given a reward? Their minds raced ahead with possibilities – until they turned the corner and the apparition was revealed…

'Oh, it's just old Spot!' cried Jean in disgust as her pony lifted his head, around which his tatty, blue, nylon head collar was fastened, and gazed at her, the hallowed turf of the cricket pitch fast disappearing between his jaws.

From then on Spot was always known as the Magnificent White Horse! complete with exclamation mark – truly a giant amongst horses, a horse hero. At least someone had thought so. His finest hour. His fifteen minutes of fame. That beauty is most certainly in the eye of the beholder well and truly proved.

Jean went on to own her own pub – as well as a collection of animals, including an unclaimed lamb one of her customers discovered upside down in a ditch. Growing into an ill-mannered bruiser, (solving the mystery as to why no-one had claimed it) but possessing a poor sense of timing, the then grown-up sheep escaped from its field one summer day and made a beeline to the pub, scattering drinkers and diners on its way to the kitchens at the very moment the health inspector, grim-faced, pen poised over his clipboard, was concluding his visit.

Um… don't suppose you could give us a moment?

That sheep worried everyone it came into contact with.

Dick, who worked at the riding school at the top of the hill, was definitely one of my horsy heroes. When I met him he was not in the first flush of youth, and had tales to tell of people and horses who had shared his life.

'See her,' he told me once, nodding to a woman who rode every week with her daughter, 'she was a stunner in her youth. We'd go out in the car and play the holiday game.'

'The holiday game?' I asked, fulfilling my obligation to ask the expected question.

'That's right,' grinned Dick. 'We'd park up and go for a tour of the interesting places…'

Ahhh, *that* holiday game…

Whenever he saw someone doing something daft Dick would lift his eyebrows and declare that education was a wonderful thing. This conclusion had been reached after witnessing the son of a local landowner who, having benefited from the best education money could buy, had run across a field with his dog on a chain lead and, upon meeting a strand of electric wire barring his path, had leapt blithely over it without considering his dog might take the easy option and run underneath. Which it did. Dick spent his days driving the tractor, ferrying hay and straw from the barn to the yards, taking water to the fields and crushing the oats in the tractor shed. Often, when we fed the horses at lunch time, the oats would still hold some heat. He was a skilled harness and saddlery maker and mender too, and made me a beautiful holly driving whip with a silver top. Dick's recommended cure-all was 'a spot of Stockholm Tar.' It might have mended a broken heart for the faith he put in it.

Dick was one of those people who got on with things, and who always had a smile and a witty word for any occasion. When he retired, his successor had huge shoes to fill, and was bound to fail.

Never meet your heroes, they say. Working for the magazines I met many of the great and good from the horse world and while most were terrific, going out of their way to help and offer advice, always wonderful with the young *Pony* readers and being jolly good eggs, others were not quite as one imagined.

Like the top three-day-eventer who, the moment a competition-winning reader, her mother and myself arrived at her yard, generously offered us all a G&T because – she assured us with a wink, she was going to have one. Except that the answer to that would be no because it was ten o'clock in the morning and one of us was twelve. Or another eventing legend who screamed insults at one of the *Horse&Rider* staff (the nicest, politest girl you could imagine) on a shoot, in front of our open-mouthed competition winners. He was crossed off the Christmas card list with a flourish. Then there was the top rider who, visiting the office to be guest editor for a day, spent most of it with his feet up on the desk, safe in the conviction that it was typical editor behaviour. How perceptive. Never did a day at the office go by without my breaking out the sherry kept hidden in the filing cabinet, taking the weight off and taking five, ten, or maybe thirty or more. Or at least I might have, had the office not been open plan.

Talking of sherry, I could tell of the famous contributor who, after sending us objectionable faxes late in the night, was nothing but sweetness-and-light on the phone the day after, with no apparent memory of the missives, leaving us to draw our own, rather obvious, conclusions.

Heroes can change with the times. Proudly displayed in one of the 1960s equine annuals aimed at the young were photographs of the great and good of the time, complete with small biographies. One was of a woman who had been the stalwart of one of the big equestrian societies. And there she was, fashionably adorned in one of those flowery swimming hat monstrosities like Liz Taylor used to wear and – wait for it – an unapologetic fag dangling from her bottom lip. I liked to imagine her nursing a can of Special Brew just out of shot, into which the butt end of the fag might be dropped once empty, prior to her crushing it with one hand. Oh the beauty of airbrushing, unknown in the 1960s.

We used to doctor images quite a lot on the mags, mainly if we'd needed to flip photographs for aesthetic reasons, so back-to-front logos on clothing had to go. Or the designer might clean up a grey horse whose owner hadn't bothered to, or smarten up jump poles which had seen better days. In one case, a hat harness was worked onto a chin where none had been before. The camera may never lie, but a designer is not only capable of visual porkies, but takes pride in fooling the reader. This explains why a throat lash may appear on the wrong side of a horse. The image has been flipped.

One of the weirdest days we ever experienced was when we greeted a show jumping personality in the role of yet another guest editor. He arrived complete not only with his cousin in tow, clearly on minder duties, but also with a knuckle-duster in his briefcase. He was larger than life and up for anything. My dog adored him. We all felt a bit limp after he left, and had to have a lie down.

Talking of dogs, Spud was Andrea's Jack Russell, and he was a regular in the office. He'd been found in a bin bag, which is how Andrea came to adopt him. After he had been with her for a short while, the mystery of why he had been found in a bin bag was no more (a bit like Jean's sheep – we can all learn a lesson here). He was a total nightmare. All Jack Russells have an attitude and Spud confirmed that you can have too much personality – in fact, I don't think they're actually dogs at all, but some separate, alien, species sent to stir things up a bit.

Spud sported a small black patch under his nose which made him look like Hitler. This, we decided, couldn't have been mere coincidence and may possibly have been the proof of reincarnation believers are always seeking. Once, when Andrea visited my house and asked whether Spud could come in I readily agreed – the only proviso being that he didn't sit on the chaise longue. It will come as no surprise to anyone who counts a Jack Russell amongst their nearest and dearest to learn that Spud raced in and made a beeline for said chaise, grinding his furry little arse into the fabric and shooting us both a look as if to say, 'Is this it? The chaise I'm not allowed on? Bite me!' I make no apologies for owning a chaise, by the way, although I lost it in a flood (which sounds more interesting than it really was so I shan't trouble you).

But Spud – like all of his kind – was smart. When Andrea, fed up with taking ten minutes to put on his collar and lead every lunch time due to his habit of thinking it a right laugh to bite and chew and wriggle as she tried to do so, got cross and told him he wasn't going anywhere, returning instead to her desk and ignoring him, Spud realised instantly that he had gone too far. Ten minutes later, he stood like a rock while his collar and lead were fastened in record time. Of course, the next day he went back to mucking around again.

I can never understand the argument for animals being sentient beings for the more time I spend around them, the more incredulous it seems that anyone might think otherwise. How arrogant of us to use ourselves as a benchmark against other species, purely by dint of our opposable thumbs and power of speech. Anyone who spends time with animals will know how our emotions are mirrored by our dogs and, to a certain extent, our horses, too. They have different agendas, different motivations, different ways of expressing themselves, but we can all think of examples of animals who display behaviour which can only be explained by emotion and learning, rather than mere instinct. What of Kentucky's sense of humour? If we were that clever, we would learn other creatures' communication, rather than expecting them to learn ours. That they do learn ours gives them the edge over us. What about the intelligence of octopuses, of dolphins, of ants?

Clever Hans was a horse trained by his German owner, Wilhelm von Osten. The horse used his hooves to correctly tap out the answers to mathematical questions posed by his trainer, to the amazement and admiration of onlookers. During an independent investigation in 1904, the wonder horse astounded the panel of examiners by his ninety-percent success rate. Clever Hans seemed to prove his master's conviction that horses could be educated in maths.

But then some bright spark (the psychologist Oskar Pfungst, if we're going to name names) noticed that Han's success rate plummeted to zero when the questioner was out of the horse's sight. Clever Hans was exposed as an ordinary horse. His trainer was as disappointed as anyone – his horse could only fulfil the brief when he could see his questioner's visual, albeit unconscious, cues after he had offered the required number of taps, now known as 'unconscious cueing'. The conclusion was that Clever Hans wasn't so clever after all.

But we might argue that Hans wasn't just clever, but rather that he was, for a time anyway, smarter than the humans around him, a true graduate of equine science. He had found a way of doing what his owner wanted and gaining his reward. This is not so surprising given that horses are masters of non-verbal communication, living their lives in equine communities that rely on subtle twitches of ears and tails, the flare of a nostril, body positions and raised hooves. Body language was Clever Hans' specialist subject.

That's the weakness with tests and experiments when analysed through our own, human, expectations and motivations, by how we see the world. You only have to watch a class of riding school horses and ponies to realise that they have their own agendas and, usually, it is they who are in charge of the riders, not the other way around. After all they're experts, they've had plenty of practice.

As humans, we often put our decisions about another person, or situations in a group, down to our 'gut feeling', something we cannot explain that goes against what the person or people say. It could be that our gut feeling is based on non-verbal communication, body language that we've forgotten but still use on a sub-conscious level, packed away and no longer acknowledged now we rely so heavily on verbal cues and responses.

Jack Russell Spud wore his heart on his furry foreleg and displayed a full range of emotions: jealousy, insecurity, anger and obsession, if not actual love – or maybe it was. The longer I knew and observed him, the more I learned about people. Spud had no need to rein in his emotions, to hide his feelings, to put on a front. What you saw with Spud was what you got – even if it wasn't always what you might have wanted.

Spud ruled the office with a furry paw for a decade and when he finally went to the great kennels in the sky to terrorise the angel dogs, everyone was bereft (why did we all think he went up, not down?). He was like a bad boyfriend, more anti-hero than hero, but unforgettable all the same.

Mo

For everyone who rides, there is always one horse that steals their heart. One horse that, out of all the horses they ride – and the total may be great if they ride for a lifetime – they wish could accompany them on their journey for ever.

The horse of my lifetime was a little coloured gelding called Mo. Mohawk was his full name, but I can't remember anyone using it. He was one of Rose's gift horses, given to her by a man who galloped him around while practising his polo technique – which explained why wherever Mo went, he went in a hurry. Chocolate brown with white splashes on his shoulder, a thick, black mane and tail and white legs, it was quickly apparent that Mo was going to be another staff horse, as his enthusiasm was just a bit too much for the punters. He had a mouth like iron and considered the front of any ride to be his rightful place. Even then, he would get excited as we turned for home, jogging in his frustrated hurry to be back. During the warm summer months when he was turned out at night, Mo relaxed and wouldn't mind walking (although going at the back of the ride with lead reins pushed him over the edge again, giving his rider an exhausting ride. He was always better as a lead horse). That he may have benefited from some re-schooling is a given (now), but at the time it wasn't really an option.

When Victoria finally moved on to her new home, leaving me once again horseless, Rose asked me to ride Mo. I wondered whether she wanted to discourage me from seeking a replacement for Victoria for I was a worker, and she appreciated workers. But I wasn't going to even glance in the mouth of my gift horse. I liked him, I liked riding him – being a forward-going sort of chap – and that's how I got to know him even better.

He wasn't a jumper. He'd freak at the sight of a cavaletto, rushing at it with his head in the air, trying to run around at the last moment, but he would jump it grudgingly if you could control the speed and steer, and he could just about cope with the small jumps in the woods. We just did them in record time, that's all. What Mo did like, however, was Bridget.

Bridget was a school horse who lived in the first stall on the yard, situated directly under Rose's bedroom. This was no accident. Whenever the grey mare suffered a bout of colic (which happened, on average, twice a year) Rose would hear her discomfort, and would spend a sleepless night with the invalid to ensure she made it to the next day. Bridget's other speciality was dropping a shoulder at canter and dumping you on to the grass. She was a good looking mare – at least Mo thought so. It was love at first – albeit one-sided – sight, and whenever you saw Bridget in the field, Mo was never far away. Bridget seemed to view Mo's somewhat platonic attentions (he was gelded, after all) with reluctance, her ears back, snapping at him like a wife tired of a boring husband, but she tolerated him. Maybe, you might suspect, because of the competition…

Dixie had come to the riding school as a chunky 14hh Appaloosa pony capable of being ridden by adults and children alike. But as she expanded widthways we realised we had a BOGOF. Bunty was born bay, but over the years turned spotted, like her mother. But it seemed Dixie hadn't forgotten being wooed, and she thought Mo was a fine fellow, resulting in a kind of equine *ménage à trois* – Mo following Bridget, Dixie following Mo. A bit sad, but it was helpful in that if you caught Bridget you could lead all three horses in from (or out to) the field with only one head collar between them, and still have a spare hand with which to lead another horse. We were quick to exploit any opportunity.

I rode Mo for about fifteen years, on and off. Ten years after my first ride on him, when I returned to the riding school in the 1980s to teach, after having gone away to do other things, Mo got a new chum. Sue and I hit it off by dint of our shared sense of humour (you know how you can laugh so hard, you think you're going to die?), and Mo hit it off with Sue's dark brown pony called Mel (this was way before Mel and Sue on the telly). About the same size as Mo, with a similar attitude to getting on with things, Mel matched him stride-for-stride so riding out together was a hasty breeze.

Mel always sported a pair of those crocheted ear muffs to prevent her from headshaking in the summer. There are various theories why horses head shake – the most common, it is thought, due to an allergy to pollen. Sue was convinced her mare was fly-phobic as Mel suffered from sweet-itch (and sported the tell-tale hogged mane and rubbed dock to prove it), and fitting the granny-cushion ear muffs seemed to cure the problem.

Sue and I also went out socially – all New Romantics, Duran Duran, Spandau Ballet and Human League blaring from the wine bars, *Iron Lady* lipstick, big hair, Beaujolais Nouveau and wide boys with Escort XR3is and David Sylvian hair – but any more about that is on a need-to-know basis and, well, you don't. Sue's other horsepower was a reluctant, old-style white(ish) Mini, held together by baler twine (natch). Its offside headlamp had a tendency to dim, flicker, and go out at inconvenient times (after dark, for example) bursting into life again only after Sue got out to persuade it with the heel of her boot. It still went like the clappers, though, even though we did feel like we were in a bit of a marked car.

One night, feeling the temperature plummet, Sue hauled a duvet off her spare bed, kicked her Mini into life and tore up to the park yard where her pony was stabled, throwing the duvet on under Mel's rug in an effort to keep her pony toasty. The sight that met her in the morning filled her with horror: Feathers. *Everywhere.* Blowing across the yard, wafting around the field gate, drifting like snowflakes around Mel in her stable.

'Oh my God, she's killed one of the yard hens!' was Sue's first thought. But no, her pony had merely stepped on the slipped duvet, never designed to be worn by a horse, and split it, the contents escaping to ride the breeze. All the bedding had to be chucked out in case we saw Mel spitting feathers, and it was another six months before all traces of eider had drifted away. Luckily, Rose thought it was funny.

Sue's famous Mini kept going for ages, until one summer night when it didn't and, with great aplomb and finality, came to a spluttering halt at the right-turn filter light on the A127 at Ardleigh Green (if you are familiar with this junction, you'll know that it is one of the *worst* places to break down. In case you were drawing breath to ask, I have no idea where the *best* place to break down might be). We were on our way to one of our great nights out, but caused instead a mile-long traffic jam behind us, until some hefty and grinning blokes pushed the Mini around the corner and up onto the kerb. We last saw it atop a flatbed on its way to the scrap yard, a tear in our eye, the end of an era.

Later, when its replacement – a silver little sporty number – came off worst after a brush with another, bigger car a male friend of Sue's, whose advances she had previously declined with no apparent lasting consequences, offered to let her store it in one of his barns where the insurance inspector could ascertain the damage.

'I'll thank you not to waste my time!' were the assessor's first words to Sue, as she phoned him after his visit.

'But… but… it's only a couple of dents,' stuttered Sue, mystified, picturing said dents, few and barely noticeable, in her mind.

'I don't know what you consider to be a few dents, Miss,' the assessor replied, testily, 'but your car is a complete write-off.'

It appeared that there were lasting consequences from Sue's would-be suitor after all, for not only had he taken rejection very, very badly, but also a sledgehammer to her car, rendering it in a far worse state than the one Father Ted had a go at. Beware of that which lurks in the hearts of men, I say.

Talking of which, romance was another interest at the riding school at the top of the hill, even if not all parties involved were always aware. As with any gathering there were meetings, pairings, matches made in heaven, others made in the other place and quickly uncoupled, and yet others made goodness only knows where. Several marriages – including Julie and Nicky's (not to each other but to their respective spouses) – were the product of introductions via the riding school at the top of the hill. Two further couples were married in the village church and, of course, there were other, darker liaisons into which we needn't delve – it wouldn't do to be judgemental as we would not be in full possession of the facts. One of our group was even a victim of stalking – before it even had a name

She began to notice a car, the same make, model and colour as that belonging to a recently divorced rider and club member, parked up in various places as she went about her daily life. It was a distinctive car, in an uncommon colour, which shouldn't have been a stalker's first choice, underlining its owner's amateur status. When its appearance became too regular to be coincidence, our friend realised she was the object of this man's desire. It didn't amount to very much – she made it very plain she wasn't interested and if he did continue to gaze upon her from afar, she was no longer aware. Case closed, thank goodness.

It could have been more sinister – but, thankfully, it wasn't.

The lurve trip

I HAD BEEN LUCKY enough to have enjoyed one amazing Spanish riding holiday, but blow me sideways and hold onto your hat if the offer of another didn't come in. Time to pack the seat saver and head for the sun! (Always take ten seat savers with you on a riding holiday. After the first day demand will be high and you'll be able to flog them all to the other riders at vastly inflated prices.)

If you have never flown to Gibraltar then I can recommend it, especially if you are the sort of person who enjoys near-death experiences. That this little piece of GB has a short runway is a given. This means the plane approaches at a terrifying angle, enabling you to get a good look out of the window as it straightens up and descends… and descends… and descends, until you try to recall whether you had actually boarded a sea plane with floats instead of wheels, your breath on hold as you wait for the splash, furiously trying to recall the safety briefing that droned on in the background, interrupting your choice of duty-free. But then, miraculously, you touch-down on a runway which has appeared out of nowhere, bouncing off the seat in front of you as the pilot reverses the engines in an effort to bring the plane to a halt before running out of land. Taking off is just as exciting as you're thrust into the back of your seat, the pilot going hell-for-leather to pick up speed. Then, just before you're bracing yourself for a dip into the ocean the plane, if not your stomach, lifts like a rocket and everyone on board stops hugging each other. I'm telling you, it's a treat all by itself.

This Spanish holiday was based on the Cape of Trafalgar, next to an isolated village where the locals tended to be spotted dozing all day, mimicking the local cockerel who limited his loud and frequent crowing to all hours of the night. We guests stayed in a darkly Germanic-style villa with its own swimming pool. Run by an Englishman, my fellow guests were three Lancastrian horse owners and a married couple with limited riding experience, but gamely up for anything.

On my first night there, I got engaged.

Well, actually, I didn't – but after a couple of beers Lancastrian Arthur did, declaring, very loudly, that we (*me 'nt thee,* if you prefer it verbatim) were betrothed. As his fiancée I would, he informed me, be giving up work on our return to Blighty, as caring for his every need was to be my new role.

Was it *eck-as-fekking-like!*

This joke was carried on throughout the week, long after it stopped being faintly amusing, and I gathered ours wasn't the first engagement Arthur had initiated, but rather he'd averaged at least one on every holiday for the past five years. This fantasy aside, we got on okay. If only Arthur had been a bit more in control of not just himself (he were a right party all by himself, were Arthur), but the horse he rode…

Gypsy was my new fiancé's flea-bitten grey mount for the week. She must have done something bad in a former life to have merited being so paired, but rising to the challenge the mare went where she liked, at whatever speed she chose, in the manner of a horse desperate to outrun its rider. Arthur had no choice but to go with her – despite protests – and our rides were punctuated by cries of, 'Arthur, where are you going?' and, more frequently, 'Arthur, you're goin' t' wrong way!' I'm still unsure as to why we told him that as it only resulted in him turning around and rejoining the party.

My mount was another coloured pony, Verano, which, I was reliably informed, means summer. Having clocked up six owners in two years his whole demeanour suggested he would rather have no further truck with humans. Like many Spanish horses he had no experience of treats offered by hand, but by the end of the week was closing his lips around a crust of bread, and had stopped flinching when I patted his neck. God knows what sort of life he had experienced. There were then still areas in Spain where horses were the principle means of transport and looked upon as beasts of burden. Verano had clearly just been getting through his days as best he could, and he was by no means an exception.

Our host's Spanish friend rode over on his huge bay, ugly-looking scars from experiences in the bull ring very much in evidence on its flanks, in order to lend a more authentic Spanish feel to our holiday experience. Señor M was delighted to pass the time of day with the ladies in our party, but the men held no interest to him and were largely ignored. Keen to demonstrate his daring-do out riding one day, Señor M headed his battle-scarred horse to ascend a pile of rocks, and for several terrifying moments I realised he intended for us all to follow him in order to ride along the adjacent crumbling and defunct one-metre-wide viaduct, where there would be nothing on either side of us but fresh air, and we might enjoy a better view of the countryside (before plummeting back down onto it, no doubt). Luckily – and uncharacteristically for a Spanish-trained horse – his bay was on our side.

'Get lost!' it snorted (or, more likely, *Piérdase*), turning away in a daring and rare protest. A line had been drawn. Señor M shrugged his shoulders in a philosophical way, and we all stayed on terra firma. Close one. It was a pity the bay didn't continue to exercise his right to protest before his rider led us for a gallop along the nudist beach.

Between cantering along the wide fire-breaks through the forest we'd happen across a bar, seemingly, in the middle of nowhere, and take five, deciding Gypsy deserved a break. It was during one of these breaks that our host told us, in response to our admiration at how well our horses stood once tied, how the Spanish teach them – by chaining them to a tree until all fight is gone, all panic subsides, taught forever that any protest is useless and that once tied only their rider can release them. There was much noisy disapproval of this barbaric method of training just as – and if this doesn't prove that timing is everything, then nothing will – our host's horse, the only one to have benefited from being taught to tie up by the more humane English style, pulled back, breaking his rope. We all watched, fascinated, as the less interesting end of the now loose horse disappeared through the trees, rope trailing, the sound of his hoof beats receding as he put distance between himself and us.

Adios.

How easy it is to judge the methods of others when one doesn't need to walk anywhere – home, for example. We watched the less interesting end of our host bolt after his horse, nodded appreciatively at our still-tethered Spanish horses, and Arthur got the beers in.

Adios, amigo.

It was a strange holiday. The swimming pool was filled with green water – nobody wanted to chance it for fear of becoming leech fodder – we'd all seen *The African Queen* – but the food was good and plentiful, even if most of it had been alive and kicking only hours before arriving on our plates. As always the horses saved it, and once again I had fallen in love. What? Oh, no, not Arthur, what are you like? I meant Verano, of course.

Who needs saddles?

I CAN'T REMEMBER WHOSE idea it was to leave the saddles at home and go for a ride bareback. I only know that it was a bad one. Actually, it may have been mine. But anyway, it was a fine autumn day when we three teenagers set off in our ignorance – Nicky on her own Carousel, Trina on her rotund Babycham, and me on Victoria. Great idea, what a hoot, we thought. Riding bareback would improve our feel, we reasoned. Who needed a saddle? We'd make like Native Americans, something I had done before, reasons for venturing out without full tack many, varied and with all good intent. It wasn't until we had gone beyond the point of no return and pressed our willing steeds into canter that we realised why saddles had been invented and what a mighty fine idea they were. Without a pommel to brace against at speed, asking your horse to slow down (or even stay at the same pace) can be totally ignored – especially when your horse isn't schooled perhaps as well as he could be. Or even if he is. You simply slide ever more forward towards the withers, and from the withers onto the neck, your mount's ears coming at you at frightening speed. In short, the brakes fail – spectacularly.

And so we whooshed around the countryside at a brisker pace than usual, our three happy horses discovering a new-found freedom in the chilly air, and taking every advantage to go at exactly the speed they liked, which proved to be much faster than we did. This freedom multiplied greatly when we headed for home. Up the Pinewood we went at an accelerating trot, into the Furry Field at an ever more spanking pace, spinning around the corner into the Avenue as though our tails were on fire and stretching into canter as the horses' blood got up, a pace which, although kinder to the riders (if you could call us that, as we were mere passengers rather than having any noticeable input), seemed less comfortable mentally. Between gasps and ineffective tugs on the reins I sent up a prayer for Rose to be otherwise occupied when we hit the yard.

No such luck.

Sparks flew off the cobbles as the clatter of hooves announced our arrival – at least Nicky had the presence of mind to haul Carousel past the yard entrance and down towards her stable, where her pony came to a sliding stop worthy of a champion Quarter Horse, catapulting Nicky off in a flying dismount in front of the water trough, but for Trina and I there was no hiding place. Customers on school horses and ponies for the 11.30am ride turned open-mouthed and clutched hastily at the reins as their horses threw up their heads in the air like llamas and slithered about on the cobbles, snorting at the sight of two mad people galloping into the yard, where we came to a shuddering and embarrassed halt.

Trina and I braced ourselves for the inevitable, any hope of appearing aloof and at ease with our lack of control evaporating as long as it took us to heave ourselves off our mounts' necks, spit out mouthfuls of mane and wiggle ourselves central once more.

What *stupid* girls we were… what were we *thinking*… if we had *any* brains… bloody stupid idea… upsetting her horses… we'd cause a bloody accident… *get ourselves killed*… The tirade went on and on – Rose never being a person to use several words when a couple of hundred would do. The really annoying thing was that having experienced the thrill (of sorts) of bareback riding, we agreed with her. I mean, *now* we *knew!* As usual, there was no opportunity for feedback. The school horses all went back to dozing in the sun and we sloped off with our tails between our legs. Again. But it all blew over, as we knew it would.

Riding bareback should only be undertaken in an enclosed space, under expert supervision, say all the manuals – none of them advise you to blithely climb aboard and go out for a suicidal ride around the countryside with your mates. Would we have taken any notice if we'd read these pearls of wisdom? Nah, of course not. That's how you learn – at least, that's *one* way you learn, providing you survive. And they were right when they said that riding bareback is a brilliant way to learn feel, the horse's movements below you becoming clearer as you understand which legs are doing what. You learn to let your body go, to stop fighting the movement and move with it instead. If you ride bareback for any length of time you will improve your seat far quicker than lessons on the lunge, or lessons without stirrups. You become a centaur, at one with your mount.

Providing you don't get yourself killed.

Of course, some years later, when Mo's saddle was being mended, Rose was fine with me taking out hacks on him bareback. Better than having him stand idle in his stable, better than me taking out another, harder-working horse for the sake of a mere saddle.

Funny that.

A decade after my hairy, bareback ride with Victoria, when Sue asked me whether I could take Mel from her paddock where she lived at Dick's, up the back lane to the riding school to be shod one day while she was at work I, of course, said yes, of course. Leading Mel onto the lane in her bridle, I decided walking a mile beside a perfectly sound pony smacked of stupidity. Even though you might have thought I'd have learned that riding bareback took stupidity to a new level (I can't help thinking that in a race to see who might learn the quickest, lab rats would leave me standing), I vaulted up onto Mel's smooth, saddle-free back in a carefree, devil-may-care manner. The sun was shining, the birds were singing and I was aboard Mel's smooth, broad and very slippery back, looking along her hogged mane to her flickering ears. It was the perfect day. I fancy I may have whistled a tune.

The perfect day continued for about fifty yards. After fifty yards, Mel began to throw her head around in spectacular fashion, causing me to glance again at those ears.

My heart sank.

They were naked.

I had forgotten the ear muffs.

The headshaking turned into a spanking trot – and Mel was no daisy-cutter. Sue was convinced her pony's family tree boasted more than one Hackney ancestor, so up went her knees and I, in turn, was thrown up even higher like a bee on a drum.

I had no saddle, no ear muffs, no mane, no brakes and no bloody sense.

As the trot got bigger and the steps got higher there seemed no doubt that I was about to come to a sticky end. Looking down, the road below me seemed to be moving at such an alarming rate, dismounting smacked of suicide. I decided to go for the lesser of the two evils and, steering on to the mud verge, kicked my ever-more-demented mount into canter.

Everything got better. The headshaking stopped. Mel's back in canter went from a choppy ocean to a still, smooth millpond as we headed for the riding school, the only problem now being the increasing speed. Mel took it up a gear as we hit the hill and, just like Victoria before her, ignored my futile tugging on one rein, my other hand rammed into her neck in an attempt at anchorage as she ramped up the speed further, flew around the corner and skidded through the riding school gates and onto the cobbles in the perfect demonstration of being totally out of control, watched by Jean, who told me later in hushed tones that she had been busy recommending my lessons to a nervous perspective pupil.

Rose was right: if brains were a disease…

But there had been a time when not only did riding without a saddle become acceptable, but Rose decided we'd go the whole hog and ditch the bridles, too. Living by her mantra of *leave that horse's head alone!* she announced that she had always wanted to demonstrate how a rider had no need of reins by putting on a musical ride without them and I, as a staff member at the time, was included in the plan.

'Six riders ought to do it,' Rose said, already certain which riders she was going to ask: Susan C with her light bay mare Tiffany, Lesley on the bay Solo (owned by an eccentric woman who seemed to drive everywhere with her newly-washed and sopping wet hair in a towel, working the car's pedals with her bare feet), Karen on the chestnut livery Shandy and Jan on Moo. Nicky and I would be mounted on riding school horses (definitely *not* Mo). All the riders were keen – some of the horses less so.

The first practice was undertaken in full tack with added neck straps. Which horses would take to the idea? In which order should we all ride? We did okay — the horses seemed up for it, so after half-an-hour or so, off came the bridles. Well that changed things rather spectacularly. Moo was all over the place (Jan pretending every move was intentional) and Solo shied at things that nobody else could see – no change there, only usually Lesley had the measure of such behaviour between leg and hand. With only leg and neck strap, the balance of power had shifted. The school horses took the piss out of their riders and exception to the liveries. Only Susan and Karen retained their control, like prissy teacher's pets.

Rose started losing it.

Voices were raised.

There was a lot of huffing, puffing and barely suppressed giggling.

Our helpers in the gallery, specially selected for their ability to keep it together under fire tried, and failed, to keep their faces straight.

The session ended on less than a high note, with a promise of better things to come – or it may have been a threat. As a demonstration of how reins were unnecessary, it could hardly have gone much worse.

For two months we practised. Horses were swapped, tried in different positions in the ride, schooled alone to give them the idea. Riders swore, giggled, swore some more and slid neck straps up to their horse's throats to cut off their air supply, the demonstration of excellent horsemanship thrown out of the window in our rush to survive. On average, Lesley (a natural and relaxed rider who could ride anything, but who was prone to fits of the giggles) slid off Solo's sleek back at least once every session as he pinged off the walls like a pin ball machine or tackled the corners like a wall-of-death motorbike. By the time we introduced the music everything was more settled and we were all more confident, with Nicky riding Bridget and me on Libby, two school horses which had proved the best of a rather unwilling bunch and able to work as a pair. The bridle-less musical ride, against all the odds, was actually coming together.

The ride began with us all in a line facing the gallery, then trotting off in single file, Susan leading on the ever-reliable Tiffany (suddenly, the benefit of dressage became apparent as Susan, when she wasn't cleaning tack, was about the only one of us who had invested any time in her pony's schooling). Performing various patterns in the school – including threading the needle, forming pairs and making two rides – we kept in trot throughout, using our legs to turn (backed-up where necessary by neck reining with the strap), and our seats to slow down and stop. The ride reached its finale as our helpers entered the arena with several white-painted broom handles which they held between them, and we jumped these individually, in pairs and finally in opposite directions, passing each other. This was the trickiest part, the broom handles being narrow, the horses tending to race each other and pull faces, the helpers holding both breath and nerve as unbridled, furious-looking horses bore down upon them. We lined up once again to face the gallery to finish, the riders bowing to the audience.

Well, that was the theory – but could we pull it off? How would the horses react to a sea of faces along one side of the school? (How would the riders, come to that?) We devised a contingency plan for if (for *if* read *when*) Lesley flew through the air, arms and legs outwards in her best starfish impersonation, courtesy of the ever-generous Solo. As we were all to be dressed in checked shirts and dungarees (no hats – come on, you know the drill by now) with our hair tied in bunches, we decided we'd all stop, point at Lesley on the ground and go *Oooo-aahhhh* in a cheerful, hopefully amusing way before she remounted (assuming someone had nabbed Solo and Lesley was in a fit state). The final part of our classy ensemble was to replace the leather neck straps with ones made from plaited, natural, binder twine. We'd found another use for it. Yay!

The day of the performance drew near and everyone in the ride felt a bit sick – sorry, excited! We were to be part of a whole evening's entertainment (!), final top billing after a jumping competition and something else I can't remember. I do remember wondering whether we should be billed as the anti-climax. But there was no going back and, as Rose was constantly telling us, we needed to *have faith*. Jan muttered something about having a prayer mat somewhere, but I never saw it. As we lined up outside the school, bareback but with bridles still in situ, I could feel myself shivering. We all tried not to stare at Susan who had morphed into a stranger by hiding her short, blonde hair with a long dark wig, divided into two big bunches so she matched everyone else.

At that moment, the zip broke on Jan's dungarees. Jan made the mistake of asking Rose for a safety pin. Rose's reaction? She rolled her eyes and declared, in a very annoyed voice, *'Oh, you've had all day to do that!'* as if Jan had known for hours, but had waited for this moment to decide to do something about it. Somebody else came up trumps, pin-wise, and Jan was good to go.

Walking into the school and lining up in front of several hundred clients and families crammed into the gallery and along the open wall, I took a long gulp and scratched Libby's shoulder. Libby reacted by doing that annoying thing she often did prior to being uncooperative – raising her head and winding it around in a circle like a giraffe, crushing any confidence I was trying to muster. Rose stressed to the wide-eyed audience that this could be dangerous (not that they cared, it wasn't dangerous to *them* – and it was the first we'd heard about it) and that there was to be complete silence and stillness in the gallery throughout. As our helpers walked down the line and removed all the bridles with an important flourish, there was some murmuring from the audience at this unexpected development. The music started (The Wurzels' *I've Got a Brand New Combine Harvester*) and Susan set Tiffany off at trot.

Lesley stayed on. The horses decided to limit their arguments to mere face-pulling, we all remembered where to go, when and with whom, and we even managed the jumps without any hiccups, injuries or deaths. As we lined up again to take our bow the audience leapt to life, giving us a huge round of applause – and that's when it almost fell apart because prior to the actual performance, nobody had clapped at the end. All the horse's heads went up like cranes, and all the riders clamped their legs around them, pincer-like, to stop them backing off in fright.

Close one!

The Bridle-less Ride was the talk of the riding school for – oh, I don't know, at least ten minutes, and the question on everyone's lips? Whoever was that strange, dark-haired girl, and why had Susan allowed her to ride Tiffany?

Riding bareback gives you an appreciation of ancient civilisations which never had saddles. Imagine hunting or going to war without the comfort of stirrups, without the security of your leather chair strapped around your warhorse. Ancient Romans had saddles but the idea of stirrups eluded them. Scholars reckon it was the Chinese who came up with foot rests which offered comfort on a long ride, as well as providing a platform on which riders could stand, allowing them to throw spears and fire arrows at enemies with greater accuracy and strength. Without them a naked horse's slippery back provided no purchase for throwing, and any energy directed through a rider's free arm through a spear was weak. But the exact history of stirrups is still hotly debated. Stirrups are not necessary, but they make riding a whole lot easier, safer and more comfortable. No wonder most of those extras playing Native Americans in western films, galloping around the wagons and firing arrows from their bows, opt for a saddle and stirrups hidden beneath a colourful blanket. I mean it's bad enough dashing over the rocks and attacking wagon trains without the added problem of no brakes and the possibility of sliding off. There is stunt riding, and there is stunt riding for the stupid.

I was once lucky enough to visit the stables of a stunt rider in order to write a feature for *Pony* magazine. He supplied horses, carriages and specialist riders for films, and being shown around his premises was fascinating: beautiful horses – mainly the photogenic and obliging Spanish and Portuguese breeds, rows of antique carriages, tack for any genre of film from ancient Roman to period English. Although middle-aged he was, nevertheless, confident of his allure to women, his latest squeeze the cliché of a beautiful blonde half his age. Men who have horses will always get dates.

After a happy couple of hours I had everything I needed for my feature.

And then I saw the mule.

I expressed an interest. The stunt guru told me how this mule's repertoire included lying down and playing dead. But wait! Fire up the camera, prepare to be amazed, he would happily demonstrate! He haltered the mule, whose ears waggled back and forth in nonchalance, throwing him a bored glance of the true professional disturbed from his downtime.

The guru gave the order. The mule – which was only about 13.2hh – stared at him with contempt, secure in the knowledge that he was anywhere but on set. An audience of one, his demeanour conveyed, albeit with camera at the ready, didn't cut it.

The guru frowned, puffed and began pitting his strength against the mule, trying to force him to his knees. Well, he was always going to be on a hiding to nothing there. The mule did a brilliant impression of bewilderment. Whatever, he seemed to say, was he trying to do? Was he mad? He had no idea what was required! He made a spectacular demonstration of playing dead in the upright position, without so much as bending a knee. I, meanwhile, hovered expectantly, camera primed, even though it was obvious that I was wasting my time. We all were.

'Please don't worry,' I stressed. 'I've got lots of lovely photographs. Honestly, it doesn't matter.'

More puffing. More bored looks from the mule who, I suspect, was loving it. I fancied it stifled a yawn.

'I really think I must be getting along…' I said in what I hoped was a soothing manner, worried now for the guru whose face had turned a deep shade of crimson. The mule seemed totally relaxed. And still very much on four legs.

He left it in the end, the guru, knowing when he was beaten. A little less smooth, a lesson learned from the little red mule.

Gift horses and other animals

I F ATTITUDE WAS THE one thing you never gave Rose, she was certainly the recipient of plenty of other delights. At Christmas, she received chocolates and biscuits enough to give everyone at the yard diabetes, and tins still containing goodies would be passed around the yard once Rose had snaffled all the ones she liked. The orange ones she didn't because, Rose explained, all the medicines she was given as a child tasted of orange.

Rose was always being given horses, and always there would be a catch – but she was never one to refuse a challenge and always gave such horses a second chance as she was usually their last. This was how she acquired Cochise and Mo, and later she was the recipient of two Arabs at different times, a mare and a stallion, together with several more horses who discovered that they could lead useful lives with people who had a bit of sense, and who would overlook the odd strange behaviours caused by dubious riding by their former owners.

She also collected dogs. They were mainly German shepherd dogs which had been bought by people thinking they'd make nice pets, before size and temperament proved otherwise – and by temperament, I mean that which had been nurtured by the inexperienced owner. Rose was never fazed. She liked the breed, and she had plenty of experience of them, and these unwanted dogs found a home either in her house or on her yards.

There came a time when someone living next to the park kept a few horses in his field – or rather, as it turned out, he didn't. The horses regularly made their escape and were spotted in the village, Rose receiving several phone calls to let her know that some of her horses were out. Which they weren't. Finally, one of these mistaken phone calls took place when Rose was not in the best of moods – she was a busy person, after all – and so, replacing the telephone receiver in what can only be described as a slam, she burst out of the kitchen with all the righteous fury of the wrongly accused and set off down the road, rolling up her sleeves as the red mist descended.

When she got to the enormous house where the-owner-who-couldn't-keep-his-horses-in lived, several big, hairy, terrifying German shepherd dogs rushed the fence, teeth bared, in a collective unwelcoming committee. Did Rose falter? Did she flinch? Did she ****! Without breaking stride our heroine hauled open the gate, bellowed at the dogs to *'GO AND LIE DOWN!!!'* and marched on up to the house to give the door knocker a good seeing-to, leaving the wrong-footed dogs to glance uncertainly at each other, before slinking off to various corners to reflect the shift in the universe.

They weren't the only ones.

'How did you get past my guard dogs?' asked the astonished house owner, looking past Rose in the manner of a gangland boss expecting to see his bodyguards prostrate and strewn about his drive.

What should we take away from this? That German shepherds recognise when discretion is the better part of valour, and can spot a pack leader when they see one? Horse whispering, dog whispering – it was all grist to Rose's mill. And then there were Rose's cats. Rickaby was a tabby who would scratch you to pieces just for fun. I'd seen him prevent grooms from leaving the hay barn merely by sitting on the top rung of the ladder and nonchalantly twitching his tail in a threatening, try-it-if-you-dare, bring-it-on-sucker, kind of way. Even when walking in the yard Rickaby was always flicking us the tail. With Rose, however, Rickaby morphed into cute cat personified. He purred, he simpered, he would let Rose pick him up and cuddle him, pushing his head under her chin and making like he was the nicest cat in catdom. What a bloody ham.

Rose thought his habit of climbing the window and banging on the glass with a paw, demanding to be let into the kitchen, most endearing. Rickaby was like an annoying older brother who pulls your hair and kicks you when your parents' backs are turned, then denies everything when you burst into tears – a total Jekyll and Hyde in a tabby fur coat. But to Rose he was the perfect cat, and she was just as protective of all the other cats that lived on the yard. The cats were the reason we spent hours on summer evenings digging out grass from between the cobbles with hoof picks. If it hadn't been for the cats we could have seen off the impending lawn with a good dose of weed killer (and Rickaby with it, come to that).

Rose even came back from a ride one day with a feline she had found, a mangy old tom whose back legs didn't work properly and whose personal aroma was so distinctive, he was promptly christened Pong. If we had any posh-looking prospective clients turn up Rose would stick an O on the end of it and call him Pongo, but nobody else ever bothered.

I suppose you could also say that Rose collected people, too. She knew when someone was having a crisis in their lives and would offer the perfect solution: to get busy around the yard and horses. This took the person's mind off their own troubles so they could put them into perspective and realise that there were other things that mattered, instead of sitting around with all those problems cluttering up their head. Rose realised the power of getting out and exercising, of doing some honest work, releasing endorphins – and all before the gyms sprang up and explained how it worked.

Rose would usually pair a troubled person with a horse or pony that needed something, too. Exercise, training, just some handling – it worked for both parties. Rose was a great believer in the power horses have to transform a human being's mental state, and I believe she knew this by instinct, rather than making any analytical conclusions.

Now charities have recognised how this relationship works and are putting it into practice. There are the inner city kids given a chance via horses to not only modify their own behaviour in order to form relationships, but to imagine a brighter future for themselves and to make it happen; the troubled youngsters who lash out through fear and frustration, for whom horses provide an alternative way to live their lives, lives without judgement, lives with purpose. Returning servicemen are discovering that horses can help heal the mental scars of war, and show them the way forward. In her own way, Rose was fully aware of the power of horses and if you thought at first her only concern was for her animals, when you looked a little deeper, beyond the gruff exterior, you realised she cared greatly for her fellow humans, too. She cared enough to make a difference to their lives.

Art and war

LIKE MOST PEOPLE WHO love horses, when it comes to pictures and sculpture it is those depicting or fashioned as horses that catch my eye. I can't help it, the horse is such a graceful and beautiful creature, and calls to me like nothing else. An emotive subject full of life and movement, a heady mix of power and sensitivity, speed, timidity – all captured in the beautiful form of The Horse. It would be easy to smother every wall and every surface in my house with images of horses (as many horsy folk do in theirs), but as I'm not the only one who lives there, balance is required.

Art is subjective, that we all know, but with The Horse, all media can be employed either to give a true representation, or a mere suggestion of the equine form. Either way, when done well they touch the soul. Much of my time as a horse-obsessed child was spent disfiguring sheets of paper, attempting to capture the likeness of that with which I was obsessed, shoe-horning my favourite subject into my art classes, disappointed with my efforts, the resulting images flat and lacking that certain something, lying lifeless on the page in obvious defeat. More talented artists can make their images come alive, dance and stare at you from their realistic eyes formed from pencil, charcoal and paint. Real artists do more than depict a likeness; their eye and hands form an irresistible siren, the suggestion of muscle, bone, skin and presence radiating from canvas, clay, metal and glass.

And what choice there is now, the ways to depict a subject wide and unlimited. Modern art divides people. Personally, I like a great deal of it – but not all. At a visit to the Tate my husband and I wasted several moments rubbing our chins and nodding sagely at something that turned out to be part of the Gallery's heating installation, so what do I know? I'm no art critic, but something needs to appeal and reach out to me. To me, it isn't enough for art to 'say' something or to make a statement. Art needs to be something I want to gaze upon every day, to live with. It has to be something I don't want to live without.

Artists need to push boundaries in order to move things along. If this were not so, we'd all still be stuck with scratching images on a cave wall, or looking at religious triptychs. It is the same with everything – we no longer ride with a piece of rope and a blanket, lean back when we jump or even believe an outdoor school is there to provide us with an area in which to sit sideways on our ponies and listen to transistor radios.

I find it incredible to think of ancient men drawing horses on the walls of caves, presumably to call on the spirits to bestow good fortune on a coming hunt. Did he admire the equine form as we do, or was it merely a shopping list? (We need one horse, a couple of gazelles and a bison tomorrow – the missus should be able to rustle up something tasty with that lot.) And the horses are recognisable, so like the Asiatic Wild Horse of today with just a few strokes to successfully depict its upswept mane, its sandy colouring still bright, hidden from bleaching sunlight, frozen in time. This ancient equine link to our ancestors is even now untamed, unchanged, clinging onto survival with man's intervention and breeding programmes, snatched from the jaws of extinction just in time – the wild horse rescued from our casual disregard for life and habitat which proved too late for the unfortunate quagga, hunted to extinction by man.

Now, with no cave walls on which to draw, we commission portraits of our beloved horses knowing that their time with us will be too short, wanting something to remind us of our friends when they are gone. And when I look at portraits, old and new, of horses long gone or recently departed, I see something of horses I have known and loved – an expression, the set of the neck, the leg markings, a parted forelock.

It is the same with living horses spied in fields or ridden at shows – something about one or two of them catches my eye and transports me back in an instant to horses I have known in my life, horses I miss, or have forgotten I miss. The heart skips a beat and the memories flood back in a rush of emotion: the coloured horse that reminds me of Mo, the grey that moves like Victoria, the small tawny pony with a mane so like Jimmy's at the riding school. So many horses – too many – nostalgia jogged by horses and ponies who are busy making memories for a new generation, yet to know the pain of loss and the bittersweet joy of recall.

There is much to love, admire and learn in the old and the true representation of horses. Horses have always featured in paintings – many noblemen and men of rank willing the attributes of the horse on which they are mounted to somehow rub off on their own persona. *Look at what a noble fellow, what a brilliant horseman I am, controlling this powerful beast, taming it, bending it to my will.* Like a small man in a big car horsepower is seen as the measure of a driver's ability, not to mention his wallet – and other things.

Whistlejacket is probably the most famous painting created by celebrated horse artist George Stubbs, painted in 1762. The image of this stallion, which was owned by the Marquess of Rockingham, is displayed with due reverence at the National Gallery, and visitors consistently vote it in the top ten of all the exhibits. As it is an arresting life-size image of a rearing horse, with no background to distract the eye, and is first sighted through the doorways of several rooms upon entering the Gallery, it is not surprising that it never fails to impress.

George Stubbs (1724–1806) made a study of equine

anatomy by buying dead horses (as you do) and suspending them from beams by block and tackle, peeling away layers of hide and flesh and getting his common-law wife, Mary Spencer, to pull on ropes attached to the limbs so he could understand how the muscles and bones worked. Mary must have been a game sort, of stout constitution and with little sense of smell, conducting a kind of gruesome marionette show at his request. Who wouldn't love to have been a fly on the wall when that was going on – after all, there must have been plenty of them about. I mean, imagine…

'Are you there, George? Jeez, what is that god-awful smell?'

'Ahh, Mary, good of you to come…'

'No worries (eyelashes fluttering, hips swaying). After all, you did promise something special for this evening.'

'Oh yes… that's right, I did, didn't I? Er… just grab hold of this rope, will you sweetheart?'

'Um… that wouldn't be a dead horse suspended from the rafter, would it?'

'Oh, you noticed. Take a mighty pull on the rope there, there's a good girl.'

'This isn't another fling at modern art again, is it George?'

'No, no, nothing like that… pull harder. Come on, put your back into it, woman…'

'Makes a change from all those lion-attacking-a-stallion pictures, I suppose. Like this?'

'Christl Not that hard, you'll have the whole bloody lot down!'

'No need to shout. Eeuuw, is that its leg moving? It is dead, isn't it?'

'Of course. Hold hard for a minute while I peel back the skin…'

'What the…?'

Stubbs's subsequent drawings in his book, *The Anatomy of the Horse*, demonstrate why he is considered the absolute master of horse portraiture. He knew how the muscles worked under the skin, he understood how the skeleton was positioned. He knew because he had seen it – and so had Mary, poor woman.

Examining old portraits of horses is interesting in other ways – the tack, for example. Fashions in tack have never stood still, and examining the saddlery adorning horses in old pictures can add another dimension to our viewing experience. At first glance you may be tempted to wonder whether the artist has got it badly wrong as the tack seems so odd – but no, they merely depicted the fashions of the time. You will see longer saddle flaps, shorter saddle flaps, square seats, long curb bits, exercise rugs which cover most of the racehorses wearing them, and more. The saddles are flat seated and sit much closer to the horse than modern examples. As you continue to look other questions arise: why, you may wonder, are horses in pictures painted around the middle of the eighteenth century depicted with such small ears? Because the fashion then was to crop them, in the way fighting-

and attack-dogs' ears are mutilated even now, snipping them into an outline considered more pleasing to the eye. Docking didn't stop at tails, it would seem. If that didn't make your horse head-shy, then I don't know what would.

Sally Mitchell's fascinating *Dictionary of British Equestrian Artists* has a section devoted to developments in equine fashions, including those of mane, tail and saddlery, and is guaranteed to sweep anyone interested in equestrian art along on a completely new and enlightening journey.

When I was a child, a print of *The Arab Tent* by Edwin Landseer was pinned firmly to my bedroom door, the beautiful mare with her delightful foal lying down within a Bedouin home clearly treasured by their owner, as the picture was treasured by me. The original is housed in The Wallace Collection, a beautiful gallery in London's Manchester Square. It's worth a visit, for not only does the original painting greet you upon entry, but the restaurant, situated under a glass roof, is pretty swish, and the armoury collection leaves one in saddened awe.

The ornate horse amour in The Wallace Collection is beautiful, expertly made, the craft of the ironsmith undeniable. It is ancient artwork to die for, to die in. It is also disturbing: the horrors of ancient war displayed behind glass, the horse rendered to the purpose of a modern-day tank for smashing and trampling, a blunt instrument used to strike fear in the hearts of enemies on foot. Glinting equine protection from arrows, swords, maces and lances fashioned from metal which must have sparkled in the sun, all housed and displayed beside beautiful weapons designed to smash, maim and destroy. We can only imagine the metal clashing in a terrible song of death, destruction and doom – as much for the wearer as for its foe.

The horse is a peaceful creature, designed to flee from danger, unused to confronting it. To plunge such a pacifistic animal into the brutality of war, where swords slashed and maimed, lances were thrust to pierce and tear and the smell of death and the cries of the dying impressed upon its instincts to turn and flee went beyond slavery. To harness equine strength and weight against enemies with which it has no argument is betrayal beyond sane comprehension.

To force horses to fight battles of the master race required bits with ports as high as the shanks were long, controlling the head in a vice of metal so strong it could, at the pull of the reins, break the wearer's jaw. Spurs spiked like stars, the length of a man's forearm, ensured mounts went forward when told. The state of surviving and traumatised horses must have required almost as much medication as the fallen, and the image of such savagery and despair fills me with sadness.

And who could invent such a deliberate cruelty as caltrops? Spiked metal stars hurled since ancient times onto battlefields, designed to lame and cripple the enemy's greatest and most powerful weapon, to leave it dead, dying and maimed on the battlefield, or throw it into agonies to run, frenzied and delirious, to wreak havoc of its own, to take over where the spikes left off. If the caltrops didn't do enough damage then adversaries armed their bows with vicious arrows known as 'horse droppers', fashioned with barbs to pierce the skin, to go in deep and stay there, no matter what.

Watching Sir Laurence Olivier in the film *Henry V*, the scene at Agincourt where the mounted French noblemen begin their charge – progressing from walk through trot to canter, and then sweeping down upon the English in full gallop, caparisons flowing, manes and tails streaming, the horses' flight instinct ignited, French lances drawn and levelled – stirs the blood in admiration and dread. But this is before the arrows, loosened from legendary English longbows, swish their way across the sky like a flock of lethal birds to fell the horses, to put the knights at a disadvantage, to level the field. We cannot imagine the carnage, the cries, the bloody awfulness of such a battle. At the real battle of Agincourt the French had dismounted, the heavy mud getting the better of their horses, but such battles as depicted in the film certainly would have occurred, with the full might of arrows and lances felling horses, or causing such injuries as to turn them mad, writhing and thrashing in agony, indiscriminate weapons lethal to both sides until someone could deliver the *coup de grâce*.

Even today, farriers in the Household Cavalry can be identified by their traditional axes carried behind them, a grim reminder that the original purpose of cavalry – now ceremonial and relieved of battle duties – was to go to war. The heavy silver spikes would have been used to dispatch fallen horses after battle, the blades slicing off hooves marked with the charger's number, supplying proof of every lost horse for army records. Horses were army property, and needed to be accounted for.

Holidaying in France aboard our motorcycle my husband and I, seeking light relief from World War I battlefields, rang the changes by visiting Crécy, the sight of a major English victory in 1346 during the One Hundred Years War. Agincourt was close by so we mounted our trusty equine substitute and headed northwest to explore another battlefield site. Agincourt eluded us. No such place existed. Had the French, in a fit of pique (which would have been ironic), erased it from the map? But no. They spell it Azincourt (no wonder the sat nav thought us mad, but they must be right, I mean it is in France, after all), and we wondered if it were a ploy to prevent the English from visiting.

Anyway, we found it by default, and it was interesting to see our hosts' take on the famous battle when our version is so familiar to us. The visitor centre lamented the terrible losses the French nobility suffered at the hands of the despised and lowly English peasants. That their own peasants went on to cut the heads off all their surviving noble descendants several hundred years later seemed too churlish to mention. This was the holiday where I lamented the loss of watching the first three days of Royal Ascot on the telly, as the date of our return would allow me to see only the final two days.

'The best two!' my husband told me cheerfully. 'You'll be back in time for the finals.'

I sometimes think he says these things just to wind me up.

You can spend a happy day in London spotting the great and the good immortalised on horses, high on plinths, on either side of bridges, in squares, riders given greater elevation and status by sitting astride their mounts – art and war combined. It is said that you can tell how an equestrian died by the way his charger is depicted: if the horse is rearing, both front legs in the air, the rider died in battle. If one leg is off the ground – as with *Coeur de Lion* in Parliament Square – the rider died later of wounds sustained in battle. If all four legs are on the ground, the rider died in more peaceful circumstances.

The *Animals in War Memorial* in Hyde Park was unveiled in 2004, and honours animals who sacrificed their lives in human wars. Two bronze mules, loaded with gun parts, share the space with a dog and a horse. Some eight million horses, mules and donkeys died in the war between 1914 and 1918 – and around 120,000 horses were requisitioned from civilians in Britain. One of the full-time staff working at the riding school at the top of the hill in the 1970s was filled with confusion when Rose and her compatriots would talk about 'the fourteen–eighteen war', discussing the local people they knew who had been involved, the tales they had told of horses requisitioned from nearby farms, shipped abroad to die in the muddy battlegrounds of France. She couldn't understand how they could possibly have remembered anyone who had lived in the fifteenth century.

One can only imagine the dread and despair of seeing one's favourite horse being led away to the horrors of war in Europe, the last conflict in which horses played a significant part. Not enough to take the men, the husbands, the sons, the lovers, nations demanded their horses, too.

According to the National Army Museum, seventy-five percent of horses who died during World War I did so from disease or exhaustion, little comfort to those forced to give up their horses to further the cause, believing they would assist their loved ones at the Front.

So many artworks depict horses in conflict. Young Alfred Munnings was a war artist, his paintings of horses serving in World War I heavy with a poignancy that touches the heart. What happened to those horses in his pictures? Did they last an hour, a day, or weeks? Did they make it through the war only to die at the hands of the French butchers, to feed the starving human survivors of the conflict, and spare the British government the expense of shipping them back home?

A visit to Dedham in Essex, with the purpose of visiting Sir Alfred Munnings's house and studio, will reap rich rewards. Later paintings of more tranquil domestic scenes mingle with those of elegant hunters and horse races, all in the artist's characteristic style. It is an elegant house in which to satisfy the senses, looking at horses no longer with us through the artist's eyes, immortalised forever in oils.

David, a trustee of the Munnings Museum and total good egg, rode all his life at the riding school at the top of the hill, a good friend of Rose and stalwart of the riding club based there. A passion for horses tenuously linked his, mine and the life of the great artist, whose work we both admired.

Images and artwork of horses have another role to play: their presence in urban environments provides us with a fix when the real thing is absent. Whenever I have had a crisis in my life it is horses – real or facsimile – to which I turn. They are my comfort blanket, a talisman, a soothing antidote to pain, to despair, or even just a bad day. Whether seeking riding school mounts in order to make a connection to the familiar while stuck working in an unfamiliar place, gazing upon a military hero on his horse on a plinth in the city, or sighting a traveller's horse grazing by the roadside, horses have the ability and power to transform my mood like nothing else. They are a drug, an endorphin, an upper desperately grasped when I'm feeling down.

Once, while walking through an unfamiliar town in such a low mood as to chance bargaining with God, I craved the comfort of a horse – any horse. If only I could spy a familiar shape amongst all this unlikely concrete, if only I could be permitted to see a horse right now, I told myself, knowing there was no logic to it, things would get better. I sought, as the desperate do, a sign. And, miraculously, as I turned a corner in this unlikely place, where new buildings promised little in the way of a traditional setting for such artwork, there stood that which I so badly needed: the grey, unmoving, uplifting, life-size statue of a horse.

The sight of this affected me in an extraordinary way. No beams of light from heaven shone down upon its smooth, unmoving back, no choir of angels sang, but I suddenly understood how, in times gone by, folk could devote themselves to religion should such a coincidence occur. Touching the solid warmth of the stone and feeling the shape under my fingers had a restorative effect. Reluctant to leave such magic I sat on a bench to stare, to take as much power from this amazing, unlikely answer to a prayer as I could.

Horses don't need to be real to work their magic.

A clip off the old block

WHEN SUMMER DREW TO a close and autumn crept in, softly and apologetically at first, punctuated by warm sunny days so that you might kid yourself it wasn't serious, before the shock of the first frost and the hunt for your gloves, work at the riding school at the top of the hill increased. Even if the weather was in no hurry to change, the sweat on the horses' ever-growing coats left you in no doubt of the passing of the seasons. The first night the school horses stayed in their stables after work instead of going out in the field, the sound of contented munching playing like music in the old coach house, the noise dulled by the abundance of straw under hoof and buffered by warm equine bodies, the easier, lighter work toil of summer became but a memory. You knew autumn had arrived when Rose got out the clippers.

If you thought your skills in horse handling were improving, holding a horse for Rose while she clipped took them to a new level. It was an education. Carried out in the corridor by the stalls in the main yard, Rose would have sent away the blades for sharpening and the clippers would be cleaned and oiled, primed and ready for action. A warm day was advisable, but with so many horses to clip Rose couldn't afford to be choosy. With the school horses and the liveries at the riding school, as well as those from the park and pub yard, and allowing for repeat clips, Rose must have clipped well over a hundred horses every year.

Clipping, as every horse person knows, is undertaken in the autumn to remove all or part of a horse's winter coat. It may seem strange to shave coats off when the temperature plummets, but horses with long coats will sweat, leaving them exposed to chills. Plus, sweaty horses can lose condition, so clipping off the coat and replacing it with rugs ensures they can work comfortably, and without undue stress. It does, however, mean that stripping the rugs off a clipped horse on a cold day can erupt in some interesting behaviour until the horse is warm, and riders need to not only mount quickly, but get their horses moving if they value their own safety. For this reason, most of the school horses were given blanket or trace-high clips, which left the coat on their backs and legs, clipping off coat from the neck and under parts where the horses sweated, in an effort to keep the client body count low.

I have never, *ever*, seen horses clipped as well as those clipped by Rose. The lines were perfectly straight, with no cop-out semi-circle at the stifle on trace-high or blanket clips. Tram lines were not tolerated, no tufts were missed, ears were shorn sharp and pointed. Heads, even acknowledging the prominent bones at the surface and delicate nature of the area, were left like suede, no masks on the front of faces left unclipped as with the less confident. Considering she suffered from arthritis by the time I worked with her, Rose's skill was nothing less than miraculous. She was scathing of bad clipping, saying it looked like someone had done it with a knife and fork, but you could never have accused her of giving a bad clip. But, of course, perfection does take a bit of time, patience – and help.

With Rose busy with the clippers it was your job, as holder, to ensure the horse receiving a haircut stood quietly and still so that the process could be carried out smoothly and safely. Some horses – usually the school's horses – were old hands at the game and stood there perfectly. Others, whose owners' more flexible approach to their horses' manners made for surly and reluctant hairdressing clients, made life more interesting and upped your skills.

'What's it doing?' Rose would enquire, bent double with her head stuck under the horse, clipping between its hind legs.

'Nothing,' you'd reply, as the horse stood as though stuffed, dozing.

'Oh don't do that!' Rose would moan, as the skin juddered involuntarily, the clippers tickling. 'It's like trying to clip corrugated cardboard!'

'Stand up,' you'd say, hoping you sounded full of authority.

'NOW what's it doing?'

'Nothing.'

'Don't let it do that!'

'It's just stretching its neck.'

'Well don't let it. It's making life difficult.'

And then, later…

'Watch out, it's going sulky on us…'

This meant the horse was getting fed up and had decided enough was enough. We might swap the head collar for a bridle or, if things got really bad, resort to the twitch. The twitch is the cord-and-stick version of a hyena grabbing a zebra's nose, releasing endorphins, calming the fractious horse as nature designed. We had to take care not to leave it on for too long (you didn't want the nose dropping off like a lamb's tail – oh I'm only kidding, but you didn't want the nose to get too numb, and Rose was in charge of applying it so it was tensioned correctly). If you were tasked with holding the twitch, you did so on pain of death. No, really. Because it was stressed that if you let go, the horse would throw its head around in an effort to sling it off and you would *get yourself, and everybody else, KILLED.*

Death by twitch.

Your fault.

If the horse did start to fidget it could go two ways: a horse Rose liked – perhaps her own Cochise, for example, or a horse she might have bred herself – would be given the benefit of the doubt.

'Now talk nicely to it,' she'd say, softly, as the horse slammed into your chest, using its head like a battering ram and forcing all the air in your lungs to be expelled with a loud *phooooof*, 'because', Rose would continue to croon, 'this horse is *very highly strung*.'

Gasping for breath, your immediate thoughts were anything but sympathetic.

If, on the other hand, it was a horse which made a habit of giving Rose trouble, or whose manners were dodgy anyway (think bronco-loving, rush-to-the-field Misty), being highly strung went right out of the window. It was declared instead to be *pig-headed*. It didn't matter if the behaviour was identical, the diagnosis depended on Rose's interpretation of the horse in question.

Horses Rose had in for clipping that she didn't know (or any horse new to the yard she had yet to name) were referred to by the generic name of *Nobby*. It was a mildly insulting form of address, said after a slight pause, ensuring we all knew she and the horse were not on familiar terms. *Big head* was another favourite for unfamiliar horses who misbehaved.

Always, throughout the process, Rose would be oiling the clippers, swearing at the blades if she didn't think they were sharp enough, twiddling with the screw at the top which adjusted the tension, or switching the clippers off to let them cool down for a while. To combat boredom you were regularly reminded to watch the lead from plug to clippers (circuit breakers? Don't make me laugh) because, Rose informed you gravely, eyeing up the smooth stable bricks underfoot, if the horse trod on it, we would all go up in a puff of smoke and you would *get yourself, and everyone else, KILLED!*

Again.

Boredom kicked smartly into touch.

As though holding a horse, gripping a twitch in a death-hold and watching out for the lead wasn't enough, you might also have to hold up a leg (equine, not your own) while Rose clipped around and between the horse's hind legs – multi-tasking taken to a new level. An octopus would have been a handier helper. We were always encouraged to be ambidextrous. Very big on us all being ambidextrous, was Rose, unwilling to restrict her teachings to those of an equine nature.

You could hear the sound of the clippers whirring (and Rose's curses) as soon as you entered the yard – a warning to anyone wanting a favour that this might not be the best time to ask. As the horse's coat succumbed to the clipper blades, it fell to the tiles and drifted about like fallen snow or autumn leaves, depending on its colour, getting into our eyes, our mouths and hair, clinging to our clothes. Horses morphed from hairy, shapeless blobs into finer, slimmer versions of themselves as though peeled, the colour under their coat often a surprise. Chestnuts might clip to mushroom, blacks turned a soft grey, palominos became cream, the contrast between the clipped and non-clipped coat giving a two-tone effect.

Rose didn't always finish clipping a horse in one go. After lunch one day, she stuck her head out of the kitchen door and yelled across the yard, 'Janet, get a head collar on that Mo so I can finish taking his head off,' to the sound of gasps all round, waiting riders' heads filled with the image of an impending bloodbath – until Mo appeared with a shaggy head and everyone sighed with understanding and relief.

You could say Rose was particular about the way her horses were turned out. Manes, she insisted, should be pulled – but not so short as to resemble a cake frill. Tails were left unpulled at the top but banged at the bottom – again, not too short. Heels were never, *ever*, left with feather intact. Gypsy cobs Rose didn't do. Whereas she might turn a blind eye to our doctored and flared Levi's, she took a very different view of her horses following such fashion. As soon as any new horse arrived on the yard out came the clippers and off came the feather, as well as any extra coat under the chin, transforming the creature in front of our eyes. I still can't quite get my head around black Friesians being ridden, as is the norm, with their legs untrimmed. Rose was always of the opinion that riding horses should never have feather, and I'm with her on that. It's just a style thing. She told us that when she had worked in a hunting stable she had been taught to pull the fine feather from the heels, as you would a mane. I'm all for clippers, me. And can I just say that birds have feathers, horses have *feather*. Singular. If you doubt this, just think of the last time you stayed in to wash your hairs.

The whirr of the clippers heralded the turn of the seasons and the start of autumn at the riding school at the top of the hill as much as any cold wind or frost underfoot. Far from lamenting the loss of summer, the sound promised days of exciting and lively riding, and evenings filled with the sound of the horses munching their hay, the stables in the big yard warmed by equine bodies rugged snugly in jute and blanket, our favourites always there in their stables for us to visit and offer a carrot, an apple or just a hug.

Donkeys... part one

I N THE 1960S, DONKEYS began to be the next big thing. No longer the poor man's beast of burden, people started breeding them as they did fancy rabbits, or show ponies. County shows held classes for them, as did Royal Windsor and Hickstead. The Donkey Breed Society was born – and it started a stud book. The Society even held a Championship Show at the National Equestrian Centre (which used to be part of the National Agricultural Centre but is now, alas, no more). Show reports appeared in the equine press.

Hmmm, a donkey, I mused in the 1970s, as I worked full-time at the riding school at the top of the hill. I could afford a donkey. It wasn't even as though I considered a donkey as a make-do horse, I really liked them. I wanted to know more about them. I decided I would get one!

Rose's reaction?

Not good.

Turned out she hated donkeys. They were useless, she ranted. They carried lungworm, they brayed a lot and horses were scared of them. Donkeys, Rose made plain, were the antithesis of horses and I would, she said with feeling, be *bloody stupid* to get one. This was a hiccup, but it didn't put me off. I obviously possessed a stubborn streak like that attributed to the object of my desire. I pressed on.

Where could I keep one? Dick supplied the answer, kindly offering me the paddock behind his house, half-way down the back lane. Perfect. Several acres with a shelter (essential, I had done my research), well fenced, handy for me to cycle down – and up again – from work. My donkey needed company. One of the riding school's pupils was getting her own pony and, when her father discovered my plan, he asked whether they might be able to keep the pony at Dick's, with no hint of the prejudice displayed by Rose. Dick approved – they were a great family, and the pony was a lovely liver chestnut mare called Minty.

I went donkey hunting.

A donkey stud in Kent provided the perfect answer to my prayers. A yearling, gelded, show quality, pink in colour – oh yes, donkeys come in pink, pale strawberry roan, in fact. His sire was a stallion I greatly admired, a previous national champion, his dam a successful show mare. I went to see him, fell in love, handed over my fifty quid and the deal was done. Mr Pickwick the donkey came home a few weeks later and was installed in his new home, settling in a treat. I was a donkey owner!

Rose was unimpressed, muttering dark things about donkeys to me whenever the subject arose. Her dislike of all things asinine had diminished not one jot, and she was never one to hide her feelings. Nothing, but nothing would make her change her mind. Donkeys were bad news, full stop. I was in her bad books.

There had never been any donkeys around the entire area for as long as I could remember, but it appeared they were like buses for it was but a matter of weeks after Pickwick arrived when blow-me-down, wouldn't you know it, a*nother* donkey appeared! This one was installed in a gated area down the back lane, next to the school horses' field. What were the chances?

This donkey was also young, but brown, tethered by a long chain behind chain-link gates. The first we knew of its arrival was when, hearing a big ride approaching, Rose at the helm, a lead rein either side, the donkey rushed at the fence, chain rattling like it was launching the Titanic, desperately braying to any equine who might be a potential ally.

As one, all the horses shot across the lane away from the long-eared, dragon-voiced monster, only to shrink back from the ditch in a spectacular about-turn, caught between a rock and a hard place – or, more correctly, a ditch and a donkey. Riders gathered reins, gripped with their heels and gasped, fearing for their lives; children wailed, someone screamed, two horses turned tail and headed back to the safety of the yard, one rider clinging on in terror, the other in floods of tears. You can imagine the language from Rose as she untangled her lead reins, yelling at everyone to calm down and to come back – not a good image. Rose had been right on at least two points: donkeys did bray, and they certainly scared her horses. The little brown donkey had introduced himself in spectacular fashion, but had done nothing in the way of public relations, taking all of thirty seconds to prove that most of Rose's prejudices were actually well founded.

Why do horses react so severely at the sight of a donkey? Most of them freak out if they're not used to them. Donkeys look a bit like horses – but not *quite*. I mean, there are those ears for a start. Donkeys don't smell like horses. In fact, they don't really smell of anything. Next time you're next to one, take a good whiff. This is probably because their coats contain no grease (they're not waterproof, so don't leave them out in the rain). The humble moke is not native to our shores – it is thought the Romans brought them along when they invaded a couple of thousand years ago – and donkeys are more at home in hot, arid regions. This is why their hooves curl up if they are left untrimmed, designed as they are to be worn down by sandy, abrasive soil, which we don't have much of. So maybe horses are puzzled by them on these two counts.

These differences might be something the average horse can get over – but if the donkey opens his mouth and brays, then you're likely to have a setback on your hands. It begins as a loud huffing sound as the donkey draws breath and then enthusiastically revs up. This huff, huff, huffing is usually followed – but not always – by a very, *very* loud *Hee-Haaaaaaw*, which can go on for a while. It is thought the ass's large ears (which can also help keep them cool) and his loud voice help him stay in touch with his chums over long distances. And if you're wondering what the difference is between an ass and a donkey then wonder no more, for there isn't one. *Equus Asinus* is the scientific name: donkey came later, probably meaning small and dun-coloured. Paradoxically, some horses – usually mares – just love donkeys and will follow them around the field in an effort to be best of friends, chasing other horses away from their new toy. Either way, whichever reaction a donkey elicits from its equine cousins, it is rarely welcomed by its cousins' riders.

So, with cousin donk installed in his strategic position, donkeys were once again a dirty word, just when an alliance was needed. Exactly why he was there, nobody could understand. The donkey was visited every day by a couple of unhorsy blokes in a van, who seemed to be working on some vehicles. What they wanted with a donkey was impossible to guess. A bad debt, perhaps? And so, for several weeks, everyone took their lives into their hands whenever they passed the yard on, or with, a horse. The little brown donkey, his chain rattling like the Prisoner of Zenda as he ran at the fence desperate for chums, gradually wore down the horses' reactions, and they grew less and less hysterical. Normality returned.

Sort of.

Then, one day, it all changed.

'Come with me!' Rose shouted across the yard. I followed her down the back lane. 'Those stupid men, one of them must have hit that donkey with the van!' she cried, striding out, a bucket full of bandages and dressings beside her. She was right. The poor donkey looked very sorry for himself, a gash over one eye, holes in his knees, a wound across his side. Rose forced her way in through the gate and dressed his wounds, her patient being just that, clearly pleased to see us out of his one good eye.

'Come on,' she said, unclipping the chain from the little fellow's head collar, 'you're coming with us.'

I don't know what the two men thought when she gave them a piece of her mind and told them they no longer had a donkey, but no argument was offered. Donk, as he was imaginatively known, went to live with Rose's mares and liveries at the park yard, and that was where he stayed, his wounds healing as he grazed with Rose's horses, coming in to his own little stable in the barn, his frame filling out, his confidence returning. He had gone from a pathetic little donkey with no friends, to landing very much on his hooves. Donk had come home.

For all her bluster about donkeys, Rose wasn't going to let one suffer. And I teased Rose about it for a good long time, bemoaning the fact that nobody could have anything original around the place – as soon as one person got something, it seemed *everyone* had to have one.

Now we both had donkeys, and no more was said about it.

Confidence

Y OU CANNOT TEACH CONFIDENCE, you can only
nurture it, provide opportunity for it and encourage
it via positive experiences. Confidence will enable you
to soar, to see you achieve, to reach heights beyond your
wildest dreams. Lack of confidence will cripple you, defeat
you before you've tried, fear and doubt overcoming your
enthusiasm, your joy. It will disable your ability and hold
you back.

I once worked with a very no-nonsense woman who
was always asking everyone, 'What *exactly* are you *trying*
to do?' in a subtle and efficient undermining of effort.
My answer was always, 'I'm not *trying* to do anything. I
am actually *doing* it!' There is a theory that one shouldn't
actually *try* when practising a skill, one should just allow
the process to take over. *Trying,* so the theory goes, can

inhibit your technique, overcomplicating and pressurising the mind, forcing the same mistakes to repeat themselves in defiance of your determination for them not to. Trying isn't quite the same as making an effort, but rather it can put you under pressure.

There is no doubt that competence in anything fosters confidence, but some are slaves to the nagging doubt of *what if*? What if I fall off? What if my horse refuses the jump? What if everyone thinks I'm a rubbish rider? Once the *what ifs* start, there is no end to them, and they creep and grow and fester. Unless you can turn things around and ask yourself: what if none of those scenarios happen? What if I *can* do this? What if I *succeed*?

Confidence is all about the games our minds play – and, more importantly, the games we can't prevent our minds from playing. Sports psychology has proved how much the mind influences the body. It's similar to replacing the *should* word (such pressure) with the *could* word (giving you choice). Even now my heart sinks whenever anyone decides I might benefit from their wisdom and insight (with the best of intentions, I'm sure), preceding their unasked-for advice with the words, 'You know what you should do…'

'A real confidence-giver' is how some ponies are described, a pony for a child with enthusiasm but little experience, a pony who will never refuse a jump, who will gladly join its rider in adventures, taking an interest, obeying the right aids and ensuring nothing shakes them or causes them to doubt. Just a single doubt can influence a less confident horse, which is why choosing your first pony (or horse) is such an important thing to get right. If neither of you is confident – well, you can imagine.

Later, if the rider is up for it (and, let's face it, some never are, some are content to be passengers, unwilling to push themselves or to learn from not only their instructors, but also from their mounts, and these riders can still enjoy riding, without changing the world), then they will choose to ride the less push-button ponies and horses, the ones which continue the rider's education with challenges to overcome. Building confidence comes not because everything always goes right, but because whatever happens, the rider knows they have the ability to cope, to improve, to realise that the challenges never stop, and look forward to them all the same.

Rose was quick to spot the riders who made an effort – although I have to say that there were occasions when we rode tricky horses not because we had no fear of them, but because we feared how Rose would react should we have refused. This way we were pushed out of our comfort zone, pushed to learn and cope and improve until we progressed to anticipating and preventing bad behaviour. If Rose thought us capable of riding a tricky horse then we believed it – and that gave us the courage to take it on.

'Can you go a bit faster?' I asked one rider who was letting Libby lag behind on a hack, allowing a gap to form which, I knew from experience, would result in Libby suddenly realising her chums were leaving her behind, and filling it at a much faster pace than her rider would have appreciated. If Rose were to notice then this would end in me getting an earful as it was my job, riding drag, to keep everyone together.

'I can, lady,' the man replied, grinning at me, 'but I'm not allowed to leave the horse.'

Fair point.

We were lucky at the riding school at the top of the hill that there were so many horses and ponies to learn from and improve our skills. Not only the school horses but the liveries because if you were lucky, an owner might ask you to ride their horse for them when they went on holiday or, if you were *extra* lucky, exercise their horse regularly a few times a week. When we became better, bolder riders, having ridden the more challenging horses, we might help Rose break in and school a youngster, or ride horses with problems which had come in for schooling. The problem usually took the same form: the horse was nappy or threatening to rear, it wouldn't go out of the yard, it wouldn't do what the rider wanted. It had behaved perfectly when the owner had first got it, but now it was all going wrong.

Of course, it wasn't hard to work out what was going on. The rider hadn't had many lessons, she had bought a horse and, after a couple of weeks, the horse had thrown in a few questions the rider hadn't even noticed, let alone answered. Quite likely, the rider was riding with the hand brake on, giving conflicting signals, souring the horse with hands that restricted, afraid to let the horse walk freely, or just riding in bits. It wasn't long before the horse realised he didn't have to do anything he didn't feel like doing because there were no real instructions coming from the saddle, and even when he did try, those hands, obsessed with getting him on the bit, held him back. It was not only the rider who had lost confidence. Better to ride the horse's body, rather than just his head.

'Get up on that,' Rose would tell one of us, 'and come up the front with me on this ride.' So we would, and after an initial, lively discussion, where the horse might object to being in front before realising it wasn't up for debate, and discovering his head was no longer held in tightly, he would walk out quite happily, the ride following behind providing company and support.

Getting back to the yard after the hour, Rose would ask how it had been. Okay would be the answer, although there may have been a couple of hiccups, possibly a shy or two, or even another try at napping.

'All right,' Rose would say, 'stay on it and take it out again.'

After three hours, the horse was 'cured', hacking out willingly and obediently, relieved to find some instructions coming from the saddle, his mouth and neck unhindered, no longer aching. After a weekend it would go back, the problem explained, with a recommendation that the rider took some lessons. The recommendation was usually ignored but we rarely saw the horse again. It was probably sold, and the rider probably took up knitting. It wasn't the horse that had the problem – trading it in for a different mount would render the same result in another few weeks of the same treatment.

There is no fast-track to this riding business.

'In this game', Rose would tell us, gravely, 'it takes ten years to learn that you know *nothing*,' (great emphasis on the word *nothing*). Ten years. Ten years before it clicks that only then have you completed the mere basics, only then are you starting your education, only then do you realise that you will never run out of horses to teach you, that there are possibilities yet to be discovered as well as people, cultures, ideas and history to learn and borrow from. Ten years and then you can really get stuck in.

The mechanics of riding are simple: imagine your hands and legs control four doors which surround your horse. Open the front door and close the back door and your horse will go forward; close either of the side doors and your horse will move in the opposite direction, close the front door and your horse will stop; close it again and your horse will go backwards. Close all four doors and your horse has nowhere to go but up, whether you want him to or not. Now all you have to do is spend the rest of your life fine-tuning all that, and learning to control your own body while you do it. And *that*, of course, is the difficult bit.

Learning to sit still, to allow the horse to move under us is the greatest challenge. We hinder our horses, twitching, worrying, moving around in the saddle, giving a thousand unintentional signals they learn to ignore; our bodyweight a hindrance – and then we blame the stoic, long-suffering ones for switching off, the sensitive ones for exploding left, right, skyward. Horses know how to move, how to dance; they just have to learn how to do it all over again with the handicap that is their riders.

You never stop learning with horses – but horsy people know this. It is a paradox that the top horsy folk are confident yet humble at the same time, open to new ideas, to new methods.

And it came to pass, sometime in the 1990s and early in the twenty-first-century, that the horse whisperers came to town. They weren't the first. Throughout history famous horse whisperers had been wowing audiences and taming horses thought untameable. The first might just have been Alexander the Great – if only he'd been allowed to follow his initial choice of career…

Macedonia, around 327 BC – 12-year-old Alexander has just tamed the mighty Thessalian charger Bucephalus, after all the kingdom's horse-breakers failed, much to the admiration of his father, Phillip II.

'Good work, son. You're a chip off the old King-of-Macedonia block, so you are.'

'Well, I just noticed that the horse was scared of his own shadow. It wasn't too hard really, I just whispered in his ear, turned his head to the sun and…'

'Shhhh, keep that to yourself. Whispering to horses will get you some right funny looks. Luckily, the finest horse-breakers in the kingdom didn't notice.'

'No, they're too used to doing things the old, forceful way. But I have some revolutionary ideas…'

'Splendid, splendid. Revolutionary ideas are just what you'll need to conquer the known world, son.'

'I mean about training horses.'

'No need, (taking a deep breath and narrowing his eyes) we've got people for that.'

'But I want to do it differently, Dad.'

'Breaking in horses is no career for a prince!'

'But I think the world is ready to take on new ideas, embrace a more humane way of training. I'd like to give some clinics, offer courses, give demonstrations of my methods around the country – or even tour...'

'Well if it's touring you're after, you can tour all you want while you're conquering. Touring is a given as far as conquering is concerned. You can't conquer anyone or anywhere without touring the world, meeting people, killing them off, slaughtering whole cities and suppressing entire civilisations – bending them to your will. That's how you make a name for yourself as a ruthless warrior and consign yourself to history. You could be truly **great**, you know, I feel it.'

'It's not what I want to do! I've patented my training ideas – Techniques of Alexander, if you will'.

'And there'll be time for all that **after** the conquering...'

'**Instead** of conquering, Dad.'

'Now don't start this again. You're going to conquer the known world and do us all proud. How do you think your mother's going to feel if you start up all this whispering-to-horses nonsense again? Huh? Downright ashamed, that's how!'

'Dad, try to understand. There's some exciting work being discovered in animal training right now – tremendous work with elephants...'

'I've heard enough! No son of mine is going to muck about chasing horses around when there's a whole world out there with your name on it. You're conquering the known world and that's final!'

'Aw, Dad!'

The horse whisperers in our time came with new thinking and fresh ideas about training horses. Magical! Radical! Revolutionary! And some certainly were that. Here were alternatives to the traditional ways we were used to. Communicating with horses was turned on its head as we had our ingrained teachings questioned, which is no bad thing. It doesn't do to think there is only one way of doing something, or that the only reason to keep doing it one way is simply because that is the way it has always been done. The emphasis shifted from training our horses to encouraging them to train us, of listening rather than telling, of putting ourselves in our horse's hooves. But not all the ideas were revolutionary – with some it was a case of a new way of telling an old story.

One of the evangelical new-wave trainers had devised a programme of progressive training for the ridden horse which I went to watch. Not only was the demonstration fascinating and correct, not only did it make perfect sense, but as I watched I realised that this particular schooling programme was nothing new. It was exactly how training has been recommended for years, just the same as the schooling by conventional trainers, taught to students in official British exams, resulting in well-trained horses and ponies. But here the steps had been re-branded and marketed in a new way, as though the trainer had discovered some amazing secret. It had been re-packaged for a new audience, the new audience who sat in awe, and then whooped and clapped at the end of it, convinced they had witnessed something radically different. A new audience hungry to discover the magic secrets that would mean they, too, could be equine gurus – they only had to buy the books, the equipment, and into the ideas.

So what? Providing the message gets across, providing horses are being trained with sympathy, with respect, with good and proven programmes, what does it matter what it is called or how it is marketed? Isn't it just an example of communication? Finding a way people will understand, paving the way for happier horses whose owners have seen the light? Anything that improves communication between and rider/handler and horse has to be positive, even if it isn't actually new.

Maybe the audience had been disillusioned by the conventional way of learning. Maybe the people who whooped and clapped had acquired their own horses before learning the basics (ten years, remember) or continuing to have lessons themselves. Or maybe they were just seeking that silver bullet, the answer to connecting with their horse where no connection had yet been made, a short cut. And maybe, with this patented programme, they would find it.

There is more than one way to skin a cat, they say. There is more than one way to ride and care for horses – and you will probably get things wrong before you get them right. We can all learn something from everybody (even if it's how *not* to do it). It is fascinating to pick up tips and ideas from different trainers, people willing to share their experiences, keen to share knowledge. Watching demos and riding lessons will always throw up nuggets to think about, to chew over and store away for future reference. Something clicks, it suddenly makes sense – *that's* what your instructor was trying to tell you!

One guru boasted of backing horses in record time – in the mere blinking of an eye (well, slightly longer, say thirty minutes). Rose had been shaving minutes off that target for years. The thing was, all the youngsters Rose bred (and she bred quite a number over the years) were handled every day, so we were hardly dealing with wild animals. The horses were all used to us, confident in their routine, familiar with the unfamiliar – farm machinery, dogs, cars coming and going, horses hacking out. On a warm summer's evening, without warning, Rose would casually suggest one of us should just lean across a youngster's back as we led it in from the field. No big deal, just give it a go when it was relaxed and full of grass. And so we did, someone else holding our legs and, if the horse made no reaction we might slowly, almost absentmindedly, throw a leg over it. If that was met with no adverse reaction, we'd sit up for a few moments and walk a few steps before sliding off again. We were light, unafraid and totally up for it. It is a privilege to be the first person ever to sit on a horse.

But here's the thing: it was slipped into everyday routine. We certainly hadn't anticipated it would happen so nobody's heart rate soared. Nobody was *whoa*-ing and *steady*-ing and giving the horse the idea that this was going to be traumatic, or that he might not like it, that something was amiss, or – heaven forbid – trying to hold him down (good luck with that). We just, quietly and gently, without fuss, did it.

Later, after twenty minutes of being backed in a saddle and bridle, and in a more official manner in the school, one of us would take the same horse out alongside Rose on one of the riding school hacks. The youngster took his cue from all the other horses around him. He was asked to go forward, in straight lines, in the approved manner, and the whole atmosphere was one of normality – no big deal. Also, controversially, he hadn't been lunged for weeks, building up fitness and muscle which he could easily have used against us. It is always a good idea to give yourself a fighting chance and in doing so, you give the horse the opportunity to do the right thing, to lay down good foundations, to instil good behaviour right from the off.

Rose was big on *just doing it*, long before a famous sports shoe brand got in on the act. 'Don't mess about,' she'd say. 'Give that horse something to do!' So we did. If we didn't give our horse something to do, Rose said, we offered it an opportunity to follow its own agenda – which could be a far cry from ours. The devil makes work for idle hooves and Rose insisted that a lot of so-called bad behaviour stemmed from horses which were bored or whose energy, for want of being channelled by their riders, had to go somewhere. Better the rider chooses where.

Years later, when my friend Diane and I broke in an Arab mare who was taking a break from breeding foals, there got to a point where I had a problem getting canter. Diane would offer some helpful advice – my right shoulder seemed a little too high, my chin a fraction too far forward – but nothing seemed to help.

I went away and thought about it. Never mind Jesus, what would Rose do? I could hear her voice in my head very clearly: *'Oh Janet, why are you twittering about? Get on with it! Push on! Give that horse something to do!'*

So I did. When Diane joined me in the field the following day she asked me, agog, what I had done. There we were, the Arab and I, cantering large figures of eight, with a simple change in the middle, happy as two Larrys, the problem apparently solved.

'I just got on with it,' I told her.

We can over-think things. 'Why,' Rose would ask, 'overcomplicate matters?' There is much to be said for keeping things simple, stupid, as instead of cluttering up your head with the technicalities, you might gain confidence with the just doing it scenario. You can fine-tune later on. Whenever I find things going awry I always try to bring things back to basics, to do what Rose would do. *Just kicking on and getting on with it* usually works. Ride through your trouble, don't store it up. If you stop when your horse misbehaves, you'll only have to start again and the problem will still be there – only magnified, for now you have allowed your horse to gain from his misbehaviour. More leg, less rein is usually the answer.

As editor of *Pony* magazine, I would organise photo

shoots at various obliging yards for the magazine, taking pictures of the children with their ponies for features and photo stories – and I was always most grateful for the efforts shown by everyone who gave up their time. However, there I found a different world from the one in which I had grown up.

Most of the girls had their mothers in tow – and it was obvious they were a regular fixture at the yard, rather than having just turned up for the occasion. So instead of a whole load of horsy kids having a ball away from the bosom of their loving family (my friends and I would have had our style severely cramped had our mums wanted to join us), there was now a whole lot of mother-and-daughter things going on.

Some mums were fabulous, enthusiastic but not interfering, with a sense of humour and fun. They supported their offspring, and it was great to see how in tune they were. But then there was the occasional other, pushy mum who, instead of letting her daughter answer the questions I asked, answered for her. The pushy mum was usually loud, usually a nightmare and, in some cases, went on to tell me what I wanted their child to do, what pictures I needed. She would talk *for* her daughter, urging her to hurry up, to get a move on. She would roll her eyes and tell me, in a confidential shout so that everyone around could hear, that she didn't understand what was wrong with her, that she despaired, that she, her mother, would have killed to have owned her own pony as a child.

It was pretty apparent to everyone exactly where the

problem lay. Mother-daughter relationships were none of my business, but it still made me think. And what I thought was that the best thing those mums could do would be to buy themselves a horse and release their children into the wild where they might find something their hearts were into. And then *let them get on with it.*

The pushiest parents at the riding school at the top of the hill were the ones who didn't, themselves, ride. They'd sit in the gallery, urging their offspring in threatening tones and with wagging fingers to jump higher, to go faster, to do it! Their children were usually quiet and withdrawn, the ones with no confidence in their own ability, the last riders to benefit from being forced into anything. The pupils I, as their instructor, wanted to go at their own pace until they volunteered to move outside their comfort zone. Were they naturally quiet, or had they had quietness forced upon them?

I know this sort of behaviour still goes on because at a riding school I visited recently a whole list of *don'ts* were pinned up in the gallery for the benefit of parents. The don'ts were pretty extensive: *would parents please refrain from telling the instructor what their child should be taught… refrain from issuing their own instructions from the gallery… insisting which pony their child should ride… suggesting what their child should be doing next week…* it went on and on. Mind boggling, really. I mean, who'd sit in the back seat of a driving instructor's car and urge their teenager to try a few nought-to-sixties away from the traffic lights, or insist that a couple of handbrake turns in Asda's car park wouldn't go amiss?

And some parents could be amazingly cavalier about

their children's safety, such as the non-riding father who, pushing his small daughter forward every week, insisted she should ride a horse taller, faster, more impressive. Couldn't she handle a bigger horse this week? How about putting her on something a bit more challenging? What reckless abandon with his own flesh and blood, urging her to do things he couldn't do, things he himself had no clue about. What better way to gamble with a person's confidence? Why didn't he have a go if he was so gung-ho about it?

Confidence is a fragile thing – difficult to build, so easy to break. We need to do all we can to ensure confidence grows with ability on an individual, tailor-made journey. Choose your riding teacher with care for what works for one rider will work against another. It may be the most important decision of your whole riding adventure.

I do posh

DURING ONE SUMMER IN the early 1980s, when Charles and Diana gave the memorabilia sellers a bumper year, I answered an ad in *Horse and Hound* for an instructor at a posh riding school in the stockbroker belt in Surrey. *Experience more important than qualifications,* the ad said. So I rang them up, called their bluff and, after an interview to which I travelled by train, was offered the job. I was pretty made up – it was a whizzy establishment and I would receive some top-notch instruction from the highly qualified proprietor, which wouldn't do my riding any harm.

On my first day said proprietor gravely informed me that she expected me to know, after three days, the names of all the horses and ponies on all the yards, a task with which I had no difficulty. Later, when I went on *Pony* photo shoots, I could name all the ponies after a few minutes, although I could rarely remember the riders. Hardly surprising, I mean, ponies all have different faces – the girls tended to look quite similar.

The hierarchy at this posh riding school was strictly imposed. That instructors were hard to come by but grooms merely two-a-penny was obvious by the not-so-subtle differences in the way the two sets of employees were treated. Whilst I and my fellow instructors enjoyed polite requests and regular lessons, grooms lived under the threat of being dismissed at the drop of a hat – or at least for transgressions such as leading a horse in from the field without having opened its stable door first. You never knew whether the people you started working with that morning would still be on the payroll by the time you clocked off at night.

One of my fellow instructors got so fed up with it all, she packed her suitcase and headed her horse towards the road, hell-bent on getting out of there. Except that half-way down the long driveway her horse took exception to his new career as a baggage handler, bucking off rider and luggage before galloping back to his chums with an indignant whinny, leaving his loving owner for dead on the tarmac – from whence we scraped her up. As an escape plan it failed spectacularly, but it did give us all a laugh. Work began on the tunnel the following week.

At this riding school, best practices were observed: all riders began their riding career via the safety of the lunge line, and young novices rode for weeks within the confines of the lower school before graduating to the larger, upper school. Safety was paramount, nothing was rushed, no corners cut. Tasked one summer day with taking some young riders out for a tame hack around the school's own fields, I wasn't prepared for what would happen: most of the riders fell off. It wasn't as though we were doing anything daring, just walking and trotting around the fields! The riders fell off for no obvious reason that I could fathom; they seemed just to give up and succumb to the lure of gravity, as though sirens called from the ground below.

They fell off when their pony dodged a daisy; they hit the deck when their pony snatched at a blade of grass; they tumbled onto the dirt when their pony stepped sideways, or took a deep breath or when another pony looked at them funny. It got to a point where I was convinced they were throwing themselves off like lemmings before the inevitable happened, just to get it over with. Getting them all home in one piece seemed an insurmountable task and I breathed a huge sigh of relief when we made it back to the yard and nobody needed medical help. My young riders were all school-bound, lulled into a false sense of security and their own competence, having always ridden within four walls where they needed only to ride one side of their mounts.

Maybe taking a few risks – like Rose's favourite dismounting at the trot – might have made a difference, a few risks taken in the school to test their seats, their reactions, their ability to think in the saddle and their nerve, just a few questions, to see how they might be answered. Would it have made a difference? (Or killed them all off?) Would it make a difference to riders today? I only offer it out there, knowing full well these ideas would give the insurers apoplexy. At the riding school at the top of the hill we all hacked out from our first lesson. The great outdoors held no worries for us – and we were fortunate enough to be allowed to stay and help, to handle lots of different horses and ponies, to learn as much – if not more – when off the ponies as we did on them.

Just as in most yards, evening stable duties meant the instructor on duty would be responsible for ensuring that everything on the yard was ship-shape before declaring everything done for the night. One working pupil was always very indignant when I insisted on doing a final yard check after she had told me all her horses were done and dandy. It wasn't that I doubted her, but I was ultimately responsible and therefore answerable to the boss. When she was in my position, I explained, she would do the same. At least, I hoped she would.

I've lost count of the number of times I've returned to a yard in order to check I've closed the bolts on stable doors, and that I've secured latches on gates – and I bet you have, too. When you're used to doing it as a matter of course you do it unconsciously and it becomes a habit, a reflex action. The secret is to tell yourself you are securing the top bolt, and now the bottom bolt, all the while watching yourself do it, so that you can recall the action when you wake up sweating in the middle of the night, doubting yourself. You have to do this because sometimes, despite your best efforts, the buggers will still make a run for it.

One Friday evening, after a hot summer day, just after we'd all retired to bed in the staff cottage we shared with spiders the size of small rats, word reached us (the door opened and said proprietor screamed urgently up the stairs) that the grass liveries had somehow escaped. They were, even as we leapt into action, running amuck, hoof-printing manicured lawns, trampling fancy fences and ransacking gardener-tended flowerbeds amongst some of the most expensive and exclusive private roads south of London.

We fumbled into our clothes – I hadn't time to take off the floor-length t-shirt I wore in bed so tucked it up into my jumper and down into my jeans. Head groom Claire grabbed a bucket of pony nuts, head collars were thrown into the car and after being driven to where the ponies had last been reported, Claire, Simon (another groom) and I were ejected into the darkness, the proprietor speeding off to deposit other staff at another likely location. With the picturesque and sleepy village green and duck pond to our right, woodland ahead and huge houses to our left, we stumbled along the tarmac in the gloom, Claire rattling the bucket and puncturing the tranquillity by screaming 'COME ON PONIES!' in her finest Clapham accent, and at the top of her voice. It could only be a matter of time before the police were summoned by anxious residents, we feared. After all, the Brixton riots were still fresh in everyone's minds.

Then, suddenly and without warning, Simon vanished. One second he was there walking beside us, the next we were adjacent to dead air. Claire screamed like she was auditioning for Hammer House of Horrors – like she hadn't made enough racket already. She screamed again when Simon popped up out of the ditch into which he had stumbled. It was Kate all over again, proving that ditches are a horse person's worst enemy and best avoided. Unfortunately, this one wasn't as dry as the one inhabited by Kate, so although our eyesight was impaired by the night, our sense of smell was heightened by *eau de water ditch*. If we'd had a small chance of catching the ponies before, they were likely to be in the next county by now – and still running.

Someone else found them – and then they found us. The walk back to their field, a pony on either side of us, was another adventure. I was issued with an ill-matched pair of ponies – one keen as mustard and still on a high from his adventure, threatening to pull out my arm as he jogged along, the other lagging behind in a sulk (possibly the ringleader), furious at having his freedom brought to such a swift end. My t-shirt kept escaping from my jumper and threatened to trip me up, and with both hands occupied I could do little to rectify it. The walk to the field took ages – and we all had a nice full Saturday's lessons ahead of us in only a few hours. I took my aching arms to bed for what was left of the night and wondered at my choice of career.

Into Africa

IN THE LATE 1990S, it was time to extend my equestrian vacations to another continent. Africa! Three holidays in one – beginning in South Africa where I was to visit two centres, and then on to the legendary Okavango Delta.

This promised to be something else.

It was.

The days in South Africa were pretty special, accommodation being in the middle of nowhere and surrounded by wildlife. Turning right instead of left on my way from the main house to my cabin on the first night, I dozily wandered off into the bush. The sudden realisation that I was in total darkness, the ground torches designed to guide my way all behind me, alerted me to my folly. Luckily, I hadn't gone too far and was able to retrace my steps. Otherwise, there's a good chance I wouldn't be writing this now, having provided dinner for something big and hungry in the bush. I'd like to blame jet lag but am willing to accept that I was just being dim.

Riding out the next day with our guide we saw wildebeest, zebra, kudu and, scarily, black rhino.

'Black rhino are bad tempered,' advised our guide, in a respectful whisper, pointing to a couple of them through the trees, 'and they are short-sighted. So if you find yourself on the ground and they charge at you, just climb one of the many trees dotted around.'

I looked at the trees. Decided I wasn't the lithe and nimble sort. There was no 'just' about it.

'Don't worry,' our guide assured me, nodding, 'you'll manage with a black rhino chasing you down.'

I supposed I would. Decided I'd rather not put it to the test, especially as the trees didn't look high enough to save me from rhino. I hoped that any rhino which might chase me might not be so much short-sighted as registered blind.

My mount was dark brown William, the South African Boerperd, a gentle and obliging sort. The terrain was scrubland and dotted with trees for the tourists to climb in a rhino emergency, so you couldn't see very far. This made riding interesting as you never quite knew what might be around the corner.

The next centre was very different. Very open, with hills to climb, game to see and a full itinerary. I slept in a *rondavel*, a borrowed and obliging dog keeping me company. We rode out into Africa and, one afternoon, we played polocrosse. The most competitive player was Gina, the cook, who, in blatant disregard of the rulebook thought nothing of repurposing her polocrosse stick in order to encourage her pony to go faster. It was a great game – but Gina's competitiveness was infectious, and I had to curb the temptation to follow her example. It is easy to forget that you have to use the stick parallel to your horse (not *on* him), for if you lean over and fiddle about trying to get the ball when it's between his front legs, you stand a good chance of tripping him up, and he wouldn't thank you for it. You wouldn't thank yourself.

My final destination was the Okavango Delta in Botswana, and I admit to having some misgivings regarding the accommodation – namely, a tent.

And this is why…

Despite my less than positive experiences with the Guides, during the late 1970s Jan and I had optimistically (some might say naively) set off in Jan's light blue Ford Escort with a borrowed tent for a three-day jolly jape around Exmoor. What laughs we would have!

A success it was not.

For a start, we couldn't work out how to put up the tent because, of course, we hadn't bothered to ask its owner for a demo. I know, *fail to prepare, prepare to fail,* blah, blah, *blah*. How do you think these sayings come about? Somebody has to volunteer to provide inspiration for the clever-dicks. Needless to say, it wasn't one of those self-erecting tents you get nowadays where you just throw it up in the air and it comes down all ready for you to move into, this one was old school. Despite Jan and I spending several hours surrounded by swathes of orange canvas, looking at both ends of every pole for inspiration and hurling pegs left, right and at each other in frustration, not one person at the campsite – of which there were many – offered to help. They just sat and watched. Sniggering. Smug. No doubt entertained. Don't talk to me about happy camping.

So we slept in a half-tent, the canvas puddling on the ground like a melting chocolate orange. The next night, having severely underestimated how cold one can be in a sleeping bag, I spent an equally cold and uncomfortable night in Jan's car. The third night I forced her, complaining (understandably) into a B&B. Camping, I no longer do.

My lack of hardiness was just the start. Deciding it would be rude to waste the Exmoor location we booked a hack from a riding stable on the moor, turning up in our best gear, appreciating the fine equine heads looking out over half doors along the line of customer-facing loose boxes, and arguing between ourselves about which of us was to ride the very nice bay, already tacked up and very obviously waiting for one of us. As the proprietor strode out, we elbowed each other out of the way like ill-mannered debs with an approaching duke in their sights, both desperate to be first in line for the bay.

'Who's the lightest?' we were asked, as a groom appeared from around the back leading a hairy, piebald, barely-awake cob. Jan and I went into rapid reverse, elbowing each other *forward*, neither wishing to volunteer. The cob was a lovely creature we were sure, but nothing like the quality of the bay and it had obviously never troubled the clippers. Besides, protruding from under its saddle was a large, three-inch deep square of yellow foam, a bit like heavy-duty building insulation. The natural state of such foam is flat, and the presence of a saddle plonked on top of it did little to persuade it to do otherwise. It stuck out either side of the saddle like Dumbo's ears, doing little to improve the cob's appearance. It was about as far away from Little Joe's paint horse as you could possibly have imagined.

Reluctantly, hoping to store up points for when I broke it to my friend about the B&B, I caved, resigning myself to seeing Jan on the bay as I settled myself on to the cob's saddle. At least, when mounted, the foam was out of my eye line. But wait, not so fast my friend, for what should appear with another groom but an almost identical piebald cob, complete with insulation saddle cloth. Jan's mount! We considered this nothing short of misrepresentation, for the piebald cobs made an appearance only after the bay had hooked us and we'd handed over our cash. Our escort (surprise, surprise) mounted the bay but, just as we were about to follow her out onto the moor, a late arrival rushed in. Could he join us for a hack?

Of course! Blow me if they didn't magic up yet another piebald cob from around the back. How many did they have? An inexhaustible supply, by the look of it – and that wasn't the only thing they had in spades for the third cob also sported the obligatory foam under its saddle. Piebald-cobs-are-us! Plenty to choose from! Why ride anything else? Once mounted we all – one astride the bay and the rest of us following on a Beverley Sisters trio of piebald cobs – headed for the wilds of Exmoor.

We took no pictures.

Let me be clear lest you leap to defend coloured cobs: I love coloured horses. I love cobs. I love coloured cobs, but when I first started riding, coloured horses were considered a bit common, not usually very refined, bargain basement even – particularly when they're as nature intended, hairy to a fault. Now, of course, coloured cobs command high prices. Ask my friend Diane: she now has a pair of lovely piebald cobs, and bargain basement They. Were. Not.

Our humiliation at Exmoor was complete when our escort turned and asked us (but not the late-comer, who was actually quite a novice rider), whether we would be okay to canter. We nodded mutely, Jan rolling her eyes, the ink on her newly gained BHS Assistant Instructor certificate barely dry…

One day, we thought, we'll laugh about all this.

That day has yet to dawn.

But I was telling you about my holiday in Botswana. Getting to the Okavango Delta meant another plane ride to Maun Airport, then transferring to a light aircraft to skim, hot and breathless, over the landscape to touch down in the Middle Of Nowhere. Truly, here we were in the wild, but our hosts didn't see why we should rough it. Huge G&Ts greeted us, the smiling staff lining up to welcome us with song.

We were shown to our accommodation: luxurious tents (phew, what a relief, a world away from my Exmoor trauma), well-spaced apart (it was a popular destination for honeymooners) complete with a proper bed, wardrobe, chairs and a veranda. A few steps behind the tent were my own toilet and bucket shower, a Pelham bit repurposed as a towel rail. Ahhh, this was the life! All I needed was a pair of elephant-ear jodhpurs, a chiffon scarf at my neck, one of those pith helmets atop my curls and a silver-sideburned Stewart Granger on my arm to complete the picture. In addition the rains had fallen upstream, which meant the rivers were swollen, and water was cascading down towards our camp. We had arrived at the perfect time: where there was water, wildlife would follow.

After dinner, tired by the journey, I drifted off to sleep in my tent almost immediately, having been sternly advised *not* to visit the loo in the night, but to use the chamber pot under my bed. The tent offered some protection, but animals still roamed the area after dark – leopards had been spotted before (no pun intended). It seemed leopards weren't the only ones. In the middle of the night I awoke to terrible crashing noises all around my tent, the world apparently coming to an end. Elephants, our hosts had told us casually over dinner, sometimes came into camp and trashed the place. The noise outside matched that description and so, still sleepy, I remember thinking to myself, 'Oh, it's only elephants trashing the place', before rolling over and going back to sleep. I must have been more than tired.

WHAAAT! Why did I do that? What was wrong with me? Why didn't I get up and watch elephants all around my tent? What an opportunity missed! I could hardly believe it myself when, the next day, elephantine footprints were very much in evidence. I still kick myself, but there is no going back.

But something else had happened in the night – which probably accounted for all the elephant action. The river had returned. The waters had flowed in to fill up the river bed which, instead of being dry, dusty and very much empty as it had been the previous evening, was now full of brown water, fast flowing, still travelling onwards to irrigate the rest of the area, thousands of air pockets making their way to the surface, the noise of them popping akin to the sound of falling rain.

And the river brought something else: wildlife. As we mounted our horses and rode out with our guides the spectacle before us took our breath away. Elephants, wildebeest, zebra, graceful giraffe, antelope, warthogs – the whole cast of *The Lion King*, minus top billing, thank goodness. Everywhere you looked there were animals, wild animals, all excited and energised by the return of the river. It was our first day in the saddle and we were totally spoilt – we could not have timed it better.

A riding safari is the most brilliant way to see game, for you can get close to the animals if you are on the back of a horse. But with this advantage comes a price – your horse slots neatly into the food chain. He knows this and his reactions reflect it. You need to be able to sit a startled and frightened horse, must have the ability to stay with him if he reacts, if he runs, if he volunteers to play the hero and get the pair of you away from danger at the gallop. If you don't… well, don't expect him to come back for you, he's not Trigger, and this ain't no film, no sirrreee!

One horse had escaped camp and had hooked up with a herd of zebra before returning, a gash on his flank telling the tale of a near miss with a big cat. We were in an area where cats were not known to roam, but even so the horses all retired at night to the safety of a barn, and when they grazed during the day it was always under the watchful eye of an armed guard. This was no hack in the park. This was riding in the raw – or as raw as you can get these days.

My mount was Selous. Dark and polite, the perfect gentleman, offering to go first or last, accommodating of my need to lug around the camera and take pictures from his saddle. The scenery was surprising: a series of huge, field-like areas and looking very much like home, clumps of palm trees the only giveaway, opening up into more open areas beyond. I don't know how our guides remembered the trails – for it looked as though none existed, and as we roamed from one area to another there seemed to be no landmarks to guide us.

But we rode for hours, spotting game everywhere: warthogs with their tails up like aerials, radio-controlled pigs, their piglets running in a line like paper dolls. Wildebeest, snorting like young bulls. I loved the wildebeest; they may be two-a-penny, they may be the takeaway of so many African predators, but they are just so underrated – beautiful, graceful and fast. And there were hyena, unappreciated dustmen, feared and disliked by animals and humans alike, and giraffe, moving in slow motion, unafraid of us on our horses but still shy. If you are lucky on these trips you can gallop alongside herds of zebra, your horse giving their striped cousins confidence, but such luck eluded us on this trip. The zebras kept their distance, unwilling to let down their guard, their instinct to survive stronger than their curiosity.

And I did see elephants! So big, almost prehistoric in appearance, extending their ears like flapping wings in an all-too-successful attempt to make themselves appear larger. Their size was a surprise – we're used to seeing Indian elephants in zoos and the vastness of their African cousins seemed almost unreal. How can they be so big? But big they are – and not to be trifled with. I felt full of respect for these amazing creatures, and grateful to see them free, sadly aware they may be the last of their kind.

The river flooded over the grasses and provided refreshment for our horses as we galloped through, mindful of hidden, sunken hippo trails which could cause a horse to trip, giving a new meaning to the word waterfall. As the water tumbled down over my boots, soaked my jodhpurs and splashed into my face I recalled the parting words of the nurse who, prior to my trip had jabbed me with my anti yellow fever injection, and furnished me with malaria tablets: 'Don't go near any water,' she had stressed, her face wearing the stern expression of the medical professional, hardly able to imagine her patient rolling around on the ground and pointing her legs skyward in an attempt to empty her boots.

Every evening we returned to the comfort of our camp, our senses a-jangle with our experiences, still more to come. We ate sitting in directors' chairs, embers from the fire shovelled beneath our seats, central heating for al fresco dining. We rejoiced when Bruce's lost luggage arrived and he could at last change his shirt – then suggested he wear everything he had when he flew back on the light aircraft as luggage was restricted – one suitcase was supposed to have remained in Maun.

We gulped down our G&Ts (for medicinal purposes, naturally), we feasted on home-made bread and delicious stews. We lived in harmony with the local colony of baboons, both parties giving the other room as we passed on the paths with polite respect. Because no food was offered they were good neighbours, even if one solitary male was a neighbour too close, his bedroom a branch above my tent, his poo hitting the canvas at regular intervals during the night, lest I forget he was there. I liked to think of him as a sentinel, should one of those leopards have rocked up.

Lo and behold, one night things took a sinister turn. As I climbed into the crisply laundered sheets on my bed and snuggled down, my feet came into contact with something that shouldn't have been there. I didn't stay to confirm my fears, electing instead to leap out of bed at roughly four times the speed I had entered.

What could it be? A snake? Some small, poisonous beastie? Something had obviously crawled in while I was out enjoying myself. The lump under the bedclothes proved it.

I thought hard.

What to do?

Hmmmm…

The way I saw it, I had two options…

Option one: I could run out of the tent towards camp screaming hysterically, *'There's something in my bed!'*

Option two: I could take a look.

Oh wait, there was option three: I could get dressed, take a look and then, if necessary, run towards camp screaming hysterically: *'There's something in my bed!'*

I decided option three had legs – and trying not to wonder whether my bed companion had them too, I got dressed. Then, with shoes on my feet and courage in my heart (I think that's what the feeling in my breast might have been), I got hold of a coat hanger and, with only slightly shaking hands used it, very slowly, very tentatively, to lift the bed sheets.

And there it was… a *hot water bottle*.

I felt rather glad I hadn't gone for option one. How kind of the management to have arranged for a little comfort on a chilly night. When I told my tale at breakfast, it seemed I hadn't been the only one hoodwinked, which made us all wonder whether it wasn't some in-joke.

Very funny.

Ha, bloody, ha.

Only a matter of time before somebody had a heart attack.

The next day, we were driven for miles to find lions. You don't want to find lions when you're on a horse – and neither does your horse. So instead, the local lion expert, Christian, and his truck, was our guide. Yes, *Christian*. Christian really was leading us to the lions – who'd have thought? Off we went, with the all-knowing Christian, and lions we found – lionesses to be exact.

I know it's a cliché, but shivers ran up and down my spine as I beheld a trio of superior huntresses. They were huge, glossy, bright eyed and full of distain for the tourists.

They were queens of their domain – and they knew it. Muscular, they looked as though they could bring down anything between them – and they didn't look hungry. I realised how different big cats look in wildlife parks, sort of bored and not quite at the top of their game, content to slob around all day in track suits. These girls were not only sleek, they gave the impression that they feared nothing, that they ran the whole show, that their coats were nothing less than designer. I sat above them in the truck with Christian-the-lion-guy and my companions, but still they had the power to intimidate me. No wonder the poor zebras never dare let down their guard.

As they walked unhurriedly into the bush to shop for something on the hoof and we turned for home I pondered on how homogenised our lives were. How safe – thank goodness.

Nevertheless, we did have a taste of potential danger at fly camp. A four-hour ride saw us reach the amazing, self-contained camp amongst the trees where we were to stay for the night. The fire crackled as we all sat around it, rifles always handy, never out of our hosts' reach. The weapons were not just for our safety for here there was no barn in which to hide the horses. Instead, they dozed in a row, rugged against the chill of the night air, tied to a rope line – the armed vigil would continue throughout the night. Lions had visited camp before: one moment all was well and feline free, the next there was an amber-eyed carnivore staring at everyone, eyeing up the horses like the specials menu. Guard is never relaxed at fly camp for there is too much at stake.

And so we sat, cigarettes lit, the G&Ts still flowing. As the evening wore on we guests, brave with ignorance (and gin), grew bolder. Bets were laid: a cigarette if you dared to walk alone to that far tree and back, a cavalier attitude from those used to the safety of civilisation. But at last it was time to retire – so another armed guard walked us all to our individual tree houses where we were left on high, sleeping under the stars, the constellation unfamiliar and what looked like zillions of halogen bulbs beaming down from the heavens. We fell asleep under a twinkling ceiling, the sound of a lone lion roar our lullaby.

What an adventure, and all because of a love of the horse. This holiday was one of a lifetime, never to be topped – the horses, the riding, the people, the guests (loud laughter when someone asked where they could fax a document to their office), the staff. The bucket showers, the sundowners, experiences never to be repeated. If you ever get the opportunity to ride a safari then I would urge you to do so. The memories will stay with you forever.

When I got back my mother's main concern was how I had got on with the food. Puzzled, I assured her it had been wonderful. Turned out she thought I'd said I was going to India.

Donkeys... part two

HAVING GOT ON WELL with Pickwick's breeder, Rosemary, I was thrilled when she suggested I might like to help out at Donkey Camp. As the name suggests, it was run on similar lines to Pony Club Camp, the obvious difference being that pony riding lessons were replaced by those in donkey handling. Even though donkeys are far from stubborn, they can't be handled in the same way as you might handle a horse, and learning the correct basics ensures a well-mannered moke that will go anywhere and do anything. Well, almost. Rosemary was the Donkey Breed Society's junior membership representative, and the junior campers were a jolly and dedicated bunch.

It was a ball and I came away more fascinated by donkeys than ever, so much so that when Rosemary asked me whether I'd like to work for her, a year after the excitement of the Queen's Silver Jubilee (1977 for the young amongst you), I made the difficult decision to leave the riding school at the top of the hill and seize a unique opportunity to learn what I could about donkeys. There was a lot to learn. Rosemary's yard was the model donkey stud with a big indoor barn, twenty stables, paddocks, a stallion yard and lots and lots of donkeys in all sizes, shapes, ages and colours, as well as show ponies for Rosemary's eldest daughter, geese, chickens, Jersey cows that were milked twice a day (if you want a cow milked by hand, give me a shout) and four lambs who soon grew into sheep.

The four geese trawled the whole stud in a menacing manner, taking their security role seriously. As I was on the yard all day I was familiar and ignored, but they would run at strangers, and even Rosemary was a target for their aggression. One day, unable to locate my jacket, I put on one of Rosemary's – and couldn't understand why the geese came at me hissing, wings out, threatening murder. The jacket must have been to blame. When the three aggressive ones died, the grey one, Grauben, was left, and she bucked the goose trend. She would follow me around as I worked, nibbling my jeans, asking me to stop and stroke her neck, which she adored, closing her eyes and relaxing like a cat. She was a thoroughly nice goose.

I worked at Rosemary's donkey stud for four years, through punk music, Kate Bush, Ian Drury and screamy Lene Lovich. We went to all the top shows in the country – all the county shows then had classes for donkeys, even Hickstead – and I learned how to handle and show youngstock, mares and geldings, looked after the three stallions and had a great time. Of course, I took Pickwick with me, so he came to top shows, too.

The first time one (very) prestigious show held classes for donkeys, they put aside a field for entrants to park away from the horses (we know why), the route to the showground necessitating a quick hop-and-skip over a narrow wooden bridge. Piece of cake – only it was anything but. All the entrants, to a donkey, decided that the bridge (the wooden slats not quite covering the sight of the running water below) was DANGEROUS. *Don't think so*, the entrants said, refusing to take another step. *It's not safe. See for yourself. Small hooves could slip through. Can't be done. Sorry.* The organisers hastily re-thought the parking arrangements.

Donkey showing is no different from pony showing. You lead your donkey around, the judge watching from the centre of the ring. After trotting individually, the judge calls everyone in for the preliminary line-up. You give an individual show before being sent around again to be called in for the final line-up and awarding of rosettes. Some donkeys train better than others. Some get an attack of stage fright in the ring and find they've forgotten how to trot, but if you do your training at home there is no reason why your donkey won't do you proud in the ring. Pickwick's dam, Maytime, was such a pro she'd practically show herself as soon as she was inside the ropes, even though at home she would tank off with you all day long.

In the spring there were foals. Nothing, but nothing, beats a donkey foal for cuteness. They look as though they've been designed by Disney. All fluff, ears and curiosity, picking up a donkey foal and taking it out for its first run in the paddock was just pure joy. The donkeys were bred quite early as, like Thoroughbreds, they take their birthday from the first of January every year. This meant mares and foals had infra-red lamps fitted in their stables to keep them warm.

The lamps also had the added benefit of bringing through their coats early. A donkey, used to the hot sun in its native, desert lands, sensibly keeps hold of its thick winter coat for as long as possible when living in the British Isles because they've learned (like Bank Holidays and organisers of outdoor events) that the weather here cannot be trusted. The summer coat is short and sleek and shows off a donkey's conformation, whereas a shaggy winter coat does little for its figure except render it invisible. Without help, a donkey will have its summer coat for only two months of the year – which explains why the DBS Championship show is held in late summer, the time of the sleek British donkey. But the showing season started with a show on Palm Sunday, and even the lamps wouldn't get the coats through that early. And so, just as with horses, rugs were the answer – both in and out.

One day, Rosemary answered the telephone to a woman who informed her that one of her donkeys was in her garden.

'What colour is it?' Rosemary asked after the expected and necessary platitudes, wondering what size head collar she would need to retrieve it.

'Green,' came the deadpan reply, devoid of humour. Not everyone seemed to realise that donkeys could wear turnout rugs.

For one Palm Sunday show, Rosemary entered her lovely stallion Philosophy for the condition and turnout class. He did look a picture: sleek, glossy, coat flattened, trimmed to within an inch of his life – hell, if I'd been a donkey mare I'd have been all over him. The judge pulled him in to stand at his rightful place, the head of the line-up. But when it came to handing out ribbons and the trophy the judge hesitated, withheld the cup, peered at Philosophy with a frown. We held our collective breath.

'Oh, no, my mistake,' laughed the judge, handing Rosemary the trophy after all. 'I thought for a moment I saw a hair out of place.'

And so I mucked out, fashioned and maintained my own (magnificent, though I say so myself) muck heap with sides so straight you could test them with a spirit level, helped train the donkeys for the shows, learned to trim them, helped with the ponies – and even learned how to drive (the donkeys, not cars – I even taught Pickwick to drive). It was great fun harnessing Samantha, who had been the national driving champion, and being towed around the fields. Whenever any other pony or donkey was harnessed, Samantha would run up and down the fence in agitation, clearly objecting to being left behind. *She* was the expert, she seemed to say, driving was *her* speciality.

Samantha was also the mother of Violet Mary. When she was born, Violet latched onto the shy yearling Laureate and made him her very, *very* best friend. They were an item, a pair, bezzi mates forever. Laureate was an introvert, happy to let his extrovert friend take the lead – which she did. Violet was a friendly, loving donkey, who would follow any visitors around (and we had a few – schools and local gingerbread groups for example) and so, whenever we had anyone come to buy a donkey, Violet Mary, with her shaggy coat, long mane and appealing nature, was always their first choice.

Only Rosemary refused to let Violet go without her best chum. She wouldn't split them up – knowing how donkeys form attachments for life. Donkeys should always live in groups or in pairs – they should never live alone as they are gregarious creatures and, as their behaviour is very different from that of horses, they do better with their own kind. Their management differs slightly, too, so if you're thinking of getting a donkey, double it – all the donkeys at the stud, apart from the stallions, were stabled in pairs. The people queuing up for Violet wanted her as a companion for donkeys they already had: they weren't in the market for a pair. And so Violet and Laureate stayed, still joined at the hip, still best mates.

Until, that is, my sister and brother-in-law bought a place with a paddock, and knew that all it was missing was a couple of mokes. Violet and Laureate found their perfect home living behind the house like a happily married couple, equally appreciated, equally loved, just the two of them.

All the donkeys had their own personalities – naturally. There was beautiful pink Hebe who, despite patient persuasion, cajoling and repeated effort, just wasn't interested in being trained for the show ring and graciously declined the lure of celebrity. She was, however, an affectionate and thoroughly nice donkey. There was the glamorous red Psyche, with an unusual white face, gentle Sophie, bossy and independent Lucinda, confident So-So, escapologist Doreen, polite and shy Hazard. All the donkeys – and there were many more – refused to be typecast. Donkeys are not stubborn; they are not stupid. Something else they are not is horses, and their care and training require a different, more donkey-friendly, approach.

About this time, my friend Jan was working for a famous three-day-eventer, and one winter, as her employer spent several weeks at the Spanish Riding School of Vienna getting some rather amazing tuition, so too did Jan – if only by proxy. Only eating and living in Vienna was eye-wateringly expensive, and she wrote not only of her fantastic experiences, but also of her hunger pangs. She was wasting away. Well, that wouldn't do so we launched the *Save Jan from Starvation* initiative, parcelling up food and sending it off to her like we were the Red Cross. She survived, but only just. Everyone knows you have to suffer for your art.

A couple of years later, when Jan had moved on to yet another top eventing yard, I would visit when she and her fellow grooms held some rather wild parties in their staff cottage. On the morning after one such wild do, the grooms rode their precious charges around to the house where I was staying. Everyone felt a little bit dead, taking on H_2O in a futile attempt to lessen the hangovers in a shutting-the-stable-door-too-late kind of way. And that's how I got to ride a four-star event horse around someone else's garden, the most prestigious pony ride ever, courtesy of Jan's colleague. If you entrust your horse to the care of others, consider that you will not always be aware of what they get up to with it.

In our teenage years, Jan, I, and all our partners in crime from the riding school at the top of the hill would make sure we went to parties suitably armed – usually with cider or, influenced by the lure of television adverts promising speedboats and other expensive and glamorous action on the Riviera, Martini, sweet or dry. Except for Jan, whose USP was to always turn up with a bottle of something called Royal Mint Chocolate Liqueur. After knocking back copious amounts of this exotic liquid at one party Jan could be seen roaming upstairs, getting down on her hands and knees and slurring, with determined insistence that Cheyenne, her favourite riding school horse, was under the bed. If he was, we couldn't see him. That RMCL must have been stronger than it looked.

Wine wasn't so hot in the 1970s, with the choice between lukewarm Liebfraumilch or the prettier and more interestingly bottled Mateus Rosé, into which it was obligatory, when empty, to shove a candle in order to turn it into the latest in chic, mid-century interior design. However, by the time I was riding (okay, I know, *sitting on*, give me a break) the eventing legend around the washing line and goldfish pond we had progressed to wine, even if that *wasn't* the fine variety. Talking of Martini, they used to be big sponsors of show jumping back in the day, as was a leading cigarette brand, and *Pony* magazine would carry full-page advertisements for both. Unquestioned at the time it seems unbelievable now, and impossible to judge by today's standards.

Meanwhile, back at the donkey stud, doing the show circuit meant deciding which donkeys would be entered for which shows under which judges. They'd then be trimmed and checked they were up on their ring craft before we packed everything into the purposely designed donkey lorry and set off, the caravan towed behind the lorry if we were staying overnight. And if we *were* staying overnight, I drew the short straw and camped out in the lorry in the space under the heads of three donkeys, all tugging cheerfully at their haynets. One morning, after a quick look in the lorry and failing to find her groom, Rosemary made an exhaustive search of the showground – only to discover me where she had first looked, having mistaken me for a bale of hay.

You prayed it would be good weather. Driving to the Royal Windsor to defend the championship Philosophy had won the previous year, we sailed past the turning on the M4, the rain falling so heavily we missed the signs. By the time we got there the showground was a quagmire (this was when it was held across the road next to the river, where drainage was a problem and where they now have the show car park). The donkeys, understandably, didn't want to play so we promptly loaded them up the ramp, turned around and drove home again. No use swimming against the tide.

Showing donkeys in the rain was never fun – for anyone. The donkeys would hunch their backs, tuck their tails between their legs and move, stiff-legged and sideways, clearly demonstrating what they thought of the whole idea. In the sunshine it was a different story, and we often came away with rosettes, trophies and, if things had gone particularly well, the championship sash.

There was one donkey stud run by a sort of Rose of the donkey world and it would be her donkeys, more often than not, which headed the line and took the top prizes. Like Rose, she also had her young helpers but word was that if she missed out on the championship, all the helpers would fight each other in order *not* to sit in the cab on the way home, bundling in with the donkeys instead, finding them better company.

It's a sad day when one is disappointed to gain a reserve championship. I mean, how many people would be thrilled with a rosette of any colour? Sometimes, with showing, you win some. More often, you might lose some. If you can't take that, then you really shouldn't be showing. You take the best donkey home, and it's only someone else's opinion, anyway. Look at Violet Mary – she wasn't the best put-together donkey in the world and she wouldn't have shone in the show ring, but a more popular donkey you would never meet.

The stud had stallions, of course. Philosophy was a stunning donkey, and he won a great deal, but he was also a very *nice* donkey, an all-round decent chap. He even visited in the house occasionally, and he would happily travel next to the mares and geldings with just a little polite *he-he-he-ing*. One of the vicars from a high church in town thought a lot of him, and decided he would be the perfect suitor for his own donkey mare, Bella, with whom he shared the vicarage.

So Bella came for her dirty weekend – or several weeks – with Philosophy, and Father M came to visit her every few days. The first visit coincided with the artificial insemination of one of the Jersey cows which, with perfect timing, took place in full view of Father M and his ancient housekeeper, who had come along for a lovely day out. Father M fully understood what was occurring, chuckling away as he rolled a cigarette, but spared his housekeeper's blushes by explaining it away as a tetanus injection. I would suggest that if your doctor tries anything similar under the pretence of administering any sort of vaccination, you get the hell out of there.

Like wise men before him, Father M came bearing gifts, only his was in the form of a bag of stale bread – gold, frankincense and myrrh being less popular with donkeys than small babies born in a stable. When he returned a few days later with another bag, rustling it as he stood at the bottom of the field, it appeared that all the donkeys had found God. Galloping down the hill they jostled about before forming an orderly line against the fence, the priest handing out offerings and looking, for all the world, as though conducting asinine Holy Communion.

Of course, donkeys have always been considered holy animals – the sign of the cross on their backs, it is said, bestowed upon them all after the first Palm Sunday when Christ rode into Jerusalem astride a donkey. Before that, the

Virgin Mary's mode of transport to and from Bethlehem was a humble ass, the same ass that looked upon the new-born Christ child in company with the ox and the sheep. Do donkeys kneel at midnight on Christmas Eve, paying homage to Our Lord? I've always made sure never to look for fear of disappointment.

In the winter, the donkeys went out in the field during dry days, and stayed in the huge barn when it was wet. But they loved the snow – galloping about and rolling, digging it up, excited by the novelty. Donkeys are famous for their sense of humour and of fun. I could go out into the field and play tag with them – something I learned from donkey guru Marjorie Dunkels, who ran a donkey training school. They'd run away from me as I played the bogey man, crouching down, my arms like an ape's, making strange noises. The donkeys would stick their noses in the air, passage-ing around the field (oh yes, donkeys can passage!), before coming back for more, their breath like clouds, loving it. Donkeys run like Arabian horses, noses high, heads parallel to the ground, drinking the wind because, as you now know they, too, come from the desert and no-one – albeit donkeys, Arabs or seven-stone weaklings on the beach – likes getting sand kicked in their face.

Marjorie Dunkels would boost her donkeys' confidence and avoid favouritism by drawing attention to their USP. 'Chester, you're the best *pink* donkey…' she would say, and to Mr Footie, '…and you're the best *grey*.' It's a philosophy we can all adopt today, especially with our dogs: '*You're* the best at disappearing down rabbit holes';

'*You're* the best at shredding the post'; 'Well done, *you're* the best at chewing my underwear to shreds!'

I was always fascinated by the difference between horses and donkeys, and made quite a study of it that isn't really relevant here. But they are very different from each other – both physically and mentally – and when you start to look into it, it's quite a subject. There are still donkeys living in the wild – the graceful Persian Onager and the northern, heavier-set, dark red Kiang of Tibet – and these are truly wild asses. Wishing to learn more about the whole equine family I would regularly bother JA Allen's Horseman's Bookshop when it was situated near the Royal Mews in London. No use looking for it now: it no longer exists. This tiny shop was crammed full of wonderful old and not-so-old books, on every equine and equestrian subject under the sun. What a place! Such riches! I'd have moved in had they let me. Once the staff realised where my interests lay I would receive letters advising me of odd rare and fabulous volumes they had discovered, which could be mine for the princely sum of, I dunno, about two-pounds-fifty – including postage. This was how one not only learned about a subject in pre-www days, but also how one acquired tomes about the equine family not widely available on the high street.

On one magical, memorable occasion, visiting a zoological park for an article for *Pony*, I was introduced to their herd of Onagers. No cuddly donkeys, they moved, agitated and afraid like a herring shoal, their wildness too ingrained to allow them to reach out and foster relations, keeping humans at bay. Even with their keeper we couldn't get close. They were, I was told, a nightmare to treat when ill. I could well imagine. I could also imagine them sleek and free, roaming and galloping the deserts of Asia, where word has it they've been clocked at speeds over 40mph.

At the same park, after visiting the Przewalski's horses and hiding my disappointment at having to stay firmly on the wrong side of the fence, I was allowed to follow the keeper into the enclosure where five Grévy's zebra mares looked our way with curiosity, ears flapping against the flies. Grévy's zebra is the largest of the fully striped equines, with huge round ears and stripes narrowing all the way down to their hooves. Wild creatures, critically endangered, whose beautiful hides, perfectly evolved to strobe and confuse animal predators, now betray their wearers to the worst of enemies – human poachers. Their habitat is shrinking, and the odds of them surviving ever-tumbles as their numbers in the wild diminish.

The keeper was suitably protective of his girls. When I, camera in hand, asked whether it would be all right to step out from behind him to take some pictures he erupted, arms waving, his impressive dreadlocks twirling in the breeze.

'Stay behind me!' he shrieked, in a furious, yet toned-down, whispering sort of way so as not to startle his charges, caring not one jot about whether he startled me. 'These are wild animals, *wild* animals. Keep still, make no sudden movements, they're not *tame*, you know.' He paddled a frantic arm behind him for emphasis. 'Stay behind me, stay *behind*.'

Well, I thought, possibly a bit of an over-reaction but I had to respect his authority and knowledge. After a few moments, when he could see I wasn't going to jump about, or use a flash, or even breathe heavily, he relented. Obviously he had experience of journalists unused to animals. I took pictures, the zebras got closer, looking anything but wild but that's probably where problems occur – it doesn't do to be complacent. As I reached out and stroked the leading mare's face I heard myself sighing. You can keep your swimming with dolphins because I've stroked a Grévy's zebra – a real live one, wild, not tame. The keeper said so.

There are so many similarities between donkeys and zebras – not least because they both come from hot climes. Zebras are not striped horses but they might just be striped donkeys.

One Christmas, the primary school Rosemary's children attended held the customary nativity play. Would we take a donkey along for authenticity? Enter, stage left, Mr Smuggins, a yearling with bags of confidence and a keen sense of adventure. Smuggins was a small donkey and he didn't bat an eye when we folded him up and put him in the back of Rosemary's Mini van. He was totally up for it – bring it on! The kids loved it almost as much as Smuggins. Donkeys are just the most accommodating creatures.

At the end of that winter we welcomed another stallion. Ra, named after the Egyptian sun god because of his beautiful red colour – a throwback from the wild Kiangs – belonged to friends of Rosemary's who had discovered him at a sale and refused to leave without him. Now they were moving, so could no longer keep him. Ra was coming to live with us.

We were advised never to turn our backs to him. His owners – knowledgeable donkey people who had several stallions at their famous and successful stud – had no idea of his history, but by Ra's unsettled behaviour when they first bought him it was clear he had not been treated with the respect and kindness he deserved. His experiences had clearly affected his temperament and they told us he had, in the first week they had owned him, picked one of them up by the collar and shaken them like a terrier with a rat.

We had been warned.

Ra was installed in a paddock behind the house, isolated from the other donkeys, with the tiny Shetland pony, Loopy, for company. There were houses and gardens backing on to this paddock, and a stable the two could share, overlooking the house. As I mucked him out and cared for him, a very different animal emerged. Ra was desperate to be loved. Whenever he saw me in his stable Ra would rush over, come on in and lift his chin up onto my shoulder. A lot of donkeys like to do this to initiate a cuddle. Ra could stay in this position for ages – only I had work to do so after a long session, we'd part and get on with our lives, only to meet up later for another hug.

We never had a moment's worry with Ra – although we were careful never to take liberties with him. He turned out to be the nicest donkey, and he'll always hold a special place in my heart. Maybe we got on so well because he didn't associate us with anything bad – and I am sure his dodgy behaviour with his previous owners was due only to experiences prior to living with them. They had not only given him a second chance, but had paved the way for his reformed character. Because we never witnessed any nasty behaviour from him, we never behaved around him any differently to how we did with the other donkeys. He even made more friends with the neighbours at the back of his paddock. Trust had been formed, on both sides.

Of course, it never advisable to blindly trust an animal you know to be a bit dodgy, but if you experience bad behaviour in a horse or a donkey then you are always going to have that in the back of your mind, and it will affect how you handle it – move around it, talk to it.

Visiting the riding school at the top of the hill some years after I worked there, I found myself holding a horse in the yard between rides. After a few minutes of us both standing there looking at each other, a bit bored, someone asked me whether the horse I was holding was Brownie – or whichever it was – to which I nodded.

'Only he never stands still,' she said, puzzled.

I can only put it down to the fact that I hadn't been aware of Brownie's little foible. I expected him to stand, I stood quietly myself, and so did he. You get, Rose would tell us, the behaviour you expect. It's why a stranger can go into a stable and tack up a horse they don't know, whereas the same horse will turn its tail to the people who open the door expecting trouble, sending them a clear message. However long you have to be with equines, it never seems long enough. There is always so much more to work out, discover and learn.

Light relief

It wasn't all work at the riding school at the top of the hill. Occasionally, as teenagers, some of our group who had their own ponies would hire a horsebox (having one's own trailer in those days would have been akin to owning an ocean-going yacht – the only people at the yard who had their own horsebox were, of course, the glamorous Mrs P and her husband) and attend a local show, with those of us without ponies of our own volunteering as grooms. Except that on arrival to the showground any high expectations would be met by the sight of the Lewis's horsebox, crushing our party's dreams of possible jumping glory.

The Lewis family were Annette and Michelle, who together with their brother, Anthony, bowled up at all the shows with various ponies, and left with all the trophies.

You may remember the sisters because when they grew up they became famous show jumpers. Annette became even more famous when, in 1985, her lovely grey Tutein decided that sliding down the Derby bank at Hickstead was too boring for words, opting instead to launch off the top like a ski-jumper, his wide-eyed rider in situ, both landing in a crumpled heap at the bottom – no bones broken.

Before all this glory the girls were honing their skills at all the shows in the area – as is perfectly right – only when you're a teenager you don't really get that and nothing seems fair. Not that their absence would have made the slightest difference to our chances. They never seemed to ride the same ponies twice and at one show, when they unveiled a tiny, shaggy pony which looked more pony-ride than pony-jumper, we were all lulled into false hope. This pony, surely, was more suited to going *under* the jumps rather than over them? We should have known better. The pony soared over all the jumps as though descended from Pegasus, another star in the making. It no doubt went on to make some small child very happy.

Anthony used to deliver all the feed that wasn't oats to the riding school at the top of the hill, and he and Rose would exchange some affectionate banter over a cup of tea. Tea, to Rose, was an essential part of getting through the day and the kettle worked longer hours than we did, steaming away on the gas hob in the kitchen, permanently on standby to replenish the workers. In the summer we'd all sit out on benches in the cobbled yard between rides, tea all round. In the winter, we'd huddle in the kitchen, unable to see out of the windows because of all the kettle-generated steam. I have never liked tea. Rose considered this a grave failing on my part, a major character flaw.

At the riding school at the top of the hill, Rose was forever thinking up ways for us to enjoy our riding and there had been a club in place, with Rose at its helm, for years before I started riding there. One event that was held every year, at the end of the school summer holidays, was the riding school's annual gymkhana. What pony-mad child hasn't dreamed of competing on their favourite pony and winning a rosette? And the gymkhana provided ample opportunities – with best rider classes, show jumping, handy hunter and a whole selection of traditional gymkhana games. There was something for everyone, livery owners and school riders alike.

The fact that it was held on a Saturday, replacing all the usual, lucrative, rides and lessons, meant that the riding school was giving something back to all its clients – their entry fees couldn't have amounted to anything like as much as a day's takings, and there was the cost of all the rosettes and trophies to consider. Plus, it was a *real* gymkhana, held in the top field, out of sight of the yard with a roped arena, two collecting rings (one for school horses and another for the liveries), a PA system, painted jumps and a scattering of straw bales for all the parents to sit on – the works. It was the highlight of the year. Everyone got terribly excited about it, and I was no exception.

You had no say in who you rode in the classes you entered – Rose and the organising committee poured over the entries and matched riders with suitable mounts. So when you were handed your number in the yard on the morning of the show you turned it over, heart in your mouth, to see which equine names were written opposite your classes. Would you have a good pony in the best rider class or be stuck with one who napped, or needed a lot of legging or, heaven forbid, might refuse to jump? The need to bag a decent mount at the gymkhana was a keen influence on your all-year behaviour at the riding school at the top of the hill.

Before that even happened, the tack all had to be polished and the horses and ponies tidied up. The greys and coloured horses were bathed the day before (Rose wouldn't hear of bathing the dark horses, they had to be dry-scrubbed) and then on the morning of the show we all rushed around grooming, plaiting and oiling hooves. All our favourite horses and ponies were transformed, totally looking the part (and somewhat embarrassed) with their manes balled up in elastic bands (sewing would have taken too long to put in, too long to take out and carried the risk of blood-letting, not to mention bits of mane being left on the cobbles by hasty scissor action), any dread felt by the ponies as they realised what was to come matched only by the excitement of the riders as we all changed into our best shirts, ties, jackets and boots.

For this special occasion hard hats were even discovered, dusty and unloved, in forgotten hiding places. Rose, too, made the effort with a black jacket over her polo neck jumper, and several male guest judges (alumni from years gone by) looked the part in their suits and ties, one aiming for added distinction by brandishing a pipe.

Competitors in the first classes enjoyed the added thrill of riding the ponies down to the field, the rest of us trailing behind, nerves bubbling up in our stomachs. This was a chance to shine. Would we, by the end of the day, have covered ourselves in glory, or would we return to the yard as empty-handed as we'd set out, with only disappointment to show for our efforts? We all knew it was the taking part that counted, blah, blah – but hell, a rosette or two wouldn't be too shabby.

The best rider classes kicked off proceedings, three classes divided by age. It must have been my third or fourth gymkhana when, just before my best rider class for which I had been allocated Libby, the ever-glamorous Mrs P noticed that some riders in the current class were riding privately owned horses, kindly offered by their owners for the event.

'Oh!' she exclaimed, from the back of her exquisite bay mare, 'what a good idea! I should have thought of that.' Looking around, her eyes, miraculously, rested on me. 'Would you like to ride M, Janet?' she offered.

Would I? I didn't need asking twice. Shamelessly sliding off Libby's cobby back without a backwards glance I scrambled up on the mare and gingerly rode her around the collecting ring, my breath held, Mrs P giving me some handy hints. It was madness, really, entering a riding class after only a few moments in the mare's saddle, and clocking Rose's expression when I entered the ring confirmed as much. I didn't do too badly – I could have done better – but it was such a thrill to ride a mare so obviously out of my league (I knew enough to realise that

I wasn't totally in control) that all thoughts of winning or even doing particularly well, paled by comparison. I think I got a minor rosette, but I was so overwhelmed by the experience it was an added bonus. I couldn't thank Mrs P enough. What a generous gesture.

I was to win the best rider class a year later. I had asked to ride Mo, despite knowing he wouldn't behave as well as some of the other horses. I wanted Mo because I loved riding him, I felt we were a team and I didn't especially want to ride anything else. If we messed up the jumps – because that was likely as Mo always tried to run out or rush them – then we'd mess up together. So what?

It was a big class, and the last year I would be eligible, and Mo was being brilliant, quite relaxed for him. But then I spotted the pipe-wielding judge pulling in a dreaded cavaletto in the manner of a medieval jailer gleefully dragging in the rack.

'Oh well,' I thought, 'this is where we go out.'

I was wrong. Mo cantered up to the jump as though he were Simon, popping over it without fuss. I breathed again. But Rose wasn't done – for now there were two cavaletti, another positioned a few strides from the first. This was surely our Waterloo. But Mo was up for it, and once again he jumped it, calmness personified. I had survived another strike.

When I looked again, Rose had sneaked in a third jump. Was she doing it on purpose, determined to catch me out?

We faced the line of jumps. They weren't large, they weren't scary, but they were something Mo was known to balk at – only he didn't on this day. On this day he popped over all three like he loved it. Was it because we were outside instead of in the school? Was it because I was making more effort with my riding? Or was it just fate? I don't know, but when we were called in first I didn't care. I wasn't thrilled so much because I had won, but because I had won on Mo. It meant more than anything. We'd done it together and my friend had stepped up, big time. It was the first and last time I can ever remember Mo jumping like that. It wasn't exactly the Olympic Games, but sometimes, magic occurs.

The Handy Hunter class was mainly contested by the liveries – obstacles included jumping a road closed sign, picking up a riding whip from a tractor while its engine was still running (couldn't do that now, especially with it being diesel), and opening and closing a gate whilst mounted. It took a while, but it was just before the break, so everyone just drifted off and grabbed a bite. And then there were the gymkhana games, run in heats, and you always hoped you'd get a horse or pony suited to the games for which you were entered – a small one if it involved getting on and off, for example, a fast one for the bending.

The last game of the day was always the musical sacks and it was only ever won by one person. This one person was Richard, on his bay mare Gypsy, who went everywhere in the manner of a medieval destrier, head into her chest, forelegs lifting higher and higher, her eyes wide, nostrils flared. Only the stupid or ignorant put themselves and their ponies between Gypsy and a sack but, luckily, Gypsy's on-board siren of loud dragon-snorting meant that even if your back was turned you could hear her bearing down upon you at ramming speed. Although the result was a foregone conclusion, we still strapped ourselves in and went through the motions of playing the game – after all, there were the minor placings to ride for. Suddenly, all that flinging ourselves off our mounts in the school at trot made sense. Richard, of course, hurled himself out of Gypsy's saddle at a much stronger pace, landing on each sack like a practised paratrooper hitting his mark behind enemy lines.

One year, in her haste to secure a sack, Topsy's rider gamely flung herself out of the saddle and ran for the target, dragging her mount behind her. With the sack secure in one hand, she turned to find the other held nothing but an empty bridle. Topsy was away, trotting back to her friends at the collecting ring, bareheaded, snorting and fed up with this whole gymkhana nonsense.

The gymkhana wasn't the only event we enjoyed. Horseman's Sunday was held every autumn on the village green outside the church – the only time horses were (officially) allowed on its hallowed turf. Again, you could take a school horse if you hired it for the hour and as there were best-turned-out rosettes on offer, we all busied ourselves cleaning tack, washing tails and plaiting manes, before dressing ourselves up to the nines and sitting astride our mounts, singing hymns and listening to the sermon. Rose and another guest judge would stalk around us, clipboards in hands, marking our efforts before handing out rosettes – one set for the school horses, another for the liveries.

Then the fun began because after the solemnity on the green there was the traditional fast ride! Led by Rose it was understood you'd need to keep up or fall by the wayside, and she'd warn you she wasn't going to tell you *when* she was going to launch off into a gallop, and that everyone had to look after themselves. It was a popular, bonkers, ride, with lightweight riders taking Sunshine and Starlight, the only time they were let off the leading rein, with predictable results. And it really was mad, with gallops over the stubble, no quarter given, liveries joining in the madness. You didn't dare fall off because A. no-one would stop for you so you'd have to walk home, and B. you ran the risk of thirty-odd riders pounding you into the ground like a divot at a polo match without a backward glance.

It wasn't the only mad ride. Bank Holidays were when four-hour rides to a big park nearby were organised, and places for these sold out well in advance. The first and last hours were taken up with roadwork getting there and back again, meaning a seven o'clock start to miss the traffic. The remaining two hours were earmarked for going a bit berserk in the park, the horses excited by the unfamiliar surroundings, and all the open space.

It didn't always go to plan. Everyone was under the threat of death if they overtook Rose as her control over Cochise was always in the balance. Once, an officious park keeper, running from his Land Rover, whistle to his lips, his arms waving, came to a halt (either in bravery or ignorance) under Cochise's nose in order to scold his rider that she wasn't keeping to areas newly designated for horses. She could, he told her, go – at this juncture he turned away from her to point in directions many and various – 'there, there and over there, but *not* over there, or here or even *there…*' blissfully unaware that behind him a skewbald horse reared, Trigger-like, his hooves dangling dangerously close to his head. It would, of course, according to Rose, have been his own silly fault if he had *got himself killed!*

On the way back the whole ride would stop at the pub and helpers drafted in from the riding school would hold horses while riders took a nature break before filling up again with a pint or two. You'd see a whole circle of horses, like a wagon wheel with Rose as the central hub, no horse daring to argue with his neighbour or put a hoof out of line while the boss was around. Suitably refreshed, everyone would once again mount up and head for home.

Nobody rides to that park any more. There is too much traffic about now, Bank Holidays being busier than at any other time. Luckily, there are new bridle paths to other open spaces, so no more roadwork is required.

One Easter, in the mid-1970s, Rose and the club decided to hold a hunter trial. This was big and exciting news – even more so as it was open to all, rather than just to riding school and club riders. A few extra cross-country jumps were added to the ones already dotted about the two fields, and repairs were made to those in the woods. Paths were cleared, flags added. Competitors would start in the indoor school, from which a panel had been removed to allow access. The course ran through this lower field, through the woods at the bottom, and back along the top field, finishing at the riding school.

Only a few school horses were capable of taking part, and these were snapped up quickly by the capable riders. Jan entered a big chestnut gelding she was then riding called Dusty, and out of the blue Mrs T (of Ouija tack box fame) asked me whether I'd ride her pony, Nathan.

Without even thinking about it I readily agreed. I have since learned to take a moment to consider all angles, to weigh up, to give offers some thought before, like all fools before me, rushing in. But that is how you learn. Nathan wasn't the most generous or forward-going pony (epic understatement), but he was a pony nevertheless, and I fancied having a go. It was kind of Mrs T to think of me. At least, that's what I thought before I'd ridden him around the course.

We got round – but I'm not sure how. I think I fell off at one point in the woods, but a little thing like that wasn't going to stop us. It wasn't the most fluent performance but we did actually make it, and without troubling the St John Ambulance, much to their disappointment and surprise. Mrs T was thrilled, so I was glad I'd said yes after all. It obviously meant a lot to her. It was a good job she hadn't seen exactly how much I'd had to persuade her darling Nathan to tackle a couple of the jumps in the woods, but once he was home again he went back to eating his hay like nothing had happened.

I haven't troubled starters at hunter trials since. Jan, of course, went on to compete in all sorts of events, as well as working for several world-famous eventers. Me, not so much. Showing is more my thing. It wouldn't do for us all to be the same.

The Hunter Trial was an exciting innovation – sadly never to be repeated. I think it just took too much work, and I dare say now the cost of insurance would be against it. The most exciting part was when one of the male riders tumbled off over a jump in the woods. As he leapt up, his belt snapped and his breeches dropped to his ankles, which woke up the fence judge. Funny the things you remember.

Oh, and I almost forgot firework night.

Most horsy folk dread firework night, but at the riding school at the top of the hill, they managed to turn it around. The annual bonfire, fish-and-chip supper and show jumping competition was organised for the closest Saturday night to November fifth. It was eagerly anticipated, and if you wanted to take a school horse in the show jumping you had to arrange it with Rose.

First, there was the bonfire – always a vast pile of wood in the dip in the field behind the school. Straw bales provided seating, the local chippie delivered fish- or chicken-and-chips and we'd all scoff away while some poor volunteer set off the fireworks. Thus fed and watered, and warmed by the fire, everyone would then repair to the indoor school where, like some gladiatorial arena, a show jumping course awaited its victims.

It wasn't a large school, so you needed an agile horse that wasn't freaked out by landing after one jump and being met with another almost immediately. It was almost grid jumping, incorporating a turn or two and a change of rein. One year I took Libby who, after a full day teaching clients in the same arena, was less than enthusiastic, rearing and squealing after refusing the first jump with the gusto of a union shop steward. I might have salvaged the situation if some joker in the gallery hadn't set off a laughing bag – which made Libby more determined than ever that someone was taking the piss. She was prone to protesting by raising her front legs – and although she *could* jump, that didn't mean she was always in the mood to do so. The more the audience laughed, the less did Rose and I was sent out in disgrace, wishing I could stuff the bloody laughing bag where its owner might never find it.

Another year Rose decided that Cochise would show everyone how it was done and I was elected as the jockey. Very few people sat astride Cochise but Rose occasionally asked one or two of us to take him down the school and show riders how superfluous reins were, stripping her horse's bridle off while we were still on board, and ordering us to ride around a bit to demonstrate. She would tell everyone to, 'Look at my girl here, and see how she doesn't need the reins – she uses her seat and legs, people.' She said this so many times, one of the clients asked us how many daughters Rose actually had, which caused great amusement.

Anyway, mounted on Cochise – wearing a bridle for a change – and aware of the responsibility on my shoulders, we started well. Over the first jump, over the next – yes, we were going to do it! And we did, clear round, mission accomplished! Only with it being such a small school everywhere we turned, at speed, there was another jump and Cochise was nothing if not honest. So around and around we went, leaping all the jumps again, not necessarily in the same order as before – not even from the same direction. Finally, believing my mount had at last come to a halt, I sat back and relaxed, only for Cochise to spot another jump, propelling us once more into space from a standstill, catapulting me even further, even higher…

I think I held the distinction of being the only person to have fallen off Rose's horse, a club with a membership of one.

So yes, *most* horsy folk dread firework night. At the *Horse&Rider* office, we received a great letter from a reader telling us how she and her friends, realising that the people who lived adjacent to their horses' field were having a firework party, had hurried to their livery yard in order to bring their horses in from the field, imagining them frantic and hysterical. Except that the field seemed empty – where were they? Had they escaped, crashed the fence in their hysteria and were, even now, racing around the countryside in panic?

Hell no. They found their horses, heads over the neighbour's fence, munching buns from the barbeque and watching the fireworks in wonder. As the owners haltered their precious horses and led them away there were disappointed protests from their new friends, begging them to let their honoured guests stay at the party. Horses, eh? They surprise you every time.

As is often the way of someone with lots going on in their lives, Rose decided to increase her work burden by forming an Activity Ride. Eight of her young pony-owners were enlisted, and work began in earnest. If you've seen the Metropolitan Police Musical Ride, you'll be familiar with some of the movements Rose incorporated. The riders rode along a line of cavaletti and displayed various actions: dropping the reins and stretching out their arms, coming over onto one stirrup, taking off their jackets, and putting them on again, all as they jumped six jumps. The cavaletti were then put into a square and the riders continued their display, riding in pairs, threading the needle without crashing into each other – it was an impressive performance achieved after many hours of rehearsal, and all to music. It ended with the riders lining up and throwing one leg over their ponies' necks to sit sideways, before performing a backward roll off and onto the ground.

The Activity Ride performed at various club events – and even took to the road to thrill new audiences at shows in the area. The riders were all much more confident in their saddles, and learned new skills. As all the riders were under sixteen, I doubt you could put on such a show now, which you may – or may not – think is a pity.

The club did enter some events outside the school, with mixed success. At one event in the 1970s, awaiting her turn in the Prix Caprilli event – a sort of low-key dressage test with a couple of cavaletti thrown in for good measure, which was popular at the time – Sylvie was struck by a sudden attack of nerves. No matter, several supportive club members assured her, they knew the certain remedy for that. Out came the hip flask and into Sylvie the contents were tipped. Much better, she assured everyone, narrowing her eyes and mentally rolling up her sleeves. She was ready! Bring it on!

Half-way through the test the judge's buzzer went, signalling that Sylvie had taken a wrong turn. Unfazed, Sylvie merely rode up to the judge's box, leant on the open window and asked her – no, no, wait a minute, *both* of them – whether they would mind telling her where she was – *hic* – supposed to go now.

No rosette that day.

The riders' club at the riding school at the top of the hill didn't restrict its events to those involving horses but extended them socially. The car rally was a popular event, frowned upon by the local constabulary but organised nevertheless with the club's customary disregard for authority. Teams would set off at intervals in their cars, following clues and answering questions which could all be found in the surrounding countryside. The fastest team home with all the right answers was the winner. Before seat belts were compulsory, quite a few members could be crammed into a car to make up a team. Cars would be seen screeching to a halt in various places, ejecting members of their teams to rush here and there looking for inspiration from the cryptic, and sometimes evil clues thought up by the organising committee. They would then hurry back to the car and attempt to jump back in before it picked up too much speed, urged on by the other team members determined to win at all costs.

At all times you had to make sure you didn't give any rival teams, which might already be skulking around in your wake, an inkling of the right answer, and laying a false trail was a much admired skill. A favourite place for clues was church graveyards – honestly, the total irreverence, unrepentantly exploiting the dead – where you might be asked the date someone died, or the name of a wife/husband of someone long deceased, or what time the mother-and-baby group met every Tuesday in the church hall. Religious attendance would rocket as the church yard filled with people all searching in a frantic yet furtive manner, everyone trying not to draw attention to the right grave or church notice. You couldn't teach us anything about enjoying ourselves.

The trick was to read the last question first – on one rally the final question asked how many phone boxes the team had passed during the whole duration, which proved hugely popular. Another question instructed them to stop at a telephone box and ring the number given to find out who Violet Mary might be. In the pre-mobile era this meant beating other teams to the telephone box (or beating them out of the way if you hadn't), and having the right change in order to work it. If nobody did, then a trip to a village shop would take up valuable time. My mother quite enjoyed her part in proceedings, and had a great time telling everyone that Violet Mary was the name of a donkey.

One summer evening, we all decamped to the Furry Field for a barbeque and a game of rounders, the undisputed highlight of which was Pete-the-park-keeper hitting the ball so hard, it soared up and over the trees to land far, far away. That this feat was accomplished one-handed made it all the more extraordinary – Pete seeing no reason to abandon his full pint, held safely in his other hand throughout, merely in order to bat. The glass was hastily prised out of Pete's hand by his delirious team mates who shoved him in the direction of first post, his rounder completed in record time. Our hero's speed was due in no small part to his eagerness to return to his beverage (a bit like how sniffer-dogs are trained with the reward of a ball), which was downed in one in celebration. Such are sporting legends made.

Never one to confuse having quite enough to do with boredom, Rose decided one summer that the riding school should throw its gates open to the public and hold an Open Day. Notices were put in the local press, word was spread. The Open Day would allow everyone to walk around the picturesque yard, and there would be displays in the indoor school – the Activity Ride, of course – but what else? How about a parade of horses Rose had bred – youngstock and those under saddle, culminating, of course, with a parade of mares and foals? How lovely, everyone thought, until the logistics dawned.

It wouldn't be too much of a problem to get the ridden horses there, and even the youngstock owned by local people, but Rose's mares and foals all lived at the park yard. That meant leading four mares and four foals the half-mile along the road – mares and foals whose usual travel route was from the barn, to the field, and back again. But Rose was determined; mares and foals there would be.

We were allocated our charges – and I was tasked with Vanity, the mare who hated anyone pulling on her head collar, meaning you had to use other cunning ways to get her attention, slow down and steer. Thing was, I really liked Vanity, so I didn't mind the challenge. We all had a few practices, and then set about tidying up the mares and giving the foals some more leading lessons, which went only so well.

If you've ever led a foal you'll know there is only so much you can expect, behaviour-wise. You sort of cajole it to stay up with mum and hope those hooves, kicked up in the sheer exuberance of being young and alive, fail to connect with any part of you. Foals, bless their hearts, are apt to see every other living thing as a potential playmate and are a nipping, kicking, rearing nightmare, cute only from a distance. You can't reason with them, you can't expect much in the way of manners. I reckoned I'd dipped in with Vanity.

On the day, which (in the best pony book tradition) dawned fair and bright, everyone wore blue shirts with their jodhpurs and boots as a uniform, and the mares and foals made their journeys without mishap – due to a huge entourage helping out and forming a rolling road-block. The sire of some of the foals, the beautiful liver chestnut Arab from nearby, was brought over by his owner, and there were even a few other mares and foals from a local breeder. The public turned up in their droves, Vanity didn't wipe the floor with me (more by luck than judgement on my part), the foals did their best to be cute and appealing and, all things considered, the Riding School Open Day was a huge success!

At least, as Rose said later, nobody died – our traditional benchmark for success.

Broken

MY LUCK RAN OUT in the late 1980s. It only happened because of a freak accident, rather than when I had been mucking about or blatantly flaunting common-sense which, somehow, made it worse. But these things often happen in the most innocuous circumstances.

Escorting a hack on a Saturday morning, not far from home and cantering through the woods on a narrow bridle path one of the school horses – a big bay mare with huge, meaty hooves – came up behind me. Then, without warning or encouragement from its rider, the bay increased speed and went for the overtake, kicking out at the mare I was on. The iron-clad hoof missed my horse, but only because my leg was in the way. There was a cracking noise, I felt an agonising pain and I pulled my mount Opal, which belonged to my pal Malcolm, to a juddering halt, my right leg now dangling below my stirrup. The whole ride pulled up behind me, silent in shock, rudderless without their instructor issuing instructions, not knowing what to do. I knew, despite being able to move my toes (old wives' tale, obviously), that my leg was very much broken. I sent the shaken and upset woman riding the guilty, yet unrepentant bay back to the yard to fetch Rose.

Minutes passed. No-one said much. I tried to breathe normally. Moaning and screaming were not options as I remembered Rose's contemptuous story about a livery rider who had fallen off in the bracken and had screamed the place down so hard, all the birds for miles around had taken to the wing like a pheasant shoot, and no-one could get their horses anywhere near her to help. Opal, bless her, stood like a rock. I was still on board, and I tried not to wonder how I was going to get off.

Suddenly, there was a commotion as Rose appeared, hurtling through the trees on the tractor. The cavalry had arrived! As I watched the trailer bouncing up and down like a wild west wagon on a rocky mountain trail I made the decision that there was no way I was going anywhere on that!

I needed an ambulance. Someone called 999 – which took a bit of time because the same someone was dispatched back to the yard where the phone lived. No mobiles back in the day (and ambulances were not in such short supply as they are now). I was lifted off Opal and the whole ride was led away, several kind folk staying behind with me. Sue turned up – and so did Malcolm – and things started to get better. Instead of being sympathetic they joked and laughed and soon, between gasps of pain, I was joking and laughing with them. Sometimes, in times of trauma, sympathy is the last thing you need and the best way to get through it is irreverence.

The ambulance arrived, gliding towards me across the grass, chalk to the tractor's cheese, together with two jolly paramedics. 'Don't worry, love,' they reassured me with a wink, 'we've got gas-and-air'.

Oh goody, I thought, that well-known anaesthetic that isn't actually an anaesthetic. Even as I was telling them it wasn't doing anything, they dropped the canister on my broken leg – before proceeding to deny it.

I wondered whether I'd made the right call, tractor-wise. Finally I was hoisted aboard the ambulance, Sue and Malcolm threatening to meet me at the hospital, and I set off, miffed I didn't warrant a siren, relieved to be heading for the sympathy and kindness of the nursing staff at my local health institution with all the confidence of a person who had never suffered a broken bone before, and who believed the spin dished out by the NHS about its caring and angelic staff.

The attitude of the nurses in A&E was less than sympathetic, kindness noticeable by its absence. They made no secret of the fact that they considered horse riders (together with motorcyclists – uh-oh – and rugby players) to be selfish thrill-seekers who cluttered up the place at the weekends with self-inflicted injuries. Frankly, their demeanour indicated, we were asking for it. I felt unjustly lumped together with all the time-wasting folk who request A&E doctors to remove objects on which they have 'fallen'.

However, they couldn't just ignore me – not for too long, anyway – so they took off my boots and cut off my favourite jodhpurs. Sue and Malcolm arrived, giggling, whispering, fiddling with the instruments and noisily munching crisps. This did little to alter the nurses' opinion of horse riders.

Two weeks I was in hospital. Three consultants argued about what to do when my plaster cast, encasing my broken tibia and fibula, needed some serious adjustment (which was difficult to forgive as they had been the ones who had put it on in the first place). Should I be put in traction? Should I be pinned (terrifying) …or could they perhaps get away with cutting a hole at the foot of the cast and shoving a couple of bits of wood in it to alter the angle of my ankle? Apparently they could, this last, simplistic and cost-effective bodge-up winning the toss. As a result my right leg has, ever since, been an inch shorter than my left. Thanks guys. Good work. So glad you couldn't be arsed.

Two weeks dragged like no other fortnight ever had or ever will. Two weeks in one of those long, Victorian-style communal wards ruled by a crisply-starched Matron, visiting hours restricted to two hours – one in the morning and another in the evening – not like it is today where visitors come and go at all hours. Bored, bored, bored, was how I felt. And I know, I totally *know,* that many poor folk suffer far more than I ever did, and I acknowledge that I totally needed a slap, but at the time I felt like it would never end.

Light relief during some mornings consisted of the ward being made spotless for the visit from (drum roll)

The Consultant. Upon his arrival there descended a reverential hush as he toured his patients and stood, for the briefest moment, by each bed (no time to linger, he had his more lucrative private patients on which he needed to lavish attention). Matron and the nurses followed in his wake, handing him notes, speaking only when spoken to, hanging on to his every word and virtually laying palms at his feet. I half believed I needed only to touch the great man's cloak and I might pick up my leg and walk. That didn't happen.

But twice a day my visitors came: noisily and irreverently playing *Ironside* on the ward with spare wheelchairs, twiddling with the knobs around my bed and shamelessly reading my notes while they reduced my grapes to stalks, sweets to mere wrappers. During one chaotic visiting hour, a grey equine head belonging to an inhabitant in the fields surrounding the hospital was enticed through an open ward window by the lure of jelly babies. The nurses, knowing how my injury occurred, were open-mouthed, believing my visitors were responsible for smuggling it along to see me. They were not, but an opportunity to exploit a situation was never missed.

My favourite get-well card was from Will. *With Sympathy*, it said on the front, above a tasteful arrangement of lilies. *May you take comfort knowing that many are thinking of you at this sad time.*

Perfect.

I healed, eventually, but my ankle, where both bones were smashed, can still give me jip and, occasionally, someone will ask me why I'm limping. As you might expect, I am always very conscious of anyone overtaking me out riding. I could have done without the whole experience but when you spend so much time around horses and in the saddle, an accident has to be considered as an occupational hazard. No amount of preparation and risk assessment can save you from bad luck – but I was lucky after all. A broken leg mends.

For ages after this unfortunate incident riding school clients and strangers alike would kindly enquire, 'Is the leg you broke all right now?' Whilst grateful for their interest I always felt I needed to set the record straight – for I didn't break my leg, somebody else did.

Mule

W**HAT DOES A PERSON** who loves horses and has made them her life, has explored and found education and delight in donkeys, what does such a person, a person who finds herself working at a donkey stud in the late 1970s, do next? It was fairly obvious to me, having studied donkeys and compared them to horses and ponies that the next part of my journey was to marry the two. A mule! A mule was needed.

I have often been asked why I wanted a mule – but to me it seemed the next logical, educational step. I had been warned that donkeys were stubborn and useless, yet I had found them to be not only charming and intelligent, but fascinating in their behavioural and physical differences to horses. Mules, too, suffered from a bad press. If donkeys were not as billed, then maybe mules weren't, either.

Plus, they were the middle-ground, the resulting progeny of both species. What would I learn about horses and donkeys from a mule? What did they take from either parent? What was uniquely theirs?

As a teenager, I had longed to be a horse owner, to be part of the club whose membership was open only to those with horses. Now, I was volunteering to take another step outside the circle, to follow a path thought strange by others for whom only a horse would do. I could hardly do this and then complain about being an outsider. So I didn't.

A mule is usually man-made (each branch of *Equus* has a slightly different mating ritual, a neat trick you'll appreciate as you read on). Mules are hybrids, the result of a mating between a horse or pony dam and a donkey stallion. If the pairing is the other way around, the resulting offspring is called a hinny. Hinnies, to my eye, look a little more pony like, but it is a rather loose rule. You can, of course, breed yourself a zorse (zebra x horse), and a zeedonk (donkey x zebra), providing you have the necessary components.

As with all hybrids, mules and hinnies are sterile – at least the males are, but with an attitude typical of the gender they just won't believe it, so gelding is advisable if they are not to make nuisances of themselves.

There have been very rare instances of female mules giving birth, but it is usually due to scientists making it happen – they're worse than bakers for trying to prove things. Generally speaking though, mules, with an odd number of chromosomes (domestic horses have

64, domestic donkeys 62 and mules 63 – even different sub-species of zebra possess a variety of chromosome numbers), have a problem producing genetic material. This is why different species have slightly different come-hither practices. If they didn't, and they regularly bred together then both species would, in effect, self-destruct.

If you are ever asked the riddle about which animal could become extinct tomorrow, yet appear on the planet a year later the answer is a mule – providing horses and donkeys are still around to get it on.

Mules are tough, strong, able to work hard on fewer rations than a horse, recover well and quickly from hard work, and are able to toil in hot and humid conditions, attributes which make them not only popular in poor areas of the world, but the perfect choice to carry guns and supplies in war-torn Burma during World War II. There are many uplifting and humorous stories told by men who worked with the mules, stories of their admiration for them, of fondness for their long-eared companions, tales of their mules' humour, hard work and courage. Those companions who suffered the indignity of being parachuted in over enemy lines, tied down on huge inflatable pads and flung from aircraft – and all that after having first had their vocal chords severed so that their loud calls wouldn't betray their position to the enemy. While a donkey brays, mule song is a mash-up between a bray and a scream. It is loud and it carries. Hear it in the dark and you'd be convinced spirits have come to haunt and kill you. War dictated that the mules of Burma be rendered mute.

After some thought, and making the decision that a mule was for me, fate, as so often happens, presented such an opportunity. *'Small red mule for sale,'* read the advertisement in *Horse and Hound*. I held my breath. If the small, red mule was in Scotland, Wales or deepest Cornwall it would have to stay there. But no, this small, red mule lived in Kent, barely twenty miles away from where I worked. It was surely meant to be!

I scuttled off to view him. He was certainly as described: small and red, with added black points which made him bay, complete with the mule's trademark mealy nose – and he was still with his mother, a dappled grey Welsh pony. The owner offered to deliver. The deal was struck. For fifty pounds (two cockney 'ponies') I became the owner of the small, red mule. What would I learn now?

For a start, I learned that my small red mule was anything but impressed by his proud new owner. When he wasn't making a point of ignoring me, he threw the odd scowl in my direction. Secondly, he didn't think much of being turned out with a herd of donkeys – even though there had been donkeys at his last home (obviously). He immediately teamed up with the only pony in the field, the chestnut Shetland with a tawny mane and tail called Noggin the Nog. Clearly, as his mother was a pony, the mule thought himself one, too, and equally clearly, Noggin was the only creature he *did* think much of. It was a bit of a one-sided relationship.

As luck would have it, at the very same time I acquired my little red mule a brand new club was being formed. The British Mule Society offered not only the chance to connect with like-minded folk, but provided a source of information which I gratefully and greedily took on board. Hearing from others who had mules meant I wasn't going to flounder about alone. Armed with some newly acquired mule knowledge, the best way for my mule and I to bond, I decided, was to bring my new mule into the secure yard as I worked, and that way we could sort of bounce off each other, meet up every now and again and get more acquainted. And this worked well. The mule seemed very self-contained now he already had one chum but gradually, as I worked with him and taught him to lead and have his hooves picked up, we reached an understanding. And he soon clocked the muck heap.

My muck heap, as I mentioned before with scant regard for modesty, was a thing of beauty. I had built it within its three-sided breeze block surround and it stood in three steps, the final being about two metres high. When the mule wanted to stale, he bounced up the three steps like a seasoned eventer and peed at the top. I'd like to say I trained him to do it, but I didn't – up there he knew he wouldn't splash his legs. Not for nothing are mules considered smart.

About muck heaps: they are easy to build well, providing you are using manure from straw bedding. You simply ensure you build up in layers, forking the walls straight, digging a dip in the centre to guide the rain inwards. At the risk of sounding geeky I must say how much I love to see a good, square, muck heap, and building one this way ensures it doesn't spread all over the place. Of course, it isn't so easy if you use wood chippings for they refuse to play ball, collapsing like a disappointing soufflé, and spreading around the yard like confetti.

Wood chippings blow around yards, too, and grip to horses' manes and tails. That some folk don't bother to brush them out of their mount's locks before they go riding leaves me smacking my forehead. Have they no pride? It looks like their horse's stuffing is coming out – poor show, people! It only takes a few moments to brush them out, and if your horse lies down again after you've groomed him, then why not put his tail in one, fat plait, to help yourself? Or tie him up until you've got your tack, or give yourself a few moments to do it all again – or even leave his mane and tail until you are ready to go?

But then I also hate to see riders with unchallenged stable stains defacing their horses. Get yourself a brush and give your horse a scrub – no need for water, just scrub to-and-fro. Put your back into it and you'll be amazed at how much you can erase. Honestly. If that fails, a dab with a cold sponge might help but remember your laundry rules: hot water sets stains, so leave it to make tea. You're welcome, don't mention it.

But what of the mule? I called him Twoy – short for Two-Persons, and pronounced 2E. Mules, so it is said, are stubborn. They kick. Well, I never found Twoy stubborn, but he wasn't one to be rushed. Whenever I asked him to do something his ears would go into overdrive. He was thinking. And what he was thinking was whether my request was reasonable, whether it was dangerous (to him), and whether he might grant me an affirmative answer. Given a second or two, he always did. You might say he was a suspicious sort of character, looking after number one and I could hardly blame him for that. Once he'd learned something, however, it was in that head for life – which is why I knew it was vital that he only learned good behaviour. He was teaching me as much as I was teaching him.

Mules and donkeys are not horses. This is obvious, but mules seem to provide a link between the two species and, when I looked hard at my shiny new equine, he seemed to me to resemble the artists' impressions of the horse throughout its middle evolutionary stages. He had an upright mane without a forelock, slender legs, thin tail, and a body and head shape which was neither horse nor donkey – yet belonged to both. Was this how prehistoric horses looked before they made redundant the toes on either side of their central, stronger and longer toe? Did Miohippus, millions of years ago, look like Twoy? If he did, maybe he had his intelligence, too. And maybe that's how he found out that running on his central toe gave him greater speed as he toured North America with his Miohippus chums…

> *'Hey Dave, whatever are you doing?'*
>
> *'What? Oh, hello Brian. Um, well, I was just experimenting, you know…'*
>
> *'I thought you were lame, the way you were walking.'*
>
> *'Oh no, just sort of… Well look, you try this, see what you think. Walk on your tip-toes. Never mind the two smaller toes you have on either side, just use the one in the middle.'*

'What, like this?'

'That's it, you've got it. What do you think?'

'Feels weird. What's the point?'

'Interesting choice of word but, well, that's just it. I'm sure I can run faster using just my middle toe.'

'Shut up!'

'No, really.'

'Let me try.'

A moment later, when Brian returns after executing a small circle at a rather unsteady gallop…

'Well?'

'Mmmm, you may be on to something. It certainly felt faster to me.'

'Hey there, what are you two up to?'

'Dave thinks we can run faster if we just use our middle toes.'

'Oh no, not another one of Dave's mane-brained ideas.'

'No, really Keith, I think he might have something with this one. Try it.'

'If we were meant to run on one toe, we'd only have one toe…'

'Oh I don't know, progress and all that. Dolores insisted her mum told her that her great, great, great, great, **great** grandfather had **four** toes!'

'Get out of here!'

'But having three toes means we're more stable…'

'Ooooooo, that reminds me, I've got an idea for a sort of shelter thing that can keep us all dry when it rains…'

'Oh have a day off, Dave. Just eat, drink and fornicate, like the rest of us.'

'You do what you like. I'm going to keep up my single-toe theory. I think it's got legs. Besides, if we never tried anything new, we'd still be swimming in the sea.'

'You don't believe all that evolution shit, do you?'

'I'm in, too. You can carry on with your three-toe running if you like, Keith, but things move on you know. Give it a couple of million years and I bet we'll all be doing it. All because of Dave, here. He's a visionary, is Dave.'

'Come on, I'll race you to that tree over there.'

'Oi, hold on, nobody said go! Blimey, you two are faster on your middle toes, aren't you? Wait for me!'

I expect it happened *exactly* like that.

Not only do donkeys and mules look very different to horses, but they have different ways of coping with the world, and individual ideas about how they interact with us. Handling them successfully requires some lateral thinking on the part of the handler. A horse has a thin gullet, and you can turn his head to regain control, but try that with a donkey or a mule and you'll find yourself being towed along, totally out of control, at walk. They just set their neck and go – in the same way Misty did when he came out of his stable and headed to the field, only he did it at the gallop. And if you think you might be able to shoo a donkey or a mule along a bit, like you can a horse, then you've another think coming for they will just turn around and face you in contempt. Clearly, with my new mule installed, a lot of thinking outside the box needed to be done – and on my part.

And how about kicking, I hear you ask? Well, mules can certainly do that – and they can kick in any direction so don't think standing in front of one will save you. Twoy had no reason to kick, so he didn't. I would say, however – and this goes for donkeys, too – that you need to watch out when they're in the field if you value your dog. Both mules and donkeys can take exception to loose dogs and can charge, kicking out with their forelegs with lightning speed and deadly accuracy. Good for guarding your sheep against foxes and dogs, not so happy for a family pet.

When I left the donkey stud I couldn't take both Pickwick and Twoy with me. It should have been an impossible choice – and in the end it was, and it wasn't, because Twoy had taken over my heart. I knew Pickwick would be fine at the stud, and he later found a great home with Mr Smuggins in a nearby village (which sounds like they became a couple, but as far as I know they were just good friends). Twoy I wasn't so sure about. He was a sensitive creature, and my plan for us to bond had been spectacular in its success. Where I was to go, I decided, Twoy would go, too. But that's mules for you; they take more effort in the initial stages but once you win their trust and become a team, it's impossible to let them go. They are the definitive one-person equine and they don't take no s***, not from nobody, no siree!

One yard we went to was a DIY livery yard, nearby to my parents' house where I was living at the time, enabling me to visit twice daily. This yard was where my old friend Diane kept her two mares, so we palled up again. One day, upon my return from the yard, there was a phone call for me from a guy with whom I was due to go on a date later that week. His opening gambit held an accusation tone.

He: 'Who's Terry?'

Me: Puzzled look – not very helpful on the phone.

He: 'I rang earlier. Your mum told me you'd gone to see... (slightly more menacing tone) ...*Terry*.'

Me: Light bulb. '*Ahhhhh.*'

We never did go on that – or any other – date. Read into that what you will.

There were plenty of misunderstandings regarding Twoy's name. He was referred to as Terry (obvs), Chewy, Louie and Trevor (!), to name but a few. My fault, perhaps, but there was no way I was ever going to saddle him with *Muffin*.

DIY livery yards can be great places, but there is sometimes a high turnover of horses and owners. And so it was at this one. One owner was a man called Nigel, with a chestnut horse he never seemed to ride. Diane always forgot his surname, assuring me as her eyes rolled skywards in the effort to remember, that it was something to do with the circus. After many suggestions involving tents, clowns, trapeze artists, ringmasters, circus acts, animals etc, she remembered it was *Smart*. I'd never have got that in a million years, but no matter. It seemed he lived up to his name for it soon became apparent that instead of Nigel getting his hands dirty, his girlfriends looked after his horse. Maybe his horse was the attraction. Maybe that's why he had it. Maybe his mum had refused to let his lily-white hands get grubby at Pony Club camp. When we noticed Nigel mucking out his own horse one day, we deduced that particular romance was off. That was when Nigel asked me out.

Now when it comes to the romantic uptake I freely admit to not being the quickest but even I had recognised the pattern by now, so I declined. I had my own stable to muck out, thanks very much. A few days later another blonde turned up, fork and shovel in hand. Whatever qualities Nigel possessed they were clearly not sufficient to keep staff for his horse (which, for some unfathomable reason, was also called Nigel. I don't know about you, but I think this takes apathy in thinking up a suitable name for your horse to new heights – or depths, if you prefer).

Another livery was a middle-aged woman who had decided, after only a few lessons, to buy her own horse and we'd often see her in the manège, cheerfully covering many miles, chugging around in never-ending circles while her horse stood in the middle, expertly lungeing her. Good exercise for one of them, anyway. We would have given her a hand but she was one of those people who preferred giving advice rather than taking it. Ten years, remember, ten years…

Nigel wasn't the only one who had life sussed. For another example of how to get people to do things for you we only had to look to a stunning young woman whose two horses I remember, but whose name I've forgotten.

She didn't have a car, but that didn't mean she walked anywhere. Various vehicles – usually of the sports variety – would pull into the car park every day and she'd alight and thank the driver, who was always male. It was a neat trick, and cost the bus service dear.

One day, she arrived early in the morning straight from clubbing, spray-on trousers topped with a lacy, push-up basque (causing Diane's husband to pull one of those cartoon eyes-bulging-tongue-hanging-out faces), barely hidden beneath one of those gorgeous Harry Hall black jackets with the velvet collar and piping up the back, causing me to rue the day I had sold mine. I'm not kidding myself, I wouldn't have carried it off with such aplomb, but I would have given it a go. I mean, we all had basques in the 1980s, and no-one wore them as underwear. I can't say it ever occurred to me to wear mine to the yard, though.

I moved on and took Twoy with me to Sylvie's yard, where I worked for a time, and Diane took her horses to a private place closer to the coast, where she got more horses, including a sweet-natured chestnut Arab called Henry. When I had to move again, Twoy went to live with Diane and her horses in the field next to the railway line with her two mares and a gelding always known affectionately as the Rat, which belonged to her husband, who would follow you around the field (the Rat, not Diane's husband). One day, Diane got so fed up with him getting in the way, she ran backwards at him (again, the Rat, *not* her husband). She supposed he might think she was going to kick him, and it certainly worked, even though she was filled with remorse after as he gave her such a 'kicked puppy' look. She didn't actually do it, you understand.

Don't the horse whisperers say we need to speak our horse's language? We could never understand why people needed gurus to teach them ways to get their horses to come to them – we could never get rid of ours. I mean, what do they do to make their horses dislike them so much? Even threatening to kick the Rat didn't put him off for long and he soon came back for more with a *I know you don't mean it* look all over his face. I wouldn't recommend you do it to most horses, you'll probably get a thump in the back for your trouble.

One day, when Diane took herself up the field for her usual evening visit to the horses she was greeted by a mystery: how come the mule was where she had left him that morning, yet unmistakable mule poo could be seen on the wrong side of the fence, next to the field where Henry lived? (Mule poo is different from horses', being smaller, rounder, and less likely to break on landing.) Clearly, Twoy was taking himself out for a visit to his chum – but he was smart enough to put himself back in his rightful place in time for tea, like a furtive equine secret agent. No problem for an 11.2hh mule with knees, who had worked out how to wriggle under the fence.

No harm done, thought Di, no action necessary. But Twoy came unstuck the following week when the clocks went forward. When Diane visited an hour earlier than the usual time, Twoy was still at large. Diane said the look on the busted mule's face was a mixture of guilt, defiance and devil-may-care.

Di and I decided that every mule should have its day, and that a local show, small but well-attended, would be the perfect place for us to have some fun, and for Two-Persons to make his showing debut. There were no mule-specific classes, but a careful combing of the schedule revealed no dire warnings about mules being escorted from the premises should they dare show their faces, which led us to consider the veteran, any-age, any-breed, best condition and turnout and best handler classes to be open season for our hybrid.

Preparations began in earnest. Twoy was well-rehearsed in walking and trotting in hand, as well as standing up for any judge to inspect him. We took a step back and cast a critical eye over our specimen. Those front hooves needed some work as Twoy still had a split in one where he'd had a touch of seedy toe. His usual farrier Richard (he with a comprehensive collection of rosettes won at musical sacks) was consulted, and after a bit of chin-rubbing, a lot of bending over and much hammering later there stood before us a tap-dancing mule, silver toes twinkling in the sun.

I trimmed my potential show mule's mane in an arch to improve his naturally ewe neck, slimmed his heels with some considered scissor action, pulled and banged his tail. His wiry coat resisted all attempts to apply a pattern to his quarters but his summer coat still shone like polished mahogany (it came through in a short, six-week window in late July, early August, taking its cue from his donkey side). His bridle was buffed up and boot-polished to a high shine. I dug out my in-hand showing gear. Thus prepped, we loaded up mule-face and took him to the ball.

We had misgivings about how his presence might affect the other competitors, what with Twoy being a bit of a novelty. Luckily, apart from a few snorts and the odd ear waggle, we entered the ring without drama – if you didn't count a double-take from the judge. Twoy behaved like a seasoned pro. He had always moved straight as an arrow, so I had every confidence that, even if the judge took against him, he would do himself proud. But the judge didn't take against him and Twoy headed the line-up in the condition and turnout class. I was amazed, and the judge offered very complimentary remarks. The local horsy press took our photograph and we repaired to the lorry. Surprised and delighted was the theme – and it continued. Twoy took second place in the veteran class and then the red ribbon in the any age, any breed, under the same judge. She really liked him, and complimented him on his movement. It wasn't the Horse of the Year Show, but hey, the mule done good!

On the basis that we ought to enter everything we could and make our journey worthwhile our last effort was in the adult best handler class, with a large entry. The man in front of us had a large, ill-trained horse which, literally, ran rings around him. He seemed to think this proved his prowess at handling a very difficult horse whereas I was of the opinion that if he knew his stuff, he'd get the horse to walk in a straight line. He kept throwing us looks, as though I shouldn't be there with my quiet old donkey, but I knew better; I knew that if we swapped animals, I'd have a serious go at getting his horse to walk straight, and Twoy would soon mirror his own horse's behaviour and start circling around him. It was one of those 'aren't you lucky your horse behaves itself' scenarios. Luck, as ever, had nothing to do with it.

We came second, next to an obviously experienced and quiet handler with a nice Welsh pony – the man at the centre of his horse's universe loudly voicing his opinion that we had easy animals, and that he had a difficult one. I'll leave you to judge that one.

And so we took our prize-winning, show mule home, smothered in glory, bedecked in ribbons and with two trophies for the mantelpiece. I showed Twoy at other local shows but we never again achieved the dizzy heights of that first outing. No matter – it was always fun to take him out, and he was always the perfect ambassador for The Mule.

Twoy continued to live with Diane's horses for many years. When it came to making that horrible, difficult decision at the end of his life, it turned out it wasn't too hard after all. He was thirty-four years old, his kidneys were failing and, as with a lot of small equines, he was bearing pain with fortitude – but he was still in pain. The vet suggested admitting him to the equine hospital, a few more days gained, but this would have been for my benefit, not his – not to mention the vet's. To be honest, I wasn't too impressed by that suggestion, Twoy being the patient, not me. I refused. It was time to say goodbye, and for Twoy to end his days quietly at home, with people he knew and who loved him, not in a strange place hooked up to a drip.

When his horse friends had said their goodbyes to his still body and Twoy was gone, Diane noticed that her horses seemed without their manager. Only then did she realise what a steadying influence the little mule had been. He had been the constant, the rock, the sensible mule from which the others took their cue. It was a long time before total equilibrium was restored.

We now know that leaving a fallen equine in his field for a while, to allow the other horses to see him, sniff him, realise the life force has left their friend and that he will never rise again, is a kindness. Otherwise, how will they know? Their friend has gone – but if they have no opportunity to learn that he has left them in spirit, how can they understand why he no longer grazes with them, why he has deserted them?

But often we do not wait for death to separate our equine friends. Instead, we move them from yard to yard, from friendship to friendship, from equine community to equine community, with no consideration for relationships they have formed. Empathic pairs, grazing cheek-to-cheek in the field, whinnying to each other when one goes for a hack or schooling, are considered a nuisance, a pain, an inconvenience to be discouraged.

When Kathy moved her horse from one livery yard to another, the first time Ben was turned out in the field he jumped the fence and galloped along the road, dodging the traffic, to arrive at his former home, sides heaving and sweating, at the stable door of the mare he loved, where there was a glorious reunion.

He'll get over it, people said. But we don't – we can't – know whether he did. How many other friendships have been severed whenever we choose to move, or are forced to find a new yard for our horses through a change in our own circumstances, as I sometimes have? Without fields and stables of our own we often have no choice and the anguish we feel on behalf of our equine friends cuts deep. Horses form lasting bonds but can they love? What is the definition of love? That you would risk death for a loved one? Ben certainly risked his life to be with his lady friend, but it is fanciful to suggest that he might have been aware of the danger. How can we know, how can we judge?

The war horses left behind in the Middle East by our government after World War I were sought out by the wonderful Dorothy Brooke, dismayed by the sight of the walking skeletons, the lame, abused and exploited horses she discovered some twenty years later, the army brands they bore a testament to their provenance. Some of those old horses, those who had survived years of betrayal in the hell of the stone quarries, of starvation and slavery, upon seeing old friends with whom they had served were reunited with obvious signs of recognition and delight. If that doesn't bring a lump to your throat, I don't know what will.

Make no mistake, it is hard to say goodbye to an old friend and some people, scared of facing the future without the beloved horse they have had for a lifetime, the horse which has been there for them while their lives have taken knocks, break ups, jobs good and bad, other losses, find the decision impossible. Panic can set in – how will they cope without their old – if not oldest – friend?

But it has to be faced. Horses rarely die of natural causes. In the wild, the old and the weak are driven away from the herd by the young and the strong, knowing that an old horse attracts predators, the safety of the herd being more important than any individual. Old horses must die alone, brought down by bears, wolves or the big cats. In our domestic settings we can do better than that for our old friends, for it is our horses we have to consider, not ourselves.

At the riding school at the top of the hill, the wonderful old staff horse known as the Chestnut suffered a heart attack one night, throwing herself around her stable, injuring herself in her frantic efforts to stay upright, her instincts telling her not to give in, not to stay down lest the scavengers came. The vet arrived at last to end her suffering and the next day we all waited, solemn and numbed by this new and frightening experience, for the old horse's body to be taken away.

Rose, however, having sat through her old friend's violent demise, had been forced into making a decision. Cheyenne, another school horse and Jan's old favourite, had been ill for a while, getting old, a thin shadow of his former self. He was led out to the yard where a single shot ended his life in a swift and unknowing instant, his shoes clattering on the cobbles as his body fell. Rose was determined his end would be kinder and swifter than the Chestnut's, and the two old horses went together.

It is not easy to make the very worst decision, and it is one we know we have to live with. It is our responsibility to let our horses go with dignity, before they are too old, too stiff, too fed up with life, before nature takes that decision out of our hands and forces a much worse alternative. Our horses let us know when it is time to say goodbye and it is our duty to be brave, putting aside our guilt at playing God, the trauma of being an executioner. What if we make that decision too soon?

Far worse to make it too late.

Epilogue

RELIVING MEMORIES FOR THIS book has brought home to me how extremely lucky I have been to have led my horsy life. And memories are still in production, for who knows how many lie in wait to be converted from future, through the present, before being committed to the past.

I haven't been able to include everything, of course. I've left out loads. Like the international press trip in Portugal where I rode wonderful dressage horses, before visiting an archaeological dig to look at fantastic Roman mosaics being unearthed. As our guide spoke to the dig's American leader he suddenly became worryingly animated, demanding to know which of us spoke English. I deftly slid behind my fellow journalists. It looked rather as though an Englishman might have been responsible for some terrible crime against his sister, which he was determined to avenge. With not a jot of loyalty our guide pointed an accusing finger in my direction and the game was up. It turned out I was safe (and so was his sister), he just hadn't talked to anyone in English for a long time, and was keen to ensure he still could. We were having a fine old chat (he was very attractive and I was rather into the mosaic) when our host dragged us all back to the mini bus to go and look at the local… ducks. *Ducks!*

I haven't told you about taking the little Arab to the London Riding Horse Parade in Hyde Park where we won the lady rider section. Judged on turnout, by the late, great, Roger Stack, I was amazed to find myself heading the line-up. Diane and I went because of ambitions to ride in the Park. Which we did – and rather jolly it was, too. Even allowing for our entry fees and diesel for the lorry it worked out considerably cheaper than hiring a horse from one of the wonderful riding schools adjacent to the park. Not that that was the point, obviously.

And then there were the pony weeks I ran at the riding school at the top of the hill. Twelve young and over-excited riders totally up for five full – very full – days of lessons, hacks, lectures and fun, even if the ponies didn't view it in quite the same way. The parents loved it almost as much as their offspring.

'Wouldn't it be fabulous,' they enthused, pushing it as they rocked up at the end of their gloriously free days to take their little darlings home, 'if all the children could stay overnight – stay *all week!*' I agreed that yes, it was a shame but alas, there was nowhere for them to stay. Such a pity. Oh, if only…

But that was out loud. Inside, in silence, I was screaming 'Dear God NO!' I mean, it was great fun each and every day – but all night as well? Not so much.

Then there was the time the tractor failed us, and Rose thought it would be a good idea to dig out the old driving collar she had squirrelled away in the house, fit it onto Bracken (she had a hunch he'd pulled something in a former life – like a cart, rather than a tendon – he just looked the sort), fasten a couple of ropes from collar to tractor and get one single bay horsepower to pull it into life. So we did that and it turned out that Bracken did, indeed, know what was expected – only the ropes broke a couple of times, which made him lose confidence, which was a pity. Before that, we were like a third-world country, harnessing up a horse to a tractor. Maybe we'll all be doing that when the fuel runs out.

I wish I could forget the top showing yard where I went to work. It was so ghastly – the horses were shut in their stables all the time, our boss referred to the other groom by the name of her predecessor in true *Devil Wears Prada* fashion and there was more culture in the kitchen than you'd find at the Royal Opera House – that I fled after only twenty-four hours. It was even worse than the time I worked at Butlin's. But you don't want to know about that. Nobody does.

The racehorses I exercised during the summer holidays for one of Rose's farmer friends turned out to be a far more successful experience. 'They're a lovely family,'

Rose told me, as she took me to introduce us, 'only a bit eccentric. Don't make a big thing of it, but all the children run around in bare feet.' And they did, all four of them. And of course my gaze plummeted immediately to their bare toes, despite Rose's warning. But she was right: they were lovely, and so were their horses.

Julie lost a whole ride once, down by the river where we seldom went. Something spooked the school horses and they tipped all their riders onto the grass and lit out as a herd, leaving Julie and her leading rein to stare at plumes of retreating tails. Rose was not impressed. Well, she wouldn't have been, would she? Neither were the riders, I imagine. It was ages before the horses all came home but, looking on the bright side, it was the last ride of the day, so at least nobody was kept waiting. And I know what you're thinking but it *was* Julie. Not me.

Today, the beautiful coach house still stands proudly in the village at the top of the hill, but the riding school, sadly, is no more. There are horses, however: the business – run by the third generation of the same family – is now restricted to housing and teaching liveries.

Rose's funeral, held in the church on the green some years before the riding school closed, was standing room only, filled with friends and riders young and old. Of course, there were horses: two Friesians pulled the hearse, and another eight horses under saddle provided an escort along the road. The riders were solemn and tearful, dressed in black jackets, a tribute to their instructor. In death, as in life, Rose was surrounded by laughter as we truly celebrated her life – good-egg-David, Jean and I all sharing memories of our friend – before everyone stood with their own thoughts, around Rose's final resting place by the riding school. She had, as she had always threatened, left nothing behind that didn't need feeding.

She is not alone in the graveyard: Dick is over to the left, my dear friend Sue, who left us too soon aged only forty-two, in a grave to her right. It is fanciful to imagine old friends watching the horses next door, but I hope the bells don't annoy Rose too much.

Rose leaves a far-reaching legacy. It is impossible to calculate exactly how many people she taught to ride, how many infants she started on their equestrian adventures, how many adults enjoyed the thrill of riding mixed with a sense of fun that was unique to the riding school at the top of the hill. Throughout a career spanning over sixty years at such a big establishment the total must run into the thousands.

Just from my generation, Rose's influence lives on: Julie runs the livery stable at the end of the back lane with a dry humour gained from her instructor. She tells me she is always advising her liveries (well, begging, really) to leave their horses' heads alone. Nicky stables her dressage horse next to Julie's gelding – and they both still hack out together in the dark.

Heather and Trina run the local Pony Club, nurturing future riders. Jan rides regularly in Windsor Great Park where, recognising herself in any horse-obsessed pedestrian children she happens across on her hacks, will stop and talk with them and their parents, inviting them to engage with her mount. Older and younger generations have their own stories, all inspired by one person, one person who made horses her life, and in doing so inspired so many others.

Rose's lessons were not limited to her pupils' prowess in the saddle. She taught us to have fun, to share experiences, to find answers to questions ourselves. She instilled in us a sense of responsibility, a sense of anything being possible, and a valuable sense of daring. She refused to give up on lost horses, dogs, cats and, amazingly, people, offering all another chance. It was Jan who provided the perfect epitaph for our friend: 'Rose taught us to be brave. We took that bravery with us to other parts of our lives.'

Not everyone can be lucky enough to have known the legend that was Rose, but I sincerely hope you can look back on a horsy life – in whatever form it has taken – as enjoyable, and memorable, as mine.

Acknowledgements

Thanks to:

Rose.

Jean – the most entertaining raconteur I know.

Jan, Julie, Nicky, Trina and Heather, and to all my other riding friends with whom I shared laughs and questionable experiences.

To my friend Diane, who loved Twoy as I did.

Thanks to Rosemary at the donkey stud for opportunities, laughs, amazing times, and all her lovely donkeys.

Thanks to Louise Kittle, editor of *Horse&Rider*, for permission to reproduce parts of my holiday features which first appeared in the publication in the late 1990s.

To Jane Badger, for permission to reproduce several chapters which first appeared on her website, *Jane Badger Books*, which gave me the idea for this book, and for her encouragement and support.

And to all the wonderful horses and other equines who taught me so much, equines I have loved and lost, and equines everywhere who so generously share our lives.

 Matador